SOULS ALONG THE ROAD

Villains, Saints and Killer Cuisine

Published by
Compass Flower Press
Columbia, Missouri

ISBN 978-1-942168-88-1

SOULS ALONG THE ROAD

Villains, Saints and Killer Cuisine

John Drake Robinson

Knowledge is love and light and vision.

—Helen Keller

Contents

Prologue: Velvet Elvis to East Jesus

The tow truck picked up momentum, speeding past a familiar silhouette along Interstate 70. From my shotgun seat, I tipped my cap to the giant plywood cutout of the King. The big wooden Elvis stood beside the Elvis Is Alive Museum, a small stone building Bill Beeny converted into a flea market collection of Elvis kitsch. An old Cadillac guarded the museum entrance. Inside the funeral room was an open casket bearing a gimcrack Elvis mannequin in a powder-blue leisure suit, surrounded by artificial wreaths and velvet Elvis paintings. The gift shop sold rolls of Elvis Presley Toilet Paper: "It's rough. It's tough. And it doesn't take crap off anybody."

Dead idols shape our lives. Sometimes they merit a museum. A gaudy garish tacky tawdry museum.

Bill Beeny is a diehard Elvis fan. A Baptist preacher and one-time segregationist candidate for Missouri lieutenant governor, Beeny believes the King is alive. He says DNA evidence proves that the body buried at Graceland is not Elvis.

I don't have a dog in this fight. I never met Bill Beeny and neither did my dog, Queenie Beanie, no relation. Queenie Beanie wasn't racist. She sniffed butts indiscriminately. Beyond that, I'm pretty sure she was a strict speciesist.

Towering over the Elvis Is Alive Museum, the sixteen-foot plywood Elvis cutout stood resplendent in his high collared jumpsuit and jet-black pompadour, bent toward his interstate fans, holding a microphone to his curled upper lip. As far as plywood Elvis cutouts go, this one rates a five. But a few years ago Elvis left the building. Beeny sold the King's contents on eBay and turned his highly visible roadside venue into the Calvary Baptist Church and Food Pantry. It's one giant leap for Bill Beeny, from crap-resistant toilet paper to feeding the hungry. The Brobdingnagian wooden Elvis got a makeover, and now the King carries an old rugged cross in his free hand, so if I squint and use my imagination, one King resembles the Other.

The tow truck passed Elvis in an instant, and I didn't bring up the subject, since I had no idea how Jack the tow truck driver felt about Elvis or Jesus or segregation or toilet paper, and we had an eighty-mile drive ahead of us.

I remember the last time I saw Elvis. He was sitting behind me in the bleachers at old Busch Stadium on a sunny spring afternoon. The bleachers were packed for a Cardinals baseball game against the Chicago Cubs. Six young men sat shirtless in the front row, each chest painted with a giant red letter so that when the lads assembled in the correct order their bellies spelled WILLIE. For the first six innings of the game, they chanted "Willie! Willie!" Their arms bowed like palm fronds to their hero, Cardinals center fielder Willie McGee, who was shy as a doe. He never turned to thank his fans. By the seventh inning the young men, drunk and discouraged, turned their attention to the man behind me with the black pompadour. "Elvis! Elvis!" they bowed in tipsy reverence to the King. I think he might've been an Elvis impersonator.

In the tow truck's shotgun seat, I rode alone with my thoughts: What's the purpose of toilet paper that doesn't take any crap? Seriously, Elvis would pick the Love Me Tender roll. But most folks use whatever is at hand. Deep in the Cascade Mountains, D.B. Cooper probably used a $20 bill, causing Andrew Jackson to choke back tears.

Earlier in the day, a morning radio call-in show was debating the fate of D.B. Cooper when my car died on a busy Saint Louis highway. D.B. Cooper became a legend the day before Thanksgiving 1971 when he stepped out the tail door of a hijacked Northwest Orient 727—with a parachute and $200,000—and vanished somewhere in the Cascade Mountains.

Some folks think D.B. Cooper is alive, and some folks think Elvis is alive, but my car was dead and we were riding a flatbed tow truck home.

We sped down I-70 in silence. Not driving, I had a rare chance to study the passing scenery and observe the wondrous monuments wrought by man, a rusty rainbow of roadside detritus in various stages of decay, jagged clusters of cholesterol along one of America's major arteries, rundown motels way past their welcome mat, shuttered storefronts and roadside trash, cultivations of clutter and crap, junk that might be a flea market, or a proud display of redneck wealth. We passed flashing neon, tinted windows, ragged banners and way more than three billboards.

I: Through a Tow Truck's Looking Glass

People in Icewater Want Hell

Maybe those movies were right, the trio of movies depicting Missouri as a haven for hillbilly hucksters and redneck killers. *Winter's Bone. Ozark. Three Billboards Outside Ebbing, Missouri.* I wasn't sure how Jack the tow truck driver would react, so I didn't bring up the movies, not wanting to spend a long drive discussing burned bones and billboards and meth murders and a lake notorious for episodes of questionable sanitation and sanity.

Are we doomed?

There are signs. Signs encourage us not to swallow batteries and Tide pods. Signs warn tourists not to pet crocodiles. Signs beg employees to wash their hands. One sign captures the decline of modern civilization: "Not responsible if seagulls eat your funnel cake."

Holy deep-fried shit!

America is morphing into a witness culture, watching life rather than wallowing in it. Too many folks only glance up from their smart phones to check a stoplight, or watch reality TV. People will watch anything: *16 and Pregnant. Trading Spouses. Hell Date. In Search of the Partridge Family.*

"The elevator only goes up," comedian Lenny Bruce said. Our culture has no reverse gear. Lenny tested boundaries of free speech in nightclubs during the '60s, salting his act with carnal phrases and f-bombs. Authorities jailed him relentlessly. He died before blue comedy took off, before reality TV branched from its socially acceptable granddaddy, *Candid Camera*, into bawdy, ribald roasts. Lenny never saw HBO or Sensurround, personal computers or microwave ovens, floppy disks, ATMs or Archie Bunker, in-vitro fertilization, email, Richard Pryor, microchips, cell phones and smart phones, DVDs, GPS, DNA, Lisa Lipanelli, Bluetooth, camcorders, wi-fi, driverless cars, artificial hearts, Roseanne Barr, high definition, JPEGs, IMAX, Tupac, Instagram, bar codes, Andrew Dice Clay, iPads, apps, Facebook, Google, Napster, Pornhub, Netflix, Wikipedia, the Cloud, tweets, texts, selfies, *Grand Theft Auto*, road rage, sliced ketchup or Stormy Daniels.

But he opened the elevator door.

From my seat in this flatbed tow truck I watched the roadside fly past.

Strewn among the cultural carnage, glimmers of hope flame up like votives in a vestibule. For a solid week, before the tow truck ride, life was a carnival: A hundred stories unfolded and the road revealed its secrets, a wow around every turn.

My car showed no signs of dying.

A week ago, Grubville was good. Moving along the western perimeter of Jefferson County, my car zagged off Highway 30 down Route W, where we rubbed bumpers with the folks in Grubville at Joe Mama's Hilltop Tavern. Cars parked bumper to bumper on both sides of this country road. We seized the only open parking spot beside the front porch where people sat around two tables framed by a pair of sleek Harley Davidsons. Near the group stood a deep fryer the size of an old tub washing machine. The cook and I greeted each other with mutual curiosity. He wondered who the hell I was. I wondered how I could politely partake in his Grubville cuisine.

"How much for some catfish?" I cut to the chase.

"No charge," he startled me. "Buy a beer, get some food." Fair enough. I tipped my cap and went inside.

This seemed to be a special occasion, but maybe the gathering was ritual in these remote hills, as families huddled together around four-top tables, taking turns refilling their plates from the mothership table spread thick with carry-in dishes. Home-grown tomatoes. Sliced cucumbers and onions. Baked beans.

Joe Mama's is the real deal. They keep it simple, and except for big feeds like today, the tavern specializes in two basic food groups: cans or bottles.

The place was crowded. But then, from what I hear, it's always crowded, this being the gathering place for miles around. There were no open seats at the bar, polished by the elbows of a dozen generations. Locals offered snippets of history about the place. It's survived almost forty years with the same name. Used to be a gas station. Before that, it was a Model A showroom.

An old country tavern might cause kids to get bored fast. Yet the Grubville children were fully engaged in games of tag and hide-and-seek, buzzing through the crowd of adults like horse flies, not an iPhone in sight.

Fortified with grub, I headed to a pirate's hideout. Rumors persist that three centuries ago during high water on the Mississippi River, the pirate Blackbeard sailed up Joachim Creek west of Herculaneum and buried treasure at what is now called Blackbeard's Cache Natural Bridge. According to legend, waters receded and Blackbeard's vessel ran aground. The crew rolled the ship on logs four miles back to the Mississippi. Sounds like a tall tale. Maybe locals got tired of telling stories about Jesse James. Today Blackbeard's Cache Natural Bridge keeps the name, and it's a great spot to hide your loot if you don't mind treasure hunters.

We—my car and I—drove through Frumet, over Flucom Creek, past Tanglefoot and Melzo, Horine and Old Ditch. We crossed Skullbone Creek, and passed the ghosts of Moontown School, Mothershead School and the old Saint Joseph Hill Infirmary for Aged and Chronic Incurable Men.

Darkness fell as my car reached the National Horseshoe Pitchers Hall of Fame. We didn't stop, since pitching horseshoes in the dark might end badly. We detoured to see the stars. Every Friday night when the sky is clear, astronomers welcome curious stargazers to Broemmelsiek Park to peek through powerful telescopes and take a gander at Orion and Polaris, the moon and the Milky Way.

I channeled the ancient mariners, the world's first abstract artists, who drew imaginary lines between stars to make pictures. All of these imaginary pictures have names, and if I spent more time bobbing in the ocean, I'd learn them all. But seriously, how does the constellation Pegasus look like a horse?

All that star power made me hungry. We drove into Saint Louis.

The Pat Connolly Tavern—if you're speaking Irish proper—may be Dogtown's most notable icon thanks to the giant neon sign jutting out over the entrance like an icebreaker's prow.

Beneath an artful logo the marquee spells one word in foot-high letters: Budweiser. Behind the neon, the sign's brightly painted red, white and green metal shows its age, wearing decades of weather on its rusty faded face. Like the Irish neighborhood in which it sits, the sign is antique, and pairs well with the elephantine Griesedieck Brothers Beer sign painted on the brick wall around the corner.

But you can't eat signs. Pat's Tavern endures because the food brings people together. Pat's fried chicken would bust the colonel back to buck private. When Patrick Connolly opened the tavern in 1942, he brought his Galway Irish values to "share food, share drink and share ideas." Pat's family keeps the tradition, serving me Reuben soup and half a chicken fried, with mashed potatoes and gravy and green beans.

Eavesdropping on a nearby table, I heard grisly snippets about a local woman accused of stabbing her best friend in the eye, neck, throat, liver, lungs and spleen. The conversation devolved to an old story about a killer dentist. His dental assistant married a victim, bought him life insurance, and led the poor man to picnic in an open field near Six Flags where the dentist, from a distance, gave him a root canal with a high-powered rifle.

Instinctively I ordered an Irish Carbomb Brownie off the menu.

Such talk is disturbing. But food and death are never far apart.

Years ago as newlyweds we lived within double-barreled slingshot range of the Playboy Club in South Saint Louis. Never went there, but we often lunched within its shadow. Famous Barr department store served the world's best crock of French onion soup. Alas, Macy's swallowed Famous, but they couldn't kill the soup. Google Famous Barr French Onion Soup and get 700,000 results.

The soup brings back cheesy memories. Even as we ate, we were stalked by the fear of exploding. Back in the '70s, car bombs rarely blasted outside Belfast, until one hot summer when cars in south Saint Louis County began exploding like popcorn, way too often to be blamed on spontaneous combustion. The blasts happened near our apartment, and the media branded the culprit the South County Bomber. Every morning I checked under the hood of our '69 Impala, in case the South County Bomber targeted me. Detectives finally broke the case: two factions of a local Saint Louis mob were hell-bent on wiping each other out.

The tow truck was not my original plan. All week my car had performed flawlessly, touring Greater St. Louis, seeking obscure faces and places left behind in our breakneck swipe-left culture, driving through Bunkum and Fish Pot Creek, Gumbo Bottoms, Lard Pond and Creve Coeur, the French term for Tom Petty mourners. Near Union Station we passed the site of the old Booker T. Washington Theatre where Josephine Baker made her stage debut while black soldiers waited for trains to depart.

We passed Saint Mary Magdalene Church, both of them, because Saint Louisans embrace Mary Magdalene's mystery: wild and faithful.

Downstream from the Chain of Rocks—a treacherous boat-smashing necklace across the Mississippi River—we searched for Quarantine Island where thousands of Saint Louisans stricken with typhoid fever were sent to die, and Bloody Island where angry white men shot each other in duels. We crossed Eads Bridge, where in 1874 a John Robinson Circus elephant was the first creature to cross the bridge, since humans were fearful to set foot on this strange span. Elephants instinctively know if a crossing is safe.

I saw a lady flip a lit cigarette out her car window, reminding me that much of America's trash is breathing.

We visited Jefferson Barracks, originally named for President John Adams but the name was changed on July 4, 1826, the day Thomas Jefferson died. On that same day John Adams died too, and his son, John Quincy Adams was president, but apparently somebody *really* wanted to name the fort for Jefferson. Hey, Jefferson bought the land.

We crossed Cold Water Creek, also known as Riviere aux Biches, and found Coldwater Cemetery, oldest in the city.

Many of these ancient names would be lost were it not for Ruth Welty, who dutifully recorded these unique appellations and the tales of their creation. It must have been a tedious project, back in 1939. I can't imagine anybody driving all of these roads to uncover their stories.

Fuzzy Fables

Early on the morning of my car's demise, there was no hint of trouble. I parked and roamed the cobblestone streets of old St. Charles among two hundred tourists who shared one common trait: their eyes and fingers were imprisoned by smart phones. I was searching for the father of Chicago, buried somewhere in this ancient Missouri River town.

Jean Baptiste Pointe du Sable—the son of a French seafarer and a Haitian mother—established a small riverbank trading post near Lake Michigan in an area Native Americans called shikaakwa, (smelly onions) or she-gau-ga (skunk weed). Either term described the pungent wild garlic that grew there in abundance. Du Sable left that trading post before she-gau-ga evolved into Chicago. He came to Saint Charles, operated a river ferry, retired here penniless, died here and was buried without a smart phone in his clutches. His gravesite is unknown because Borromeo Cemetery has been moved twice since his death in 1818. But the new cemetery honors him with a monument.

More than a century after du Sable died, down the street from this peaceful cemetery, armored battle tanks rolled out of an old railroad foundry, testing their mettle on these cobblestone streets before the tanks were packed off to fight World War II. The tanks liberated the world. Then social media came along and captured us without firing a shot. Anyway, the old tank factory now harbors world class artists as The Foundry Art Centre, in a transformation that turned swords into plowshares.

It wasn't the town's first transformation.

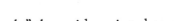

"That there's not a skunk," the guide pointed to one animal pelt on a table, "That's genuine Alaskan sable." It *was* a skunk, the guide admitted, but to the European fur market in the early 1800s, the term Alaskan sable sold better.

"See that coonskin cap over there," the guide continued. "Nobody around here wore coonskin caps. But they were sold back east as genuine frontier wear."

Frontier fake news.

When Missouri's first legislators met in Saint Charles, they walked into this dry goods store stocked with skins and hats, powder and pelts and fabrics. On the way upstairs to the capitol, they might stop to buy a brick of tea, the way suppliers sold it around here.

Upstairs the tiny governor's office and the senate chamber flank the house of representatives with its rows of benches facing an 1804 King James Bible. Legislators stayed warm beside a stove at one end of the room, a fireplace at the other. Beef tallow candles offered dim light in these chambers, the cradle of democracy in a frontier state that would launch a million prairie schooners west.

Saint Charles was the waistband in the hourglass of westward expansion. If your ancestors migrated west, it's a good bet they passed through Saint Charles, whether they were traveling by boat or overland trail.

The old customs house stands proudly on Main Street, just as it did when all westward travelers were obliged to stop to register. Sometimes they would spend the night in the customs house, especially on weekends, since the law prohibited traveling on Sunday.

The Missouri River was the first westward highway, for trappers and traders, explorers and settlers. But overland trails evolved quickly. In 1825, President John Quincy Adams authorized a bill by Senator Thomas Hart Benton to survey the road called the Highway Among Nations, better known as the Santa Fe Trail, but locals called it Boonslick Road, because it led past a central Missouri salt lick, a business operated by the sons of local judge Daniel Boone.

Part of Boonslick Road became a plank road. Shortly before the Civil War, a unique road-building phenomenon swept Missouri. Builders laid seventeen wooden toll roads, roadbeds made of hewn timbers, secured together like long, bumpy, cellulose Venetian blinds over muddy trails. The Western Plank Road, a ten-mile stretch from Saint Charles to Cottleville began to warp and rot soon after it was laid in 1850.

Nearby, a century later, builders paved the first mile of interstate highway. Over the years it began to warp and rot, too. Any time my car hits rough pavement, she shrugs it off. Riding rubber tires on rough asphalt is a cakewalk compared to iron wheels on wood planks.

On this oldest American interstate, headed for home, my car was about to have a heart attack. As we passed a sign denoting the first mile of federal interstate highway system, we were running smoothly.

Then things went bad.

The Good Badass Samaritan

It was Friday, already scorching hot, and the sun's heat shimmered on the highway ahead. My car, Erifnus Caitnop, pointed her nose toward Columbia, and we both looked forward to some rest after a grueling week on the road. By the time we returned home, Erifnus would show 290,000 miles on her odometer.

Not so fast.

Cruising along I-70, we fell into the rhythm of the road, rolling without incident until Erifnus shot me a stark SOS. Her battery light came on, and I knew what it meant. Her alternator had quit, and she wasn't making electricity. Without her pacemaker, she would die soon.

I turned off the radio, shut down the vent fan, and we kept driving toward the safety of home. I called her mechanic to give him a heads up. "Think we'll make it?" I asked him.

"Not likely."

The car kept running, 70 miles per hour, and hope springs eternal in old bones and brains. Maybe we could make it on the juice left in her elderly battery. But Erifnus was doomed, and the problem reflected in her eyes. The precious battery charge bled out through her headlights, shining in safety mode as they'd done since I drove her off the lot seventeen years ago.

In my mind, I prepared for the worst. If the car lost all power, we'd glide to the side of the road and I'd start making calls. The nearest mechanic. A tow truck. My wife.

We kept driving, and I tried to steer clear of thick traffic. But this was I-70.

Erifnus was showing symptoms of a heart attack. Passing Warrenton, her dashboard's brake light came on. Two miles down the road, her headlight indicator began flashing. When the speedometer and tachometer started swinging wildly between zero and infinity, I knew her time had come. The big green highway sign told us the Wright City exit was a mile away.

Long mile.

We stayed in the right lane and I coaxed her like a thoroughbred rounding the final turn. She rolled up the ramp and we coasted into an empty parking lot.

Erifnus was dead.

Our landing pad bordered a typical interstate gas station. The mechanic bay was long gone, replaced by aisles of snack foods and Slurpee machines. At the side of the gas station, a man crouched, airing a front tire on a car which looked more seasoned than Erifnus. I approached him carefully because, well, you never know.

"Where's the nearest auto repair shop?"

He jumped up from his crouch and pointed. "Just down the service road. You broke down? Wait a second, and I'll give you a lift."

The guy looked older than me, with a backwoods ponytail pulled back from a weatherbeaten face covered by a beard that some folks would label "Taliban" but in rural America was more akin to *Duck Dynasty*. His wiry frame moved like a crab through the car's floorboards, picking up beer bottles and trash to make a spot for me.

"Oh, that's okay, man," I answered. "You're busy...I can walk...."

A cigarette hung alternately from his lips and fingers as he spoke. "I'll take you. I know the mechanic. Good guy. They got a wrecker. I always jump at the chance to help somebody."

His enthusiasm was disarming.

Still, riding shotgun on this new adventure might turn out badly. I hadn't hitchhiked much since college. In fact, the last time I stuck out my thumb, a hearse picked me up, reminding me the end is near.

"Vietnam vet," he said proudly. "Always glad to help an American." He sized me up, too, figuring I was a long-haired T-shirted ball cap-wearin' good ole boy. He wasn't wrong, really, since that's how I was dressed. Truth is, on my travels along the back roads, I can play the good ole boy role, especially around banjo music.

He kept talking, a helpful trait that would give me clues. "I was a badass in my younger days," he said. I believed him. "Came back from 'Nam and painted cars. 'Vettes. Mercedes. I own a Mercedes right now." I didn't ask why he was driving this old beater. He continued. "I don't like to fight, but if they come at me.... Wife left me a couple years ago, ran off with another man. I thought about beating his ass, but I just let it go. The guy's dead now, anyway." He took a deep drag on his cigarette, through teeth the color of his fingers. "Women..." He rolled his bloodshot eyes. I agreed because, well, I was in survival mode.

"Let's get you to the mechanic."

I walked over to Erifnus, opened the door, and changed into

running shoes, just in case, but left my camera and overnight bag and notebooks in the back seat. I cranked up Erifnus's windows, locked her doors and gave her a goodbye pat, lest she never see me again. With a sigh I climbed into his car and began the next leg of this adventure. Seat belt for me, none for him.

He drove out of the lot and onto the street. I hoped this mission would not change from rescue to recovery. Images flashed through my mind. A body bag on a cold morgue slab. Cheryl. The grandkids. Would I ever see them again?

As we drove slowly toward the repair shop, the Samaritan kept talking through another cigarette. "Worked at a body shop fer forty years. Even painted commercial jets...dangerous stuff. Some guys got sick and died 'cause they took their masks off while painting. That jet paint hardened in their lungs and they suffocated. I'll be sixty-eight next birthday. Got cancer and the doc says my days are numbered. So I'm just glad to help folks when I can."

"Man, I really appreciate the ride...but I coulda walked. You got things to do...."

"Got nothin' better to do than helpin' a brother out."

I agreed.

We got to the mechanic, but he was busy until Monday. Erifnus would have to lay over. Worse, the mechanic's wrecker was stationed at an all-day off-road mud race. "Sorry," he said.

"That's okay, I'll call AAA." I whipped out my phone. The AAA agent reminded me that the tow was free for up to one hundred miles.

"You can get my car to Columbia?"

"Sure." Done deal. But the wait for a wrecker was two hours.

"I'll drive you back to your car," the Samaritan said.

"Oh, man, I can walk."

"Bullshit," he said. "Get in." I got in.

Erifnus was still there when we arrived, and the badass good Samaritan hung around the two hours we waited for the tow truck. I asked him if he minded if I took his picture. "No problem," he straightened up a bit. "Just don't use my real name. There are people wanna kill me." I believed him.

A big guy rolled up to us, riding a Harley chopper with a dramatic sunburst paint job. "Hey, I noticed the camera," he said. "I'm out shooting pictures of old barns. Know any good places?" I told him a few places to try. "Name's Curtis Plunk," he introduced himself. "People call me Curplunk." [rimshot]

My two new friends began a passionate conversation about choppers and cool paint jobs and gangs and fights and bars and the law.

The Samaritan finished his dozenth cigarette as a flatbed wrecker backed up to Erifnus. Jack the tow truck driver tipped the flatbed and cranked Erifnus onto its deck, chaining her down like a French criminal. I said goodbye to Curplunk, and turned to the Samaritan to hand him five bucks. He refused. "I don't take charity."

"It's for gas...or beer. Anyway, it's only five bucks." He refused.

Then I got an idea. I climbed the flatbed and dug a book out of Erifnus's backseat and scribbled on the title page: "Thanks for saving my life. There *are* good people in the world."

"Here," I handed him the paperback. "You'll be in the next book."

"Don't use my real name," he said. "People wanna kill me."

The tow truck rolled away from the Samaritan and Curplunk and Saint Louis, away from forgotten stories we'd found earlier in the week, none more obscure than the tale about two great American literary bookends who grew up on the same Saint Louis street.

Two Tom Cats, the Westminster Poets

They grew up a half block from each other. Two of the world's greatest purveyors of felinity—one associated with New Orleans cats, the other with London cats—spent their wonder years on Westminster Street. Both left this street more than a century ago, but the residue of genius remains. When Tennessee Williams and T.S. Eliot lived there, Westminster was a tony neighborhood bordering a world's fair park.

Eliot lived there first.

Thomas Stearns Eliot attended Smith Academy, the forerunner to Country Day School, an academy founded by his grandfather, who also co-founded Eliot Seminary, the forerunner to Washington University. Thomas studied at Harvard and the Sorbonne. At age twenty-six he ended up at Oxford and married a Cambridge governess. He became a British citizen at thirty-nine and renounced his American citizenship. Yet flickers of his youth emerged when he wrote that the "Missouri and the Mississippi have made a deeper impression on me than any other part of the world."

Although his ashes are scattered in East Coker, the British honor him with a stone inscription at Poets Corner in London's Westminster Abbey. Few Brits realize Eliot was born and raised at a different Westminster, a street in Saint Louis.

Tennessee Williams's father moved the family around a lot. They lived at several Saint Louis addresses, and came to Westminster Street sometime during Thomas Lanier Williams III's youth, a time of anguish and turmoil. His father, a frustrated shoe salesman, ruled the household with angry intimidation, and kept his mentally ill daughter, Tom's sister Rose, imprisoned upstairs. Tom used his experience at Soldan High School to pen *The Glass Menagerie*. He went to the University of Missouri School of Journalism and then everything went south from there. During a stellar playwriting career Williams returned home a few times—once to receive an honorary doctorate from Mizzou. My parents hosted him for that weekend. I was too young to be impressed by one of history's greatest playwrights. He came back to Saint Louis one last time to be buried at Calvary Cemetery and await his beloved sister Rose, who would join him three years later.

Eliot never came back.

In the shadow of the Chase Park Plaza Hotel, Westminster Street stretches from the park to a burned out '50s jazz district called Gaslight Square, so cool it was hot, where Miles Davis mesmerized drunken white people, barely masking his disdain, and Kerouac and Lenny Bruce held court. It's a street where I lived as a fledgling copywriter for the ad agency that created the brand for Busch Beer. I had no heady part in promoting the beer, certainly not in creating it. But I drank enough of it to fill an elevator shaft with piss.

Gaslight Square is long gone, victim of greed and drugs and whorehouses and crime and the fear that comes from it. Somehow the stately mansions on that street survived.

When I lived there in the '70s, I often awoke to gunfire. The mansions were struggling from the neglect that happens when landlords won't invest in upkeep. Families wouldn't risk living there, for good reason. The neighborhood had turned apocalyptic outside my bedroom window. Prison-like iron bars blocked the window's fire escape.

One morning I went out to the curb to start my car, turned the ignition key and nothing happened. I opened the hood to find my battery gone. I missed work for an entire morning, riding buses, tracking down a battery, installing it. Next morning, I went out to start my car. Nothing. My new acquaintance, the thief, got a brand new battery. What a dumb ass, I cursed myself. From that day until I left the neighborhood, I parked the car behind a backyard fence, a tight squeeze through the alley and a narrow gate, but safe from the clutches of the grab-and-go auto parts merchants.

Still, the mansion I shared with six other tenants showed the grandeur of the Gilded Age. Gas lamps on the walls had been converted to electric, but they still wore tiny linen lampshades. Every room felt the warmth of a fireplace, even the bedrooms. The upstairs floors had been divided into apartments. Mine had a walk-in closet with an octagonal window, and a poem, an ode to the closet window, scrawled on the closet wall and signed by Ogden Nash. I never wrote down that poem, and can't find anything similar in Nash's anthology. It was an unrecorded one-of-a-kind poem, and if, in the intervening years, it was painted over or the wall was knocked out, the poem is gone for good. What a dumb ass, I cursed myself again.

Today the neighborhood has stabilized, and life along the street is safer, like it was back when two young poets lived in houses on either side of the Ogden Nash poem.

The playground for Westminster's privileged children is Forest Park, big enough to fit New York City's Central Park in its lush verdure. On these grounds, the 1904 World's Fair unfolded, surrounded by the several hundred Gilded Age dwellings that survive today.

As the tow truck carried us home, I thought about that big park, and how it changed your life.

Fast Food First

More than any other spot on earth, Saint Louis is the birthplace of fast food.

In terms of speed and convenience, Saint Louis has made the single biggest impact on your gastrointestinal tract since cave people first burned meat, more than White Castle or pizza jockeys or Cap'n Crunch or Dairy Queen, more than McDonald's.

Argue if you want. You can point to ancient Romans who popped into a popina to get quickie servings of wine, food and other earthly delights. You can nod to the Earl of Sandwich, whose namesake innovation loafed in obscurity until more than a century after his death. You can thank the ancient Turks who stuffed the portable pita.

And of course, we owe a debt of gratitude to the ancient Mayans who invented the tortilla, which eventually encouraged Americans to think outside the border.

All these primitive packages—the taco, the pita, the sandwich—evolved into a menu offering 1.2 billion alternatives for instant grab-and-go gastro gratification. And while most of the following examples of success have a thousand fathers, Saint Louis is secure as the undisputed heavyweight champion of the fast food world. Nowhere in history did so many shortcuts to food foist themselves on the world at the same time in the same spot. Forest Park is the grandmother of modern convenience, the birthplace of fast food.

Here is compelling evidence.

Some historian will point out that the hot dog was created at Coney Island, not in Saint Louis. Likely it was neither, since Germans have been eating bread-wrapped dachshund sausages for centuries. No matter. The importance of the hot dog sizzled with the introduction of the hot dog in a bun. Some say that unique bread package was introduced by a German at the Saint Louis World's Fair (aka the 1904 Louisiana Exposition). But a decade earlier, a German who owned the Saint Louis Browns baseball team began the tradition of ball park hot dogs. The sausage gets top billing, but if you're talking portability, the bun is the star. Fast food.

Still skeptical?

Try this experiment: Boil some tea. Now, drink it fast. Horrors, think proper Victorians, who know that sipping hot tea is a time-honored royal ritual that shouldn't be rushed. So when somebody dropped ice cubes into tea, it stirred a revolution as habit forming as any tea party. This time around, the guilty party emanated from the 1904 Louisiana Exposition, and iced tea took the world by a storm that's still brewing.

There's a pattern here. Saint Louisans didn't invent the food. They just made it easier to eat. Portable. Efficient. Fast.

Whole wheat has been around since before cultivation. But when a Kansas farmer developed a way to keep whole wheat from turning rancid, a Saint Louis entrepreneur named William Danforth packaged it as Ralston Whole Wheat Cereal and sold it in Saint Louis grocery stores.

While the happy meal was created by a Kansas City ad agency, the idea—first called the Fun Meal—was envisioned by a Saint Louisan. Such recent innovation only pays homage to the beginning of fast food more than a hundred years ago in Saint Louis.

Oh, everybody plays a part. For example, Chillicothe, Missouri, touts the world's first commercial bread slicer. But a Saint Louis invention—a collapsible bread tray—kept bread slices together until they could be wrapped.

Ravioli existed before the 1904 World's Fair. But toasting ravioli at the fair made them easier to carry in your pocket.

You think you had problems with M&Ms. Think about holding ice cream in your palms. The 1904 World's Fair came to the rescue, and *voilà*…the cone. It seems so simple. Ice cream got a geometric boost into the fast food era. Never mind that somebody has recently found a two-century-old engraving of a woman eating what looks like ice cream in a cone. And yes, a guy patented a cone mold in 1903, and an earlier London cookbook told about putting ice cream in a wafer cone. No matter. The cone came into its own during the Saint Louis fair.

The implications boggle the mind. The 1904 World's Fair popularized peanut butter, first patented in 1895 by John Harvey Kellogg. This led, eventually, to the phenomenon we know as Elvis. Just as important, the portability of the peanut butter and jelly sandwich launched a resurgence in the carpet cleaning industry.

That same world's fair claims credit for introducing Dr. Pepper, cotton candy and the Hamburg steak in a bun. The invention of the hamburger has many mothers, from Texas to New Haven to Hamburg, New York. But the world learned about the portable burger in a bun from its Forest Park debut.

Clarence Birdseye, the father of frozen fish, was born on the East Coast. But Saint Louisan Harry Hussmann provided Birdseye the first frozen food case, shortly after the Saint Louis World's Fair. Three decades later, Hussmann scored again on the convenience meter, providing shoppers with the first self-service frozen food display case, and the first self-serve display cases for meat, dairy and produce. These frozen food cases launched the chilling invasion of pot pies and frozen pizzas.

About the same time, Pet Milk Company, the Saint Louis creator of Our Pet Evaporated Cream, began irradiating evaporated milk to kill germs, long before the process became common in the food industry.

Pets of every stripe enjoy a support system of Saint Louis-based fast food. The folks at Purina didn't invent dog food. But Cat Chow, yes, and an ark full of other chows, too, including that happy meal for young dogs, Puppy Chow.

The city introduced soft drinks named Vess and Howdy and 7-Up, Provel cheese, prosperity sandwiches, gooey butter cake, and the precursor to Dairy Queen's blizzard—the concrete. In honor of this rich heritage, Hardee's moved its headquarters to Saint Louis in 2001. Well, maybe that's not why Hardee's chose Saint Louis. But they're here.

Some folks think fast food is one of the signs that civilization is nearing the end. If this is the case, don't blame Saint Louis. After all, the city had nothing to do with inventing Twinkies or turducken, or the corn dog, for that matter, which evolved during the 1940s in Illinois or Minnesota or Texas, depending on who's telling the history of this battered pig on a stick.

If that's too much heartburn for you, wash down a Tums, a 1928 Saint Louis invention.

Even the original fast food got some face time at the Saint Louis World's Fair during a speech by horticulturalist J.T. Stinson, who first uttered that famous phrase you can still hear in your mother's voice:

"An apple a day keeps the doctor away."

Erifnus Never Met Lenny Bruce

From the tow truck's shotgun seat, looking through a shoebox-sized side mirror at my car in chains, I had time to reflect on the journey with Erifnus.

Her air conditioner long since lost its cool. She has no GPS to assure our course, but her radio still plucks the forecast from the sky, and she trusts me to read the thumb-worn maps in her shotgun seat to guide us past danger. Or into it.

She accepts her fate with quiet dignity.

You wouldn't pick her for World's Greatest Car. Her headlamps have filmy cataracts. Her doors are dented, and she suffered the insult of a salvage title after her complexion was pocked by a hailstorm. She smells of antifreeze. Her transmission whines. Her brakes squeal. She's blue-collar in a red dress. But she's a keeper.

I met her in a car lot seventeen years ago. She was sleek and new and lipstick red, and even though I didn't realize it at the time, she would set course on a journey no other car has made: She's driven every mile of every road on Missouri's highway map. She's felt every crack in Missouri's pavement.

Her name reflects the auto company that built her, a company that folded and faded in the rearview mirror, leaving Erifnus Caitnop to fend for herself. Yet she remains strong, reaching an age when 99 percent of her peers have been pounded into refrigerator magnets.

With little planning, Erifnus and I began a string of shortcuts that lasted beyond a dozen years, a journey that left our tire tracks along every inch of state-maintained pavement, every county road from AA to ZZ, thousands of miles of gravel and dirt, trouble and stories. Tracking those roads was like mowing a 64,000 square mile lawn.

Erifnus and I covered more miles than the combined travels of Marco Polo and Magellan, Columbus and Zebulon Pike, Lewis and Clark and Dr. Livingstone. The only difference between us and those other explorers is that their amazing feats of bravery changed the world. We just drove around. A lot.

For what? Now Erifnus was strapped to a truck bed, and as I looked out the tow truck window, life's random questions kept surfacing: Is there really an entertainer named Joe Buck Yourself? Lenny Bruce would not be surprised.

Civility is on life support.

Technology hits us so fast from every angle we all have PTSD. And we've chosen sides. Red rover, blue rover, if you ain't like me don't come over.

We emerge from our safe houses to a middle ground—schools and churches, shops and malls and highways—where clashes of rage and carnage can trigger at any moment, at any speed.

So we seek safety wherever we can find it, retreating to our tribes, our colors, our neighborhoods. On the way we hit the drive-thru for a buttermilk cinnamon pretzel iced latte, then curl up at home in the scent of a candle called Freshly Signed Divorce Papers.

An avalanche of inventions bombard us on TV, offering to spare us from the chore of survival. Canned sandwiches. Electric scissors. Automatic dog ball throwers and TV remote beer bottle openers, self-stirring mugs and selfie sticks. Buy a bed that makes itself, and an automatic banana slicer. Clap off your bedroom light, and Roomba your dirty floor. And when all this shit wears you out, take a nap on your inflatable tie.

From your safe place, order all this stuff via app and it will be dropped on your doorstep.

I was still a couple of hours from my doorstep.

Jack the tow truck driver barreled toward Columbia, eyes alert. No cell phone distraction. Refreshing. Jack was all business as he carried my car to its destination. I wondered how often he hauled cars with their drivers riding along. I sensed that he preferred to drive without passengers, like the hundred truck drivers we'll pass along this route, cowboys at heart, diesel jockeys on the open road. It's easier than branding cattle. Jack didn't look like a cowboy. His cowboy hat was a ball cap, his footwear steel-toed work boots, his red beard flecked with enough gray to betray impending retirement.

He's probably picked up a thousand wrecks on this Godforsaken highway, seen enough dead bodies to stack on his flatbed like cord wood. I don't know. I didn't ask.

I would spare the small talk with Jack the tow truck driver.

In the side mirror Erifnus balanced on the flatbed. She bit into the wind like she always does. But her wheels were not turning. She was racking up miles while her gears sat still. Her gurney, this flatbed, was rushing her to a trusted family physician who would excise her alternator like a bad gall bladder, and fix her with a new one. For Jack the tow truck driver this delivery is just a job. For me it's another setback in caring for an aging family member. Some folks would give up on her. They've told me so. "Get a new car. New car smell. And GPS."

But my allegiance runs deep.

This 1999 Pontiac Sunfire became my Trigger, my Lassie, my Old

Faithful. She's crossed Skull Lick Creek and Rabbit Head Creek. She's climbed Long Tater Hill, descended to Devil's Well and the Little Grand Canyon. And three Toad Sucks, for Godsakes. Oh, and the Garden of Eden. No shit. The real Garden of Eden, according to Mormon prophet Joseph Smith.

She's witnessed the toaster-trading frenzy at OcToasterFest and the fruits of mass castration at the Testicle Festival, and a mineral springs with two iron pipes that deliver separate healing waters to Democrats and Republicans.

She's outlived the company that made her. But I wouldn't trade her for the Mona Lisa.

This car won an Emmy.

Oh, I went along for the ride, but the car was the star of the show.

Erifnus doesn't care. Even as she nurtures a small patch of rust beneath her passenger door, she's a workhorse, performing like a gymnast as her driver shifts through her five forward gears. She handles like a thoroughbred through curves and mud, dodging texters and tweeters and assholes infected by road rage and drunks and texters and squirrels and deer and terrapins and texters and assholes.

Erifnus remains non-judgmental. She groans if I grind her gears, and screeches when I slam on the brakes. Yet most of the time she's responsive, and dependable. She's dauntless on dirt roads and fearless among forty-ton truckships on the interstate.

Blame her brushes with danger on driver error.

I drove into danger because I was curious. Erifnus did it because she had no choice.

I never planned to drive every road. But in jobs requiring constant travel, I quickly tired of seeing the same old scenery along the interstates. So Erifnus started taking the back roads. And I kept track, wearing out a stack of highway maps.

I kept sifting through my mental Rolodex for topics of conversation with the tow truck driver. Nothing.

Oh, I could tell him about two nights ago, when I thought I would die before Erifnus did. It was late night when we stopped at a South Saint Louis convenience store for gasoline. As two men got out of a pickup truck and followed me into the store, an ominous feeling rushed over me like a rancid fart. Bright lights and cameras didn't feel safe enough; ten dozen twerks lurk within a mile of this cash register. Walking dead. They need money for meth. The lady behind the counter was pleasant, helpful. She told me a backroad shortcut to my next stop. I thanked her and left, expecting to read her name next morning in the crime section of the newspaper.

Convenience store clerk may be the second most dangerous job in America. It was the last job for Shirley Drouet. Nobody thinks much about Shirley Drouet anymore, besides her loved ones. But her story affected me deeply. She was a forty-three-year-old convenience store clerk in Port Arthur, Texas, working the graveyard shift on April 20, 1980 when two men entered the store. At the counter, a dispute over a six-pack led to murder. J.D. "Cowboy" Autry was convicted of shooting Shirley Drouet in the forehead, right between her eyes. News reports said her heart kept pumping and swelled her head with blood. Autry claimed the other guy did it. On the way out the door they murdered a priest and maimed another innocent bystander. Autry was sentenced to death. He wanted his execution televised, even though he claimed it would be a sissified lethal injection. He made clear his preference for hanging or beheading because it would be more manly. Of course, nothing is more manly than shooting an unarmed innocent woman between the eyes.

I rubbed my eyes. Why would I bring up a story like that?

Jack the tow truck driver was accustomed to driving in silence, and so was I. Aside from a few curious reporters who rode shotgun with Erifnus and me, we mostly drove alone on these long treks into the middle of nowhere. Cheryl, who married me forty years ago, tolerates my travels, but has no desire to spend whole days crisscrossing county roads for the simple reason that they exist, checking off an alphabet soup of road signs, intent on discovering nothing in particular. Our two daughters have real lives of their own. They agree with their mother about my foolish compulsion to take needless chances in the middle of nowhere.

As for Queenie Beanie and her brother Baskin Robinson, our Yorkshire Terriers, they had no interest in travel, unless they could escape through the back fence and change their names to something respectable, like Wolf. And pee freely.

The tow truck raced toward home. I looked into the mirror at Erifnus. Queenie Beanie and Baskin Robinson would have loved our travels earlier this morning, before the car broke down. I would've felt compelled to keep them on a tight leash while we roamed Bellefontaine Cemetery lest they try to mark their territory on the headstones of Saint Louis legends. A smile came as I envisioned Baskin Robinson pissing on the headstone of the father of Budweiser. Nothing against Budweiser. Hell, I've pissed a lot of it myself.

The Last Man to Beat Bill Hickok

Bellefontaine Cemetery is a history lesson. I'd seen this sprawling marble orchard from the air every time I landed at Lambert International Airport. But I'd never visited the graves, in the shade of 5,000 trees, including three state champions.

Confederate General Sterling Price lies here. So does Susan Blow, the American Mother of Kindergarten, the explorer William Clark, teacher and abolitionist John Berry Meachum, poet Sara Teasdale, and a litany of storied Saint Louis names: Barnes and Benton and Busch, Eads, Maritz, McDonnell and Danforth, Lambert, Lemp, Wainwright and Mallinkrodt. Eleven Medal of Honor recipients.

Bellefontaine Cemetery holds stories that forged America. Good. Bad. Wild, like the story of Captain Bill Massie, the world's greatest riverboat gambler. His unmarked grave belies his prowess. In the parlors of his riverboats, Captain Bill Massie could read the deadest poker face. His ability to count cards was the same skill he used to memorize every bend and snag on the treacherous Missouri River. From the wheelhouse he could read the signs on the water's surface—ripples, colors, stream lines—and tell whether they hid snags or sawyers, planters or preachers, those sneaky hazards lurking beneath the waterline, closer to Hell, and he knew how they changed depending on weather. Other pilots paid Massie so they could follow his course, and sometimes he'd lead a string of six or eight riverboats. In sixty years of piloting, Massie sank only one boat, when the giant sternwheeler Montana hit the Wabash Bridge at Saint Charles.

After Massie retired from the river, luck dealt him a strange hand. On August 2, 1876, Massie sat at a poker table in Deadwood, South Dakota, with Wild Bill Hickok and two other players. On this day Hickok's back wasn't against the wall, as was his custom, and Massie apparently refused to change seats with Hickok not once but twice.

Massie was winning and Hickok was losing. In Hickok's last game,
as Massie laid down his winning hand, an assassin's bullet smashed
into the back of Wild Bill's head. The bullet exited through Hickok's
cheek and lodged in Massie's wrist. Wild Bill's fists still clutched his
last poker hand with two pair—aces and eights—known to modern
poker players as the dead man's hand. Massie carried that bullet in his
wrist for thirty-four years, and took it to his grave in Bellefontaine
Cemetery.

All of these iconic Saint Louisans buried in close proximity share
one thing in common: each knew that the lifeblood of this land flows
through the confluence of two great American rivers.

Adjacent to the protestant Bellefontaine Cemetery, I found Dred
Scott's grave in catholic Calvary Cemetery. Scott has two headstones,
one explaining the landmark Supreme Court decision denying his
freedom from slavery. The other is his traditional headstone, its top
covered with pennies, all heads up, a thousand faces of Abraham Lincoln
reassuring Dred that emancipation is real, or at least Constitutional.

In that same cemetery—not far from an eighteen-acre corner of
virgin prairie with the most diversity of bees in the city—Thomas
Lanier Williams lies beside his dear sister. On the back of his
headstone under his more familiar name, Tennessee Williams, is a
line from his stage play *Camino Real*: "The violets in the mountains
have broken the rocks." Nearby are writer Kate Chopin, and William
Tecumseh Sherman, remembered more passionately in Atlanta than
in his hometown of Saint Louis.

Saint Peters Cemetery in Velda Village holds the remains of Allen
Britt and Willie Lyons. You may think you don't know these guys.
But you do. You know why Frankie shot Johnny. He done her wrong.
Johnny was actually seventeen-year-old Allen Britt, and twenty-two-
year-old dancer Frankie Baker caught up with him in a barroom in
the rough and tumble Tenderloin district of downtown Saint Louis.
Artist Thomas Hart Benton depicted the shooting in a mural at the
Missouri State Capitol, a mural that survived protests about Benton's
vivid scenes.

And Willie Lyons? You know him as Billy, one of two men
who gambled late on Christmas Eve, 1895 at a tavern on Delmar
Boulevard in Saint Louis. They were shooting craps, and Willie swore
Lee Shelton threw an eight. Shelton said it was a seven. They argued,

and Shelton shot Willie so bad the bullet broke the bartender's glass, according to the ballad "Staggerlee." In reality, Shelton was a high-profile pimp in the Tenderloin District, and he argued politics with his friend Willie. Willie snatched Shelton's hat, and Shelton, in no mood for teasing, shot Lyons.

In nearby Hillsdale, I found Greenwood Cemetery. Conch shells accent some graves in this oldest African American cemetery in the city. The conchs represent a Caribbean tradition: the spirit of the sea, from which we came, to which we will return. This hallowed ground teetered on the edge of obliteration until a few determined descendants and archaeologists uncovered its history, including the final resting place of Harriett Scott, Dred Scott's wife. The cemetery dodged the bulldozer.

I suspect my dogs would have hated today, since the car broke down. And they wouldn't care much for Jack the tow truck driver. But Baskin and Queenie would've loved yesterday.

It started with steak.

⸙

The Gateway to the West doesn't have stockyards like its western sisters Saint Joseph and Sedalia and Kansas City. Still, one prime Saint Louis cattle drive steers my tastebuds to Lindbergh Boulevard.

Kreis' Restaurant has been kicking steak house butt longer than I've been alive. Seriously, my friends Ruth and Cris think this steak is better than any chain. Oh, the dining room's atmosphere may be a bit too upper crust for comfort, a rich interior with dark wood paneling and deep red trim, sporting oil paintings of ships and hunts, all in gilded frames, spotlighted for effect. The snooty clientele and assertive butler service fit hand-in-glove, causing an otherwise restrained pinky to stick straight out from a cocktail glass. But really, a restaurant's décor is just a frame for the painting. Let's talk marbling. These midwestern steers and heifers practiced a rigorous regimen to develop superior shanks and shoulders, rumps and loins. Their posthumous reward is to hang for a couple of weeks to finish their conditioning, and earn the status symbol that less than three in a hundred bovines achieve: prime.

The rare three-inch thick prime rib with a twice baked potato and fresh creamed spinach left me just enough room for warm apple strudel, a family recipe with Granny Smith apples, cassia cinnamon, baked in flaky pastry served warm topped with a drizzle of brandy crème sauce.

Okay I lied. I couldn't finish that monstrous meal, and I asked for a doggy bag. As a patron of less regal stature, I was not ashamed to save uneaten portions of my ample prime rib and take a bag of bovine home to my neighbor's canines, who truly appreciated the gesture. It appeals to the wolf in every dog. And every dog has the instincts of *canis lupus* at its core, no matter how much breeding has altered your pooch's outward appearance.

For the most remarkable display of selective breeding this side of Windsor Castle, Erifnus took me to Queeny Park, where old Jarville mansion morphed into the American Kennel Club Museum of the Dog. There's no taxidermy in this doozy of a dog house since the subject of this museum is the greatest animal ever: your dog, and hundreds like it. For dogs who like looking at dog pictures, the museum puts out the mat, a veritable Met for a mutt, exhibiting spiggydogg artwork dedicated to man's best friend. The museum originated in New York more than 330 dog years ago, an effort by the Westminster Kennel Club to "improve the life of the dog." By 1985, the museum outgrew its Manhattan quarters, and moved here.

Alas, we're losing the dog museum. The American Kennel Club is yanking its leash, and walking its dog paraphernalia back to New York. Son of a bitch.

Feeling wild, we drove down the road to see some pups. Not just any pups, these are the children of the canids from which every other breed springs. Wolf pups.

The Edge of Wild

The howl of the wolf fell silent in Missouri's remnant wilds when westward expansion pushed wolves from their habitat. Because humans and wolves compete for lamb chops, chicken and veal, they never mix well, behaving like Black Friday brawlers at Walmart. But in one local neighborhood, the howling wolf comes alive. Calling itself "the alternative to extinction," the Endangered Wolf Center sits just off Route 66 in Eureka. It began back in 1971, shepherded by Carol and Marlin Perkins. Marlin was director of the Saint Louis Zoo at the time.

Five Mexican gray wolf pups were born recently at the center, to proud parents Perkins and Abby. Only forty-two such Mexican gray wolves live outside captivity in the wilds of New Mexico and Arizona. Along with Abby and Perkins, the other residents—Anna, Apache, Bob, Frijole, Rocky and Picaron—are doing their best to propagate the species. Nearby, one lone red wolf named Inapa walks on three legs, due to a mysterious injury to her left foreleg.

Human contact is kept to a strict minimum. But from a distance the wolves strike a presence, and a chorus.

A full moon peeked over rugged hills. Around a campfire visitors heard wolf tales—not the tales your mother read to you. Suddenly from the woods came a full-throated concert—the world's most sincere *a capella* voices sang in nine-part harmony. As most dog lovers can attest, it's easy to get a canine to sing. The howls you hear from this choir are the genesis.

This nonprofit center deserves credit for helping avoid extinction for wolf species. But like the wolf, the wolf center is endangered, and limited resources jeopardize this menagerie of canids who depend on the kindness of strangers. Some folks are just fine with that, wondering why we protect wolves. I know why we protect them, every time I think about Baskin and Queenie.

My pups tried to teach me a lot of things: how to eat poop and lick my balls, and more importantly, they taught me how to love unconditionally. No religion. No politics. Just pure love.

Not a mile from the wolves, as the crow flies, Rio slept through high-flying dreams. Rio is a retired actor who grew up performing at Reptile Gardens in Florida. When he arrived at the World Bird Sanctuary, his rap sheet said he was "territorial and an unreliable flier." But the folks at the sanctuary saw promise in this bright red macaw with stunning blue and green trim. Now this talkative teen lives here with Nemo and Guapo and the other parrots, not to mention owls and eagles, and the world's fastest animal, a peregrine falcon.

It's no accident the World Bird Sanctuary sits so close to the Endangered Wolf Center. This bird haven was hatched in 1977 by ornithologist Walter C. Crawford, Jr., who worked with Marlin Perkins. Crawford recognized a need to care for birds of prey, especially injured raptors, and exotic birds illegally smuggled into the United States. His hospital takes patients with broken wings and aviary ailments. But the worst malady suffered by incoming patients is neglect. The parrot rehab and placement program has successfully relocated more than 900 birds, including abandoned parrots who outlived their welcome, or outlived their owners. Parrots live a long time. And they remember things. Standing next to these amazing birds is the closest I've come to a pet who can pronounce my name. Up close, I saw eagles and owls who survived gunshot wounds, and red-tailed hawks who survived tangles with cars.

Bad cars.

———— ⁂ ————

In the tow truck's rearview mirror, Erifnus rested uncomfortably, chained to the speeding flatbed.

"Ever been to Branson?" I broke the silence. Not sure why I picked Branson as a topic, but riding shotgun in a tow truck seemed comfortable to pursue this line of questioning.

"Been fishing at the lakes around there," Jack the tow truck driver answered, "but I haven't been on the Branson strip since Boxcar Willie died."

"Yeah, Boxcar Willie was great."

"Yep."

More silence.

I started to tell a Branson story, but wasn't sure how the driver would react. Back when Branson was growing so fast it had stretch marks, Boxcar Willie ran a lively show from his theater on the Branson Strip. Country Music Boulevard was fresh on the national scene, capturing the hearts of fans and wry smiles from critics, even a president's wanton fascination. And petty thieves came out of the woods like ticks. That seedy story wouldn't sit well with some folks.

But it was on my mind.

Back Door Branson

It bothered him like a gnat, the red dot on his chest. He knew it wasn't a rash because the dot danced in a tight circle on the outside of his grimy wife-beater undershirt. He tried a few times to brush the red dot away as he climbed out of the steep wooded ravine and reached a long row of garage doors, storage sheds where renters pack old furniture and vehicles and junk. And maybe valuables. He picked a door and from his pocket he pulled out a small crowbar to bust the padlock. As he wedged his tool against the lock, a violent force pounded him to the ground, knocking him out.

He regained consciousness lying face down in gravel, hands cuffed behind his back. He could see only his captor's baggy black cargo pants stuffed into paratrooper boots.

"Can I have a cigarette?" he asked the boots.

"You picked the wrong day for a break-in," a voice atop the boots ignored his request.

"How'd you find me?"

"We've been watching you since you entered this ravine," boots replied. "I jumped you from the roof."

On the other side of this low row of storage sheds, President Bill Clinton's motorcade paraded down Branson's main drag. The Secret Service had secured the route for days. A sniper atop the storage sheds had taken aim as the burglar climbed the ravine.

"I wondered what that red dot was," the burglar was resigned to another stint in jail. "Can I have a cigarette?"

Not everybody who visits Branson is a thief or a president.

I was neither when I first visited that tiny Ozark hamlet. Now it attracts eight million visitors a year, mainly because Branson is a candy store for the country ear. And eye. Miles of neon along the main drag announce theaters and hotels, restaurants and go-kart tracks, pottery shops and T-shirt vendors, and museums that have nothing to do with Branson or the Ozarks or country music. The Branson strip looks a lot like the commercial boulevards in Maui, without the ocean or the weather. Maui and Branson do, however, share a propensity to erect gaudy signs.

Beauty is in the eye of the beholder. Nowhere on earth does that phrase ring true more than Branson, a town built on the banks of a river, and the backs of fishermen, and their wallets. Seventy years ago when Branson was small and sunset stopped most fishing, locals would entertain fishermen with hillbilly music and homespun humor. Over the years, other entertainers flocked to the area's remote beauty, and its fish. They built bigger and bigger monuments to their music, and the town ventured onto the glittery sands of hype and greed. The town grew so fast it became a subject of a *60 Minutes* story about the safety of many of the new buildings. Branson fought back hard and secured the confidence of its target audience.

I have a love-hate relationship with Branson Nation. I love them. They hate me. But the tow truck driver wouldn't care about all this horseshit, so why tell him? And if I did tell the story and he got angry I might be compelled to jump out of the tow truck at 75 miles per hour and then what would become of Erifnus?

The thought was unsettling, more unsettling than most Branson behind-the-scenes stories, which mostly remain untold, probably for good reason.

Beautiful scenery still exists along the drive into Branson, away from billboards where the Mark Twain National Forest covers both sides of the highway. There, Missouri's old tourism slogan sings: *Where the Rivers Run.* The Branson glitterati hated that slogan. Hated it. It had no relevance to their country music theaters on the strip. I had one opportunity to persuade Branson Nation they could turn the phrase into a positive. After all, a trio of man-made lakes surrounds the city, so this is where the rivers come to vacation.

Branson didn't bite. They'll just have to make their millions without my help.

A disciple of James Taylor, Erifnus Caitnop hates the pace along Country Music Boulevard. Hurts her motor to go so slow. So I showed her another side of Branson.

We left the glitter and headed to old town, driving down Main Street, Chick's Barber Shop on one side, Dick's 5 and Dime on the other. Chick's and Dick's is a metaphor of sorts for Branson's struggle with the reality of human desires. A couple blocks away is a karaoke bar where some of the show dancers gather after hours, a rainbow coalition in deep red country.

To fulfill the two most basic human desires, the town built a monument to shopping and tax breaks: Branson Landing, a rural version of an urban renewal project. Branson Landing sprawls along the banks of Lake Taneycomo, a thirty-second drive from old town. It employs all the latest shopping center tricks to please the eye and relax your credit card in places like Jock's Nitch or Victoria's Secret.

Branson Landing is a far cry from the run-down appearance of the old lakefront, which offered amenities for campers and fishermen, but not much bling. Now, the Landing helps attract conventions.

Branson built another new landing, too, a modern spacious airport. Shortly after the runways opened, a Southwest Airlines jet from Chicago to Dallas made a scheduled night stop at Branson. It mistakenly landed at the wrong airport, the much smaller—but brightly lit—runway at the nearby College of the Ozarks.

The jet screeched to a stop just before plunging off a cliff at the end of the runway, and passengers deplaned with a story to tell about God, their copilot.

As the nonessential copilot on Jack's tow truck, I dozed off and fell into a recurring dream: Jesus sneaked into Branson. He pulled his hair up under a John Deere ball cap, threw on a shabby baby blue polyester leisure suit and rode an old red Western Auto Flyer bicycle down Country Music Boulevard to revel in the love and tolerance among His flock.

His disguise worked, since His flock would be looking for Him in a flowing white robe.

He bought a ticket to a gospel show and there to His surprise He heard more pleas for military prowess than for fishes and loaves. At the next theater He cried when an actor portrayed a sad old man, then made it clear he didn't like snakes and spiders, and at least one political figure. Jesus made a note to Saint Francis.

Waking from that strange dream, I wiped the drool from the corner of my mouth and glanced at Jack the tow truck driver to see if he'd noticed I fell asleep. It didn't matter to Jack. Or Erifnus. As our tow truck cruised toward her mechanic, other drivers thought we were headed for the junkyard. They saw an old used car chained to a flatbed. They didn't know her story. They couldn't see beyond the parking lot dings and the hail damage, the dents and scratches from hauling a canoe. They couldn't see her backseat, a disheveled file cabinet preserving an accurate record of her wake.

Erifnus didn't care. She has passed them all, one way or another, somewhere along her 290,000 miles. And she's not done passing them, this Best Pontiac Ever. Anyway, none of them have ridden on the Toad

Suck Ferry or spent the weekend at turkey camp for Godsakes.

But Erifnus has.

Wish we were at turkey camp, instead of hauling Erifnus home. Jack the tow truck driver probably would like turkey camp.

"Hunt turkey?" I asked.

"Yup." Silence.

Deep in the woods, our turkey camp is the perfect venue to hunt turkey. But the turkeys are safe, mostly. The closest most camper-hunters get to birds happens when folks take a pull on the fifth of Wild Turkey passing from hand to hand around the campfire, bathed in the warm glow of bluegrass ballads. And every morning in the wee hours, when the fire burns low and the last refrain of "Let's Talk Dirty in Hawaiian" fades into the woods, and the Big Dipper sets over the horizon, two or three hunters wake to hunt, greeting a dozen pickers and grinners stumbling toward bed. It's a changing of the guard.

Turkey camp forces attendees to choose their passion: Get up early or stay up late. Hunt or hoot. It's a metaphor for lifestyle.

I generally hang around the hooters.

One morning I crawled out of my tent as one hunter returned with a pair of squirrels he'd bagged. He cleaned the rodents and prepared them for the evening meal.

I'd never tasted squirrel.

I felt entitled. For years my tomato plants have fattened the squirrels who roost in my backyard trees. Payback.

So when the dinner bell rang, I sampled a tree rat. "Delicious," I complimented the chef. Later that night as we picked and grinned around a giant campfire, I remarked about the feast. "Squirrel was tasty. Meat was fatty. Reminded me of bacon."

"Well, dumbass," the cook said, "that's because I seasoned it with bacon."

My fork had only snagged hog side. Closest I came to tasting squirrel was a strip of squirrel-infused bacon.

Jack the tow truck driver would think I'm a dumbass, too, I suspect. But Jack has no idea the places this car has been. Within minutes of this truck's giant spinning tires, Erifnus has crossed Lost Creek, Skull Lick and Skunk Branch, passed Unanimous School and Wide Awake School, Washbowl Hollow, the Whosau Trail, and the Hoozaw River, Beaver Slide and Gunboat Landing and Slingtown, named for heavy imbibing of a drink called gin sling. She's been through La Charrette, where Daniel Boone died. She's passed Devil's Boot Cave and Western Orphan Asylum and Emmaus Asylum for Epileptics and Idiots, White Way Camp and Shake Rag, so called because the residents danced a lot in ragged clothing.

The stories behind this strange nomenclature would be lost, were it not for Eugenia Harrison, who dutifully recorded these unique appellations and the tales of their creation. It must have been a tedious project, back in 1943. I can't imagine anybody driving all of these roads to uncover their stories.

Jack the tow truck driver doesn't care. Neither does Erifnus.

Sure, she's had a few minor breakdowns. Like today. But she's a stalwart. In the rearview mirror she looked strange, not accustomed to riding. This was the longest ride she's hitched since the week she was born, when an auto transport trailer delivered her to Columbia. Since then she has racked up the stats of a hall of famer.

On her journey she's stopped at 8,277 cafés and restaurants, greasy spoons, diners and dives. She's bathed in the glow of a hundred campfires and stood guard outside 800 motel rooms. She's catalogued the dead, enduring stops at a thousand historic sites and cemeteries. She's cringed at the living, pinballing past 4.2 billion front yard artifacts on display—old refrigerators and washing machines and rusty cars mounted on cinder blocks. Almost every drive down a beautiful road inevitably led past at least one yard full of junk, so the first working title for this exploration became *Please, God, Let This Be a Yard Sale*.

She was a regular witness to my most frequent discomfort: Out of necessity I've watered damn near every "State Maintenance Ends" road sign while Erifnus idled in the gravel. It's a practical matter. Every day of our journey, in the minutes before dawn's early light, I'd fortify myself with a water tower of coffee from whatever roadhouse woke me, then leave civilization's handy indoor plumbing in the rearview mirror. After zigzagging back roads for two hours, we'd reach a remote spot where the pavement ends, and Erifnus would stop to let me disgorge my hydrant. One morning, standing beside one of 4,000 State Maintenance Ends signs, the angel and the devil on my shoulders debated naming this book *Pissing All Over Missouri*. We left that salty suggestion in the damp underbrush, since the title would raise questions about my love for this "land of the giant canoes," warts and all.

Erifnus refueled 761 times, gulped forty-one oil changes, wore through a dozen brake shoes, five batteries, two windshields, two side mirrors, four mufflers, two radiators, three starters, and finally, one clutch. She's been sidelined by two dozen flat tires, and her donut spare has traveled more miles than your neighbor's Lexus. Now she's taking a $250 tow truck ride to get a $20 alternator.

She was stopped nine times by the Missouri State Highway Patrol. Mostly she was guilty of speeding, and officers would smile when I told them she likes to go too fast. It's true. In our effort to trace the capillaries on our road map, we'd fall into a driving rhythm, sometimes covering 600 miles in one day. It was a challenge to break her out of this driving trance, but we did, and filled forty steno notebooks with the stories herein.

As our tow truck raced home I saw a turtle crossing the interstate and wished him good speed. His long neck stuck out of his shell like a finger poking through toilet paper, and moving at a breakneck pace for a box turtle he scurried across the pavement. It reminded me of a tragedy.

————— ∞∞∞ —————

Morning rush hour murders your nerves. Worse for turtles. I saw a box turtle the other day, stranded on the center line of a busy expressway. He was upside down, legs fully extended, grasping at the sky. His chances for survival were slim as he wriggled in the morning sun, cars whizzing by. So I pulled over and stopped, waited for a hole in traffic and trotted out to pick him up. As I neared him, I saw the small pool of blood, and the gash in his right rear leg. It might be a fatal wound, but one thing for sure: I would not let him die on that center line.

Picking him up, I carried him to safety. Walking down into the woods, I built him a nest of grass and leaves, and carefully placed him there, to regain his strength and wits, and perhaps survive his wounds. I left him, trotted up the hill to my car, and zoomed onward to work.

I thought about that turtle all day. He was big, as box turtles go… probably older than me. Maybe he would survive.

Erifnus drove home over the same road, and we stopped at the rescue spot. His makeshift nest was empty. I walked back to the road again, thinking maybe he was okay, when I saw him a few yards away, his hard shell crushed on the center line. He had tried to make it across the road again.

My earlier act of kindness had delivered him to the wrong side.

Our flatbed tow truck collided with a cold front, one of those late summer storms when the sky grows black behind eerie green clouds rolling toward us like Armageddon. These rollers seemed to speak with urgency, as if Mother Nature were frustrated by our intransigence.

I looked out the tow truck side window as we passed a familiar landmark, a symbol for motion and movement and fun, a metal monster unlike any of the country windmills or cell phone towers that puncture the sky. Barely more than a ring toss away from the busy interstate sits a solitary Ferris wheel, in the middle of an empty field, a half mile from the nearest exit. I'd seen this Ferris wheel a hundred times as I passed during the night, a beautiful sight, the familiar kaleidoscope shape lit in the colors of a carnival, gold, green and red, a lone wheel rising out of dark nothing, standing motionless, shining its geometric neons against a black night sky. But it always stood by itself, oddly out of place in a farm field next to no ticket booth, no midway. I've never seen the wheel turn, never any passengers, since its big broad people buckets are missing. It's a decoration with no purpose but to change electricity into color patterns, and become a golly along a dull superhighway. But this time was different. This time the big Eli wheel was surrounded by friends. Not people. Just the tools of carnival desire: a dozen trucks packed with pig iron painted in candy colors, a cornucopia of bulbous arms and garish gondolas and unmuffled motors.

The trucks were parked around the Ferris wheel in no pattern, signaling that this is a carnival at rest. The trucks and their thrill ride treasures sat poised to jump, to form a caravan and spring the carnival into the next town.

A complete carnival. Except for one ingredient.

Around these trucks, there was no motion. No flags or banners, no bally cloth or flashing lights, no arch for an entrance, no back end either. Nobody coming or going. There were no carnies or talkers or troupers, no roustabouts or ride-jockeys, no Marlboro Reds rolled up in greasy T-shirts, no shills or sharpies, no blade glommers or lot lizards looking for a party, not one possumbelly to trade a hummer for a dime bag, no patch money to juice the local gendarmes, no green help standing around waiting to become wise, no forty-milers who won't travel too far from home, no marks or moochies with a poke to peek in, full of sawbucks and c-notes, no hammer-squash customers for the butchers to fleece. Even in a group, the trucks looked lonesome, with no camp, no warm yellow lights shining out of the boneyards, those silver trailers where the floaters and the geeks and gunners, the gazoonies and goons and grinders sleep.

I've never stopped to inspect that lonesome Ferris wheel, since there was no seat, no motion, no ticket. We didn't stop today of course because a stop at a sleeping carnival in a driving thunderstorm probably isn't at the top of Jack the tow truck driver's bucket list. So at 70 miles per hour, as the storm lashed us I saluted the captive carnival, tied tightly to flatbeds and custom carriages that sleep those giant mechanical thrill rides. Maybe we'll see them down the road.

I turned away from the slumbering carnival and shut my eyes, silently repeating the mantra, "Life Is a Carnival." From a thousand miles away in Woodstock Cemetery Levon Helm sang an eternal message of hope: "You can fly off a mountaintop. Anybody can." Down the road, there's always something. Maybe not the carnival you want, but a golly just the same.

McMoonshine Junction

The tow truck approached the New Florence exit. Even in a raging storm McDonald's golden arches shouted up and down the highway, big baited trolling hooks for the eyes. Most people who pass this spot think about French fries. But just a punt from this exit, as Highway 19 leaves the taint of McGrease and meanders toward the fertile Missouri River valley, sits an international shrine to the great spirits. It's the home of French wines, if home means the glorious casks which lend a layer of flavor to the ferment.

Independent Stave Company started locally. Now it's a multinational conglomerate on six continents forging the barrels that cask your fine whiskey and wine. In the Ozarks, prized Missouri white oak trees grow tall and sturdy, offering deer stands and birdhouses and squirrel nests until the mature oaks are felled and hearsed to a factory to meet their maker in a blaze of sawdust and fire. They're sliced and steamed, twisted and belted with steel, their insides scorched to a charcoal skin. Worldwide, the best vintners and distillers pick these barrels to cask fine wine and age whiskey. The New Florence outlet recycles old barrels for decoration or planters. Nothing is wasted. This is the Ozarks.

Until recently in the remote Ozark hollers south of here, whiskey stills were more common than bathtubs. Nowadays, moonshiners still dot the landscape, although they're outnumbered by pot patches, and outgunned by meth labs.

The rain subsided as the tow truck charged into the wind. Not far from my view of the golden arches, beyond the old churches of New Florence, downwind from Laddonia, a chip shot from the signs pointing to Routes K & KK, just past the '50s ambiance of the Shady Rest Motel, stands a steam-belching company that smells like 80-proof corn chips. But it doesn't make corn chips. It's a ten-story whiskey still that makes liquor for your car.

For a while ethanol production was the fastest growing industry in the Midwest. Grain farmers pooled resources to create giant distilleries, with their side benefit as air fresheners. Cattle farmers hate corn distilleries, since cows and cars must compete for grain, and corn prices have risen sharply. So now you pay less for gas, more for steak. It's caused a stir among farmers, and just about everybody else in this rural agricultural setting. But cows love this ethanol plant since cows have a much easier time digesting grass than grain. Erifnus is ambivalent. She tolerates a small mix of alcohol in her diet but would perish if she imbibed too much.

Downwind from the distillery, the inmates at the pink prison at Vandalia smell the fake corn chips. Pink is a bold approach to cruel and unusual punishment, or so I thought. It turns out the inmates chose the color, and it's really mauve, and it's soothing to them, I guess. So the Vandalia women's prison is not quite pink, and it's not quite home. The mauve exterior is striking, and softens the harsh reality of the purpose of this cluster of buildings that resembles the Branch Davidian compound. It's certainly prettier than the old dead trailers west of town. But everybody, fettered or free, smells the fake corn chips.

The tow truck raced past Graham Cave, the world's most bypassed state park. Within spittin' distance of I-70, the cave entrance resembles Mick Jagger's lips. For eons, folks took shelter beneath this stiff upper lip and sat around ancient cook fires drumming the ancestral syncopations to "Sympathy for the Devil." Once, around a roaring campfire voices told me the story of people who lived here before us. A century ago a farmer was feeding his hogs in the cave when he noticed ancient artifacts. Eventually University of Missouri archaeologists excavated the cave, and it became America's first archaeological site to be named a National Historic Landmark. Now it's a state park, and under the giant bur oaks and the Kentucky coffeetrees the most prevalent artifacts are beer cans and Cheetos bags. Send in the goats. The end is near.

People who say they've figured out how the world will end generally include caves, those fissures from which evil seeps. Many caves were named by people who were obsessed with Hell. The art director for the judgment day, Hieronymus Bosch, painted vivid vignettes depicting the pits of Hell. Dante mapped the nether regions and warns, "All hope abandon, ye who enter in!" Plato describes the cave as a prison. Early Roman Christians buried their dead in the Catacombs, the scariest place this side of the *Book of Revelations.*

Poe and Twain used caves to trap heroes and villains. Vincent Price used caves to give bats a bad name. Several caves became Ku Klux Klan hangouts.

Ozarks settlers named caves after the Devil and creatures they didn't like: Devil's Well, Snake Pit Cave, and ten holes in the ground named Bushwhacker.

In Texas, don't stumble into Putrid Pit, Coon Crap Cave, Toad Frog Falling Floor Fissure, Left In a Lurch Cave, or Big Mutha Caverns. Georgia offers Dead Dog Pit, Miss Ing Pit, Not Dan's Birthday Pit, and Missing Evan Well. Don't drink the water. In Alabama, avoid Glenn's Hazardous Double Shot, Hurt Tree Pit, Meek Shall Inherit the Cave, and Crypt of Terror Pit. The Tennessee landscape hides Milk Horror Hole and Dead Dog Drop.

Graphic accounts of the 1907 Monongah Mine Disaster defined the horrors of an underground explosion and cave-in. In that West Virginia mine, 361 miners met their fate. That year 3,242 Americans died in mines.

No wonder some folks fear caves, using terms like claustrophobia, spelunkaphobia and bathophobia. Yet it's puzzling that the million-word English language dictionary doesn't appear to contain a word for the fear of payday lenders.

We rollercoastered down Mineola Hill past a place where the Devil appeared regularly on a rock outcropping imprisoned between the eastbound and westbound lanes of I-70. The outcropping forms a huge platform, called Slave Rock by historians who say humans were auctioned right there on the rock, halfway up giant Mineola Hill, overlooking the Loutre River. Slave traders delivered the slaves from the Loutre's mouth at the Missouri River, hauled them up to the rock, sold and split family members and sent them in different directions. There's no sign to designate the spot, no park or scenic overlook at Slave Rock. It just sits there, a bald canker in the hillside. One African American historian says the highway department can't figure out what they'd do to make the site accessible. So it sits silent, and only a few passersby know the stories about the inhumanity that happened here. A few years ago the Missouri legislature passed a bill with a floor amendment—with no public hearing—to name it Picnic Rock. Supporters said the name recalls the many picnics there before the interstate was built. But the governor vetoed this attempt to whitewash history.

"I heard that's called Slave Rock," I broke the silence with Jack the tow truck driver.

"Yeah, some people call it that." Silence.

Shameful scenes. They pop up along this road. At the Williamsburg exit we passed a lone gasoline station that's all business and no pleasure. No law requires purveyors of petrol to be friendly, but the only time I stopped there, I came away with the grimy feeling they did me a favor by suffering my presence. The station sat a quarter mile from the interstate, its petrol prices missing from the towering price sign. At the pump I realized its gas prices were higher than anywhere else. I eschewed their gas, and walked into the grimy shack where the clerk sat inattentive behind the counter. Plastered on the door was a yellowed sign with a blunt message: Restrooms are for customers only. The attendant raised his head from reading, looking at me like I was a moth. "I stopped to use the restroom," I told him, "but I see your sign there, so I'll just go piss in the parking lot." I didn't, of course. Hey, I didn't see a sign saying "no bathroom humor."

—————∞∞∞—————

Jack the tow truck driver probably knew the guys who ran that station. So I kept my mouth shut. Mom always told me, "Never miss a good chance to shut up."

Highways helped train me to keep silent, mostly, and listen. And watch, because highways are teachers. They teach about routes and ruts, and highs and lows. They lead to Success and Freedom, Tightwad and Liberal, dead ends, burnt ends, drive-ins, Tom'n'Hucks, tommy guns and one-armed bandits, Frankie and Johnny and Staggerlee, Paradise, lost and found, Conception, Calamity, pride, prejudice, Shakespeare and Dickens, Churchill and Elvis, Chester and Lesterville, Hoppy and Popeye, carp and crappie, bees and Monarchs, snowflakes and deplorables, floods and tornadoes, hello, goodbye, come in, keep out, go to Hell, save your soul, cell towers, fire towers, water towers, wilderness, cleanliness, bathrooms, barrooms, back rooms and attics, Lithium, Licking, toads and spiders, jail and bail, Watchtowers and witnesses, elk and Rotarians, Carver, Cuba and Cairo, chips and salsa, Ethel & Elmer, crop dusters and liquor stores, poachers, Devils, assholes, noodlers, murders and meth, massacres, missionaries, grave robbers, bank robbers, squirrels and turtles, skunk and rabbit, Babbit, billboards, ziplines, trotlines, hemlines, whores and hemp, hooters, hellbenders, hillbillies, whiskey, barrels and murals, morels, Moses and Jesus, Yogi and Mickey, midway barkers, burgers, Bald Knobbers, barbecue, buffalo, bucks, beef, hogs, hot dogs, fish and chips, chickens and members of Congress. And breaded pork tenderloins pounded to the size of manhole covers.

—————∞∞∞—————

Erifnus carried me without radar, sonar, Pixar, Pulsar, Dagmar, Bolivar, Telstar, Avatar, NASCAR or a minibar. We relied on maps.

Compared to GPS, maps are lazy and they won't work on their own, preferring to doze, folded tight as a sleeping dog, gravitating like spiders to dark out-of-the-way spots like glove compartments and magazine racks.

But if you coax them from hiding, they'll open up like a Georgia O'Keefe flower and draw you into every pistel in the Ozarks, every bend in the rivers, every drive down the main drag of every town. The map sets the stage for a remarkable discovery:

Highways have souls.

Like the travelers on its back, a highway may be black or brown, tan or white or red. Even blue. Its face may be smooth. Or it can be pocked, pitted, patchy. Its makeup may be fresh and bright, or worn thin.

A highway always follows, even as it leads.

Its shoulders can be broad and supportive, or narrow and difficult. It can be tough to mount, if so inclined. And dangerous, if crossed.

It whines beneath low tires. It can sing. It can screech. It can scrape and skin and maim and kill. It might be beautiful. Or homely. But always, it's the way home for somebody.

Highways have souls. And all unfold into stories.

Like Crane's Country store. Across the interstate from that inhospitable gas station, in the rainy distance, Williamsburg waits warm and inviting. The town is a speck compared to its colonial counterpart, Williamsburg, Virginia. But the speck boasts one big attraction. Crane's Country Store lures travelers off the interstate into the smell of waxed wood floors and countertops eroded by a million purchases, old candy counters and cash registers with gears. The store is one of the few buildings left standing near the intersection of two rural roads, the only real street corner the town ever had, even before the big superhighway bypassed it, sealing Williamsburg into the past.

My last visit was a month ago. Entering the old store with its stamped tin ceiling, I first spied a box of yams on the floor next to a box of oranges. Folks were milling about—locals picking up supplies or tourists who'd heard about this place. It's Marlene and Joe Crane's personal museum, with old tools and toys hanging from the ceiling and racks with Filson rucksacks and Dickies pullovers for purchase. Business was brisk. At the counter, they'll build you a sandwich with one meat and one cheese for two dollars. I ordered a Braunschweiger with pepper cheese on wheat and a bottle of cream soda, and took a comfortable seat in the reading room, a small space between supply racks where a semicircle of unmatched upholstered chairs offer a chance to relax by a potbelly stove, enjoy a cup of coffee, and read the *Fulton Sun* or the *St. Louis Post-Dispatch*. Looking for the bathroom, I squeezed between boxes of copper fittings, sidled past a giant burlap bag of seed corn, open at the top with a scoop stuck in it. I turned left at the stack of store receipts from the first half of the year, and found the restrooms, labeled Reuben and Rachel. The whole place had an attitude of cheer. But today Jack the tow truck driver sped past, and we kept our eyes on the rainy road ahead.

Jack doesn't need a map. Not today. He has me to direct him to our destination. Even without me he wouldn't use a map. Jack has GPS. Doesn't everybody? Not Erifnus. She's too old.

For our purposes, not having GPS has saved Erifnus and me from endless nagging and aggravation. Driving without GPS is liberating. No matter how smart the technology, GPS would have no clue where Erifnus is driving, or why, and that soothing voice would countermand our noodling direction so many times that finally she would say, "I give up, asshole. You seem to know everything. You're on your own."

But Erifnus *does* have airbags. So my old Ozark airbag is history.

The Ozark airbag fixed the one thing duct tape couldn't fix: old cars without air bags. Back before airbag technology dipped down into the everyday lives of poor people, car wrecks would endow a fair number of sternums with steering wheel implants. My contribution to world peace was an add-on feature for cars built before airbags became standard equipment.

The Ozark airbag is a byproduct of the supercenter, where buying big really saves. In this case, it saves lives. An 18-roll package of toilet paper sits snugly in a driver's lap, and fits comfortably under the chin, between the arms. Granted, the Ozark airbag is almost obsolete, a dying art, and most folks are content to let it die.

Erifnus has implants, airbags of her own, and she has never had to test them. She's grateful. I'm grateful I no longer wear a bag of toilet paper on my chest.

The rain intensified, pelting the windshield. The flatbed tow truck cut a wake through standing water on I-70. It was mid-afternoon but it seemed like nighttime as the rain turned the truck's cab into a bubble.

Erifnus disappeared from the face of the mirror. Cars pulled to the shoulder and turned on flashers, hoping the deluge would pass before they were smashed to bits by a rain-blinded 18-wheeler. Jack the tow truck driver kept driving.

"All this rain," I attempted to strike up a conversation, "you'd think we'll always have enough."

"Yup." Silence.

Jack the tow truck driver didn't elaborate. No matter. When the war over water comes, he'll be for water. You will, too.

As we sliced through torrential rain, it was way past lunch time, and hunger reset my circuitry, and hunger wouldn't let me think about anything but hunger. My stomach hijacked my mind and took me back to a tour Erifnus and I completed last summer, in search of the world's greatest tenderloin. Ah, tenderloins. The mere mention set my salivary glands to work.

The list of great pork tenderloins I've pooped took over my mind as the mile markers passed. Smith's Restaurant in Collins. Kitty's Café in Kansas City. The Toot Toot in Bethany. Lucky's Café in Edina, where the giant fritter makes the bun look like Charlie Chaplin's shrunken hat.

And this.

The Tenderloin Hunter

Maybe it was a mistake.

The server set the platter in front of me, stepped back and smiled, "I told you."

Dominating my field of vision sat a breaded pork tenderloin the size of Eldon. The bun perched atop the sandwich like the postage stamp on your tax return. Panic crept in. I must've ordered the family sandwich.

"Nope," the server assured me. "It's all yours."

I ate for an hour, never finished it. When I returned a month later, Jefferson City's Dinner Bell Diner had closed. I never knew why. Maybe they would rather shutter the business than yield to the economic pressure to reduce the square yardage of that table-sized tenderloin.

When talking tenderloins, size matters. The bigger the tenderloin, the more it invites conversation. Sure, taste is a consideration. And tenderness. But the true pork tenderloin is a visual art form, butterflied and pounded paper thin, dipped in golden batter, the breading fried to a crisp finish.

Since most pork tenderloins are lactose intolerant, the sandwich cannot qualify as a balanced meal. Cheese rarely covers a breaded tenderloin, applied only by people who believe Elvis is a gourmand, and wrasslin' ain't fake.

True tenderloin lovers dress the sandwich like it's a family member. They follow the guidelines of the World Tenderloin Federation, squirting mustard on the bottom bun to cement the raw onion rings in place. They carefully apply dill pickle shingles atop the mixture, and use the mustard squeeze bottle to write their sweetheart's name on the protruding lobes. In some instances, rogue ingredients may be approved, like Heinz red relish.

There's one more key ingredient. Like most fine dining, the tenderloin experience requires a healthy slathering of ambiance. I recall my first bite, as a wide-eyed child in a scary old Hannibal tavern, down by the railroad tracks. The open grill at Abe & Higgie's pumped out hot air currents saturated with the aroma of grilled onions and grease. The tavern's dark wood paneling absorbed the dim light offered by a hanging lamp that somehow had trapped a tiny team of Clydesdales. The little plastic Clydesdales trudged round and round inside that greasy lamp, trapped in horse Hell, pulling a beer wagon to nowhere. But nightmares in horsehide vanished when the server set a breaded pork tenderloin in front of me. I can't recall if there was a plate beneath it. Never saw one. "It could smother a snappin' turtle," said a voice from a distant table. The voice came from the silhouette of a verifiable descendant of Huck Finn. "The sandwich was so big, ol' pap had to pay property tax on it."

During college, when loins were tender, a legendary Columbia restaurant beckoned across from the classrooms where I slept through journalism school. In the dim light of the Old Heidelberg, we'd sit in a time capsule disguised as an old wooden diner booth, ruminating about bad wars. We were young reporters with noses and arteries that had yet to become hardened. And although none of us would admit it, the tenderloin became our *raison d'être*, at least for lunch.

Today the Heidelberg's old booths are gone. The new booths show fewer tattoos and scars than the originals, but the ambiance is much the same. The music hasn't changed since Mad Dogs and Englishmen opened for The Band. Best I can tell, the tenderloin hasn't changed much, either. And despite the tenderloin's bad reputation, this one has healthful benefits, with what I suspect is cayenne pepper sprinkled in the breading to pester parasites lurking in the colon.

Like a greasy snowflake, each tenderloin has its own unique charm. Dressed in the costume and character of its host, the sandwich presents a feast for the senses.

Tenderloin hunters know the dangers. They become enslaved to grease and gigantism. To excel, the tenderloin must be breaded and deep fried. The bigger the better. I'm looking for a fritter big enough to let me read *War and Peace* in one sitting. It should be capable of launching tactical air strikes from its deck, and win the blue ribbon at the state fair. It should carry a surgeon general's warning, and attract wildcatters to drill for oil.

Any fry cook worth her bacon welts knows that breading seals the flavor. Flavor is synonymous with juice, which is code for grease, the arch enemy of people bent on saving me from myself. But danger and tenderloins spring from the same mindset. A disproportionate number of cigarette smokers infiltrate the ranks of tenderloin lovers, while nearby diners wring their hands about second-hand saturation.

If you live long enough, something will saturate you. It might be grease, or smoke, or dogma. The road ahead contained all three.

And rain.

Wide Spot in the Road

Buckets of rain overwhelmed our windshield wipers as the tow truck passed the sign pointing to tiny Calwood. It's an insignificant blip on a traveler's screen. Not long ago I stopped to discover the spot where a hundred farm boys met Armageddon.

Calwood's biggest promoter is I-70. Two-foot-tall letters shout the name Calwood off the big green exit sign. It does no good. A million motorists fly past Calwood every week. Hidden a mile from the busy interstate, a grain elevator dominates Calwood's skyline.

Across the street a property teeters between junkyard and used car lot, its vehicles awaiting their next chapter, maybe as useful steeds, more likely as organ donors. This unincorporated village is the poster for "wide spot in the road."

But bloody history happened here.

At the only intersection in town, the Wright Brothers store does a brisk business selling gas and sundries. The store sits on the site of an old country store that witnessed a deadly clash of armies.

Just south of that country store Erifnus pulled off the road at a monument to the Battle of Moore's Mill. It was summer, 1862, and Confederate Colonel Joseph Porter was sweeping through the area enlisting farm boys to fight for the South. Meanwhile, a Union order declared that any Southern sympathizers would be "shot down upon the spot." A subsequent order for all men in the area to take a Union loyalty oath had the reverse effect. The loyalty order motivated Southern supporters to join Porter's ranks. Missouri State Militia Colonel Odon Guitar's cavalry caught up with Porter and rode into an ambush along a creek at Moore's Mill. After fierce fighting, Porter's troops withdrew, low on ammunition. Guitar's cavalry was exhausted and didn't pursue. After the armies parted, folks quietly gathered dozens of casualties—lifeless bodies both Union and Confederate— and buried them together in a single mass grave.

America's Civil War scholars pay scant attention to the Battle of Moore's Mill. But it was the beginning of a Union campaign that eventually would scatter Porter's volunteers, and hamper recruitment of Southern sympathizers in this state where the Civil War began.

It couldn't happen again; it will happen again.

Beyond this peaceful spot with its turmoil interred, on my autumn afternoon drive a fortnight ago, the Great Impressionist had turned expansive soybean fields to giant green and gold palettes. Some fields, planted earliest in the spring, already had turned buckskin brown, the beans ready for harvest. The drive through the patchwork of soybean fields was reminiscent of a Monet canvas, or a Van Gogh landscape, green speckled with bright yellow, bordered by golden browns, and surrounded by hardwood forests, themselves changing colors as chlorophyll retreated to roots, leaving a forest splashed with red and gold, orange and maroon. On some of the fields, farmers were beginning to harvest the grain, and a dozen red-tailed hawks followed the combines as they chopped up the cornstalks and exposed the secret trails of a thousand mice.

Back then I knew if I returned, and stayed long enough among these beautiful fields framed by forests, I'd see young boys play soldier, as boys always have.

Someday they'll learn what horror happened here.

The rain beat heavy on the windshield. Ahead a billion brake lights glistered through the downpour. Traffic had stopped dead. Maybe a wreck. Our tow truck veered onto an exit ramp to Kingdom City.

"Might as well get outta this jam fer awhile," Jack the tow truck driver looked like a man searching for relief. "Hope you're not in a hurry."

"Nope! I may get some food."

A voice crackled over Jack's CB radio: "Pileup on I-70, marker 144. Casualties."

"Looks like you'll have plenty of time." Jack was matter of fact. He added, "We might as well take the back road to Columbia."

Water poured from an angry sky, filling a labyrinth of potholes in the parking lot at the Iron Skillet Truck Stop, our refuge while this monstrous thunderstorm churned unapologetic above dead people on the highway.

The yellow light from the diner windows looked warm and inviting. The truck stop bustled with energy. Travelers buzzed, electrified under the spell of Mother Nature's almighty fury. And the smell from deep fryers stuck like fish hooks in my nostrils.

Quietly, I observed truckers and travelers taking a break. Families and couples and messengers and locals flowed into this fuel center, this nerve center, this pit stop. The wall behind the service counter bore backlit photos of the Gateway Arch, Mark Twain Lake, the state capitol.

Round the clock, there's food, souvenirs, and food. And souvenirs.

A family entered the main door, shaking off rain, engaged in a lively debate. Mom and dad wanted to head to the Lake of the Ozarks, two hours southwest. The kids, a brother and sister, begged to travel to the land of childhood adventure in Hannibal, a two-hour drive in the opposite direction. The children were close enough in age that I guessed they might be twins, about Tom Sawyer's age and attitude.

I wanted to offer a suggestion but stayed silent.

Instead, I filed through the buffet, piled my plate like a professional and sat down in a booth with mounds of so many different foods that it can only be compared to grandma's dinner table. I'm a gluttonous sucker for buffets, which offer an irresistible challenge: lower the cost per bite.

The family debate followed me through the line and settled into a neighboring booth. The young boy was adamant: "We're *this close* to Tom Sawyer and you won't take me?"

Mom knew the problem: Dad was itching to play golf.

The young girl rolled her eyes. She caught me smiling as I watched them out of the corner of my eye.

"Well, what would *you* do?" she drew me into the debate, challenging me with all the unfiltered frankness of an eighth grader.

With a sympathetic shrug to mom and dad, I answered. "I'd stay an extra day and hit 'em both."

Silence.

I took a bite of broccoli. My eyes scoured the buffet table for a to-go box. The four family members looked at each other to size up the battle lines.

"Works for me," Dad said finally. Mom looked relieved. The daughter gave me a thumbs up sign. I relaxed and shoveled into my baked beans.

"So if you had one day, what would you see in Hannibal?" Dad put me on the spot.

That was easy. "Look for Mark Twain."

My words sounded silly. Quickly I explained.

"Climb Cardiff Hill to the lighthouse, and get an angel's view of Mark Twain's soul, the Mississippi. Downriver, drive up to Lover's Leap for a good scare, then search for the Devil in Mark Twain Cave. Jesse James signed his name on a cave wall." The children's eyes grew wide and they stopped texting. "So did Elvis," I lied.

"Eat a loose meat sandwich at Mark Twain Dinette. Check out the museums, and ride the riverboat if you want. Buy tickets to Planter's Barn Theater and watch a live portrayal of 'Mark Twain Himself.'"

"And the Lake of the Ozarks?" Mom asked.

"Ever seen *Ozark*?"

"On Netflix?"

"Yeah. Wasn't filmed there."

I started to point to a brochure rack near the truck stop entrance, but changed my approach. "Google it." The parents laughed. The kids already had returned to their smart phones. Through their meal, eight thumbs danced on personal electronic devices, and the family communicated in the new normal.

I ate in peace. Jack the tow truck driver emerged from the men's room and sat across from me. Within seconds a honey-haired veteran of the truckstop opry brought him a cup of black coffee. "Here you go, hon."

"Thanks, Phyllis." He grabbed the porcelain cup with both hands and took a sip.

"You from around here?" I guessed.

"I live in Saint Charles," Jack said, "but grew up in Auxvasse, just up the road."

"Exercise Tiger Highway."

"Yeah. Honoring a World War II battle, I think."

"Do you know the story?"

"Nah. And I musta passed that road sign a hundred times."

He's not alone. On the road between Kingdom City and Auxvasse, thousands of travelers pass a sign that designates a stretch of Highway 54 as Exercise Tiger Memorial Highway. Most of them don't know what Exercise Tiger means.

"Yeah, the story was kept top secret for fifty years," I said. "Hundreds of local families never knew why their loved ones didn't come home."

"How do you know?"

"I interviewed two survivors."

For the first time on our journey, Jack the tow truck driver was intrigued. "Do tell."

So I told him the story about the ambush that left the fate of hundreds of local soldiers and sailors shrouded in mystery for a half century. Exercise Tiger.

Decades passed before Leonard Bruns learned what really happened. He remembers that cold April night in 1944, when he was a nineteen-year-old Army corporal, just one soul doing his part to prepare the world for peace. Under cover of darkness, his squad stormed a beach with advance troops and engineers. The beach was Slapton Sands, on English soil.

At the time, he wasn't aware of the scope of the mission. This event was a rehearsal for D-Day, the pivotal invasion that would turn the tide of war in the Allies' favor. "I was in the signal corps," Leonard recalls, "attached to the engineers. My job was communications, setting up phone lines on the battlefield, and signals from ship to shore. When this thing occurred, we were already in on the beach."

"This thing" turned into a bloody German assault. Allied commanders picked Slapton Sands as a practice area because it resembled the D-Day target at Utah Beach. Just off that English coast, in the darkness, a random patrol of nine German naval torpedo boats discovered eight U.S. LSTs (Landing Ship Tank) carrying soldiers to the landing area. The hourlong attack left 749 Allied troops dead, including soldiers and sailors from Missouri, especially Boone, Callaway and Audrain Counties.

Meantime, on shore, "We didn't know about the attack," Leonard remembers. "We didn't know until months later that something had happened."

In his book, *The Forgotten Dead*, Ken Small suggests that Exercise Tiger "was never covered up; it was 'conveniently forgotten.'"

David Troyer knew about it. He was an Army private first class among "the first army units to take amphibious training. In Southampton, we boarded ship and headed for Slapton Sands, but we didn't know why at the time. We were onboard a landing craft away from the LSTs that were attacked."

Troyer has spent much of his life piecing together the details of that night. "Everything went wrong that could possibly go wrong," he said. "We only had one gunboat escort. One other escort had collided with another ship, and had left for repairs. LST531 was hit by two torpedoes, sank in six minutes. We didn't have the right training wearing life preservers. Some of the men put the preservers around their waist instead of their shoulders. When they hit the cold water, pretty soon they turned upside down and drowned. The British and American navies were on two different radio frequencies. So when the LSTs called for help, nobody came. LST515 went back to pick up survivors, against orders. The captain was court-martialed and demoted.

"When we hit the beach, British machine gunners were supposed to be shooting over our heads." The training had been designated a live fire exercise. But in the confusion, "they began mowing us down like ducks on a pond. Friendly fire."

"Next morning, they moved us off the beach right quick. We were sworn to secrecy," he said. "We bivouacked five weeks in an isolated area, and we couldn't talk to anybody outside our company. We even had escorts to the bathroom. Eventually we were shown a big billboard map with our next target. It was Utah beach. The night before D-Day, they served us steak with cherry pie and ice cream at midnight. Then, because of weather, the landing was postponed for twenty-four hours. So our 'last meal' ended up being K-rations."

Jack the tow truck driver said nothing. His eyes expressed anger, as if he'd just learned that his neighbors had been murdered.

They had.

The sky brightened. The storm lessened. Time to go. "Have fun!" I offered to the family of dancing thumbs. I think I saw Dad nod in response.

"Thanks, Phyllis," Jack shouted.

"Love ya, hon. Be careful out there."

Before we jumped back into the cab, I stood and surveyed this crossroads of two major American highways. Kingdom City's economy revolves around travel. The usual suspects crowd three of its four corners: gas stations, all-night diners, fast food drive-thrus, and gaudy bespangled curio shops that sell concrete bird baths, walnut bowls and hillbilly windmills. Everybody needs one of those. The fourth corner supports two unique structures behind its obligatory gas station. One is a monument to firefighters. The other is a tourist information center. The gas station sees more traffic than the other two combined, sad proof that travelers are prisoners to the interstate serpent and its three commandments: Speed. Convenience. Familiarity.

Kingdom City is neither a kingdom nor a city. Heck, the town's population barely reaches three digits. But it shares a common trait with famous small towns like Branson and Lake Ozark: tens of thousands of travelers touch it daily.

Kingdom City gets its name not from a witness to Jehovah but from the area's claim that it was a secessionist holdout during the Civil War. Fact and legend mingle to portray the Kingdom of Callaway

fending off Union incursions. Ruggedly defiant residents defended
the area using negotiation and sleight of hand, including tree logs
carved into fake cannons and thousands of untended campfires built
to overinflate troop strength.

As the tow truck left the interstate behind, my mind drifted a
dozen miles ahead, to another campfire in the Kingdom. It was late
night 100,000 miles ago when Erifnus led me deep into the dark
woods of Mark Twain National Forest.

I had spent the morning coaxing Erifnus down isolated back roads
through thick fog that unfolded inches ahead of her bumper. As the
fog lifted, a dog ran across the road to terrorize a yearling calf lying
peacefully beside the roadside fence. Startled, the calf jumped straight
up and hit the ground at a gallop, into mother's pastoral safety. Mission
accomplished, the dog trotted back to her porch to curl into her sentry
spot.

A mile down the road, cresting a hill we couldn't avoid a giant
snapping turtle, the size of a manhole cover. Erifnus's oil pan ticked the
top of his shell. We stopped to check on him, prepared to administer
Goodyear euthanasia, if necessary. He appeared dazed, lumbering
around in a circle, obviously not in command of his body, but soon
steadied his course and headed off the road. I knew then that he would
survive, tough old soup bone.

That night, enveloped in forest and fog, we camped near Dry Fork.
Camping alone always sharpens the senses, smelling for fear, looking
for motion, listening so hard I can hear ants. Not far from my campsite
were unmarked paupers' graves. Exhausted, I crawled into my sleeping
bag. My eyelids soon became silver screens to a dream that drifted into
a poker game with Bill Hickok, Cap'n Bill Massie and the snapping
turtle. Hickok was dead, face down on the table. Massie kept flailing
his wrist like it hurt, and the turtle, chomping a cigar, calmly laid down
a full house and said, "Gimme a bite of Wild Bill."

It was a wild phantasm. But the Kingdom of Callaway produces
more fantasies per capita than anywhere on the planet, fantasies that go
way beyond fake cannons and empty campfires and snappers that talk,
and enters the sacred realm of Shakespeare and Milton and soap operas.

The tow truck passed Fulton toward our detour. I gazed out the
window through the mist in the direction of this small town with big
stories.

Fulton is landlocked, so naturally it adopted the name of a steam boat inventor. Its city limit surrounds 12,000 proudly independent citizens, and 1,200 citizens with limited independence. The latter are residents and outpatients of Fulton State Mental Hospital.

Before the Civil War it was called the state lunatic asylum. At that time people treated mental illness like demonic possession. They called the mentally ill lunatics and idiots, and if these unfortunate souls had no family, they lived on the streets, in abandoned shacks and remote caves. The hospital was a step toward more humane care of the mentally ill, but it only happened because of one tragic event.

Depression—the economic kind—had gripped the country after the Panic of 1837. Missourians stubbornly resisted spending tax dollars on anything, much less a lunatic asylum. But the result of another type of depression—the suicide of a popular governor—helped bring attention to the debate over mental health treatment. The legislature approved the first "state lunatic asylum" in 1847, and began admitting people with mental issues caused by "epilepsy and tuberculosis, religious anxiety, disappointed love, intense study, jealousy and indigestion," according to historians. One prominent psychiatrist said the hospital initially planned to house the "feeble minded" as well. But eventually feeble minds were turned away because bed space was taken by increasing numbers of indigent insane.

Fulton became famous as the setting for a pair of dramatic portrayals by two world-stage conservative icons. Ronald Reagan called *King's Row* his best movie. Filmed in 1942, it's a fictional story about folks in Fulton. Four years later, Winston Churchill delivered his Iron Curtain Speech on the campus of Fulton's Westminster College, and set in motion the American visual of the cold war, which consumed the attention of an octet of presidents, including Reagan.

The Winston Churchill National Museum sits in the Church of Saint Mary the Virgin, Aldermanbury. The old church gets around. It was built nearly 900 years ago in the middle of London. Sir Christopher Wren redesigned the chapel after the 1666 Great Fire of London gutted its interior. The Nazi blitzkriegs of 1941 destroyed the old church again. The ancient stone walls survived enough that in the mother of all pilgrimages, loving hands picked up the church, jumped the pond and plopped it down in Fulton. They reassembled it using a numbering system that's part paint-by-numbers, part Rubik's Cube. Beside the vestibule, hidden by a door, seventh-century stone steps descend to a million stories buried by time. Having undergone a facelift worthy of Wren, the church houses a museum celebrating Churchill's life and achievements.

This place has become the American Westminster Abbey, without the dead bodies. Before the old church made its big leap, before the tragic fire, and the awful bombs, it was the place where William Shakespeare prayed for good reviews, and where John Milton got married. Milton hints about his marriage in his epic, *Paradise Lost*. During an earlier visit to Fulton, I searched in vain throughout the college for a Paradise Lost and Found. The Kingdom holds no such treasure.

It took ten centuries for the church to show its first world premiere movie. *Darkest Hour* is a deep Shakespearean study of Winston Churchill, his range of emotions played powerfully by Gary Oldman. Outside in the churchyard sits just enough of the Berlin Wall to give a creepy feel for the reality of the Cold War standoff. I hope we're not headed there again.

❧❧❧

"Ever heard of Henry Bellamann?"

Jack the tow truck driver drew a blank. "From around here?"

"Fulton. Wrote a book about local goody-goodies who led secret scandalous lives."

Silence.

The words sounded stupid, even when I uttered them. But there was a time not long ago when scandals were only whispered, and not televised as reality shows. Henry Bellamann changed all that. It's ironic that nobody talks about Bellamann. Oh, Fulton historians treasure him. But considering how he changed America, it's sad people don't honor him as the grandfather of the soap opera.

Bellamann was born and raised in Fulton, and when he moved away to teach music at Julliard and Vassar, he dabbled in psychology and poetry. Yet his lasting legacy is a dark tale of psychological terror and taboo: the novel *King's Row*—the same book that later boosted Ronald Reagan's career—about a small town with whitewashed fences and whitewashed reputations hiding dirty little corners, and seamy obsessions with money and status, class and racism, sex and sadomasochism, profit and plunder, and a cornucopia of mental afflictions. The novel begins by advising readers that the story is fictional, and could be about any town, anywhere. But there's little doubt that Bellamann's setting is Fulton. In the sadly sanitized movie adaptation of the book, Ronald Reagan received accolades for his performance. The movie bears little resemblance to the novel's deep disturbing Dostoyevsky themes and subplots. Literary critics call this book the blueprint for *Peyton Place,* and every soap opera since. "They made a movie out of it," I said after a long silence.

"Last movie I saw was a video of my own colon," Jack said.

I laughed. "I tell 'em to knock me out. Gimme a double."

"Yep. After I came to, they showed me…" He paused. A voice crackled over the CB radio with an update on the carnage on the interstate: "Gonna take a while to clear both lanes."

"Glad we took the back way," Jack said, happy to change the subject.

Me too. We'd be at the garage in a half hour. Our awkward conversation would come to a merciful end. Our trip was business, not an interview. I realized that almost every topic I started to discuss might lead to a strong difference of opinion. Even the goddamned weather. In the back of my mind I heard my mother's voice: "Never miss a good chance to shut up."

Jack the tow truck driver turned away from Fulton and drove the backroad toward Columbia. In the rearview mirror, Erifnus, lashed to the deck, remained unfazed by drama.

She's been assailed by deranged road ragers, bombarded by road hazards, buzzed by fallen power lines, assaulted by strange car doors in parking lots, and gang felt by undergrowth on dirt roads that warned her to get the hell out.

Her bones are iron, her skin plastic, tin and glass. Her blood is black. But in the grand scheme of the cosmos, both of us follow the same rhythm of existence: the new car smell at birth wears off as we seek to perform for those who invest in us, and as we both grow older and more brittle, we do our damnedest to stay relevant and dodge the tripwires of doom.

"Doesn't everybody?" I blurted out loud.

Jack the tow truck driver shook his head ever so slightly. He said nothing.

"Sorry. Talk to myself sometimes."

He laughed, nodded in a way that signaled he talks to himself sometimes too.

The stories along these roads reflect life's uneven rhythms. Breakdowns and revelations. Close calls and car wrecks. The beauty of violent storms. The aromas of September sycamores and campfires and forest fires and kitchen fires, and the old tire fire outside of Salem, a massive mountain of smoldering rubber that clean air laws finally extinguished. These are the tastes and touches and sounds you can't coax from a tweet. Sometimes Erifnus and I happened upon good people acting bad. We bumped into a few unsavory characters, boozers and bruisers, ruffians and renegades. Our hapless ass got rescued by badass Samaritans. We spent a lot of time wandering graveyards uncovering triumphs and heartbreaks, but mostly assuring that the badasses who lurk and troll in these stories are dead. Some are dead, but before they died they made more.

The words of the badass good Samaritan echoed in my head. "People wanna kill me."

Maybe that's true. But they can't kill the stories.

Home

It was late Friday when Jack the tow truck driver dumped Erifnus and me. Handshake and Jack was gone. University Garage had an alternator waiting, and slapped it on in minutes.

On the way home we heard a radio wag blurt that Columbia shouldn't spend city money to preserve the home of Blind Boone because damn few people know who he was.

Technically the radio spin quack is right. Most folks don't know about Blind Boone. Same with Carl Stalling and Cliff Edwards—great Missouri composers who never posted a cat video that went viral. No matter. Sooner than later you'll hum one of their songs.

A century ago—before legendary singer James Brown was born—John William "Blind" Boone was the hardest working man in show business, the Elvis of his era. He showed up in more places than Jesse

James. And Jesse James was everywhere, if you believe all the hype.

Erifnus took a detour and we passed Blind Boone's home.

Sandwiched between a bank and a church, the house can't get any closer to God or money. Yet the house sat neglected for years in downtown Columbia after its last tenant—a funeral parlor—folded. Such details would not worry Johnny Boone. He was an optimist, and maybe America's greatest piano player during the early twentieth century.

Boone's troupe toured by train from town to town. His concerts featured a precursor to "stump the band," and Boone fast became famous for his ability to play a tune verbatim after hearing an audience member play it just once. Folks loved his music. They loved his style, the rhythmic sway of his torso as his arms and elbows flailed and his fingers flew. They loved it because he loved it.

Sympathy could have ruled Johnny Boone's life. He was born in Miami, Missouri in 1864 to Rachel Boone, an unwed cook for the Union troops of the Seventh Missouri Militia. His father was a bugler who went AWOL, surfacing to blow reveille for another Union unit at the Battle of Shiloh. Historians suspect Rachel had been owned at some point by descendants of Daniel Boone, likely Nathan Boone, who had settled between Ash Grove and Walnut Grove, north of Springfield. When her infant Johnny developed brain fever, a doctor removed his eyes to relieve pressure and save his life. Rachel settled in Warrensburg to raise her child.

Young Johnny moved easily among white families and black families, black playmates and white playmates. At five years old, he organized his first street corner band. Everybody loved Johnny's music, the way he beat rhythms on a tin pan, and played the harmonica using a china teacup as a mute.

The townsfolk believed he was a prodigy. They raised money to send him to the State Institute for the Blind in Saint Louis.

He got his education, but not the way the townsfolk had planned. Johnny was a good kid. He soaked up the curriculum at this historic school, the first in America to offer Braille to students. The school also required students to learn useful skills, like making brooms. Johnny knew what he wanted, and it wasn't making brooms at school. He escaped the school and lived for days on the streets in Deep Morgan, a tenderloin district of barrooms and brothels in downtown Saint Louis, an area dominated today by an imposing Edward Jones sports dome. There, in a setting that would later produce Stagger Lee and Frankie and Johnnie and the Pruitt-Igoe housing complex, he experienced raw life...and music. He played his harmonica on street corners, where a Frisco Railroad conductor fetched him off the street and arranged with a conductor from the Missouri Pacific Railroad to let him ride back home to Warrensburg. His ticket? Playing the harmonica for passengers.

That set the stage for young Johnny Boone's early performances, riding in railroad cars between Laddonia and Vandalia, Glasgow and Clark, Centralia and Mexico. He played harmonica for tips. An early forerunner to the subway performer, Boone and others became such fixtures in railroad club cars that railroad management banned them as nuisances.

Johnny learned to sharpen his hearing, and count change by the sound of coins dropping into a tin cup. And he knew what he wanted to be...not just a musician. He would be a performer.

Piano legend Eubie Blake called Boone phenomenal. But his popularity was due to another Johnny.

A legend in his own right, John Lange was the world's greatest tour manager. A friend and confidant to Boone, Lange also was from mixed heritage: Mexican, Creole, African American. His mother was owned by Kentuckian James Shannon, who moved the family to Columbia when Shannon became president of the University of Missouri. Shannon later founded Christian College, now called Columbia College, where instructors helped Boone refine his mastery of the piano. By the time he met Boone, Lange was a successful contractor who built damn near all of the roads in Boone County, as well as the first black Baptist church in Columbia. It was for that church that Lange first hired Boone to play at a Christmas concert in 1879. The event was a success. The pair bonded into a tour de force that was bigger than the sum of its parts. They relied on each other, Boone with the talented touch, Lange with the talent to keep in touch.

———— ∞∞∞ ————

As the talk show guy ranted about why we shouldn't spend taxpayer dollars honoring John Boone, I sent the blab a telepathic message through the radio: read more, bitch less.

Erifnus pulled to the curb at our house, glad to be home. Me too. Cheryl gave me a welcome kiss, then immediately dispatched us to the store to pick up a few ingredients for chicken Parmesan. On the way, trouble hit us head-on.

He was going the wrong way down Broadway, holding a can of Budweiser, rolling by his own power in a wheelchair, one leg skittering along the pavement, the other leg missing. There was no sidewalk, no shoulder on that stretch of road between shopping centers. So he rolled his wheelchair into the face of oncoming traffic. He didn't care, daring traffic to hit him.

Approaching him on a collision course, we dutifully stopped. He didn't look up, didn't acknowledge my presence. I shouted, "You okay?" He shook his head no, and muttered something unintelligible. Erifnus, in the middle of the road, made a big visual target so the afternoon rush hour traffic would avoid barreling into us.

The man in the wheelchair was an ex-marine. Beneath his Semper Fi ballcap, a tattoo on his forearm labeled him a member of the First Marine Division.

He was close to delirium.

"Vietnam?" I asked. He nodded. He told me his roommate had "gone postal" and thrown him out. So he was headed downtown.

"That's two miles," I said. "You'll never make it."

"I know."

He was too proud to go back, too weak to go forward, fueled only by a paper bag of Budweiser cans in his lap. His amputated leg might be because of a war injury. Or maybe diabetes. By my guess, he was sixty-something years old. He didn't look healthy.

Another pulse of traffic whizzed past us. I convinced him to move out of the road, and helped him to the shoulder. Meanwhile, a car pulled over into a nearby parking lot. The driver and his wife jumped out of the car and approached us. "Let me help you," the driver said to the vet. He wheeled the man into the parking lot while his wife called police for assistance.

Confident that the vet was getting attention, I left to finish my errand. When I returned, the couple and the vet were still in the parking lot, waiting for the police. The couple was agitated. "If it was a heart attack, they'd have been here fifteen minutes ago. Nobody wants to help an old drunk vet in a wheelchair."

Maybe. Maybe not. At any time in a growing city, emergency personnel may be overwhelmed with calls. This was not a life-threatening situation, an old disoriented vet in a church parking lot. After all, the situation had been downgraded from the earlier crisis: an old drunk vet in the middle of a busy highway.

It's hard to tell whether this guy fell through the cracks, or jumped. I don't know his history, don't know his name. Maybe he made some wrong decisions. Maybe he won't follow doctor's orders or stay on his meds. Maybe he resists help.

I get a warm vibe from organizations who send veterans to see the World War II Memorial in Washington, DC. But unless I'm wrong, most of those vets get a seat on the trip because somebody's watching out for them.

Meantime the old drunk vet is out on the streets, no telling for how long.

Intermission: Yard Bargains

"How much for books?"

"Fifty cents."

I didn't quibble. I knew what I wanted. Hardback classics. I rummaged through several cardboard boxes and plucked out a half dozen keepers. A collection of Jack London short stories. Aldous Huxley's *Brave New World*. A 719-page story that begins, "Scarlett O'Hara was not beautiful, but..."

My eyes grew wide when I snagged a four-pounder. It may have been my best catch of the day, an 1853 *Works of Lord Byron*, complete and unabridged, even as it sat without a cover on its back and spine. That's okay, when I'm 160 years old, I won't have a cover on my spine either. I held it tight like a new toy, even though I knew that for the rest of my life, I won't sit still long enough to get through its 1,100 pages. "Reference," I whispered to myself, justifying the acquisition.

You never know what you'll find at a yard sale. I'm not an expert, since I don't work the sales religiously. Some people do. They scour the newspapers. They search websites. They plan their weekend strategies like Sun Tsu. They rise with the deer hunters and the milk trucks, and like an army they do more before breakfast than most people do all day. Not me.

"Good selection," the owner said as she accepted my money.

"I never read *Gone with the Wind*," I blurted. "But I did see the first half of the movie."

She looked at me with pity.

"The Byron!" I changed the subject, clutching the old book with both hands like it was the Stanley Cup.

"Yeah," she sighed. "I'm an English teacher..." She explained she was getting ready to act on her life's goal and launch into serious creative writing. I wasn't sure why she would want to get rid of these classics. But she *is* an English teacher. She probably memorized most of this stuff...sees it in her dreams. Now she's changing course, from full-time teacher to full-time writer.

Many of life's transitions are marked by yard sales.

I thanked her for the treasures, and wished her success in her literary career, and took off down the street on my bicycle, two bags of books hanging from my handlebars like the scales of justice.

I smiled to myself as I rolled up to my back door. It was only a split-second impulse that I even stopped at that yard sale. It was late afternoon, so my timing wasn't good yard sale strategy. "The bargains are long gone," I can hear the members of the Serious Yard Sale Society chide me.

That's okay. Professional yard salers, the ones who show up at 5:30 a.m., usually aren't after a battered book of Byron. Neither was I, until I stopped, and flipped on my OCD switch labeled "books."

Every yard saler's switch is unique. Like a fingerprint. And every yard sale is a psychological study. The sellers organize clues to their past and spread them on a grid for buyers to pick over like blackbirds. A carny of card tables and cardboard boxes serve up a mix of function and folly, kitsch and utensils.

Yard sales operate on the simple principle that beauty is in the eye of the beholder. A good friend of mine used to buy anything with a poultry theme. Egg timers and poachers. Prairie chicken salt and pepper shakers. Rooster lamps. A cast iron skillet with a laying hen lid. Everybody needs one of those.

Over and over, yard sales offer the best proof that Elvis never left the building.

During my wasted youth I never cared much for spending time at yard sales, until I found the mother lode. A few years ago, I passed a row of boxes on a residential curb. Somebody had cleaned out a roomful of dusty old books and set them beside the road. Maybe the books ended up curbside because of a marriage breakup. Or maybe the owner of the books died, and the spouse could finally unload all those dust magnets. I don't know.

I pulled to the curb, parked my bicycle and dug into the boxes. I culled four dozen hardbound beauties–Conrad and Kafka. *Crime and Punishment*. Hugo and Hemingway and Harold Bell Wright. Things I should have read in my formative years.

As I stood there—a stranger in a strange front yard—I resolved to comb every yard sale and collect the classics and read as many as I can.

Other drivers began to stop to pore over the boxes. Alarm shot through my body, much like a '49er must've felt when he saw other prospectors climbing the mountain toward his gold mine. From deep in my DNA the early bird shopper gene emerged, and I packed my selections into one cardboard box, guarding it like a goalie. The box was big enough to hold a sheep. Loaded with books, it was heavier than a window air conditioner. Balancing it on my bicycle's handlebars, I attempted to pedal this unstable pyramid toward my house. Alas, my balance fell short of the Great Wallendas. I ended up walking my bike and booty home.

I welcomed the books into our house like new pets. I built more shelves. And I began to read. *Sons and Lovers. King's Row. Genghis Khan.* The more I read, the more I collected. The more I collected, the more I realized I'd never have time to read them all.

Hoarding? No. This is a special brand of punishment, a self-imposed penance. In high school, I faked my way through English literature. Reading *Silas Marner* was harder than staying awake in church. Memorizing Shakespeare was drudgery. The scarlet letter on my chest was a big S for slacker. My ambivalence continued through college, where I skimmed a whole library of *Cliff's Notes*.

It's poetic justice that I just confessed to an English teacher that I took cheap shortcuts through literature, even as I plucked a Byron out of her outbox.

Someday my family will have to dispose of my lifetime collection. I hope they find good homes, these books, where their pages will get a workout and their backs and spines will wear.

Passing on knowledge is the most satisfying form of recycling. That and yard sales.

———— ∞ ————

That afternoon Mizzou's football Tigers hosted some special guests at Faurot Field. The buzz and the color of 70,000 fans packed together attracted some adherents to flower power. They weren't hippies or Krishnas or my friends who stand on street corners with signs reading "Honk for Peace." They were bugs, big beautiful bugs. A hundred thousand monarch butterflies rode the breeze above the open stadium, assuming from a distance that on their long journey to Central America, this big bowl was a rest stop with enough pistels and stamen to fortify their resolve to travel on. Alas, as they drew closer, they realized it was a ruse, perpetrated by the reds and golds and greens of the crowd. The vibrant black and orange Monarch Air Force flew over us, just out of the collective grasp of the spectators.

The bugs inspired me to keep traveling on my long journey. If they can do it, so can I. I stayed to watch the rest of the game, not wanting to start too soon on the road lest my windshield get plastered with these beautiful winged miracles.

II: Gourmet Elvis to the Promised Land

Oh, the Trumanity!

"Give me the Elvis."

I hadn't expected to encounter food fit for the king. Not here, within a wedge shot of so much history. But that's what makes the journey so rewarding.

I finished my Elvis, a peanut butter sandwich slathered with marshmallow crème and bolstered with bacon and bananas, served on grilled whole wheat. It's a big seller at Clinton's Soda Fountain on the Independence town square, although young Harry Truman never sold one in his first job there, since Elvis didn't put his first peanut butter in his diaper for decades after Harry worked there.

"Where's the Harry Truman?" I asked my server across the counter. She pointed to the menu on the wall. "Right there: The chocolate sundae with butterscotch." I had one, in due course. Thus fortified with the favorites of the king and the leader of the free world, I set out to scratch the surface of this historic town.

Guarding the courthouse, Truman's statue shares the grounds with the county's namesake, Andrew Jackson. In America there are more counties named Jackson than there are rabbits or zucchinis. This Jackson County has a wild history. Old Hickory couldn't care less, by the looks of his statue, mounted on horseback, sitting slim and grim. He looked pissed. But Andrew Jackson always looked pissed. Today he's pissed because people want to kick him off the $20 bill. In contrast, Harry Truman's statue is smiling as he strikes a walking pose. He's not wearing a hat. A hatless Harry is something locals rarely saw.

And locals saw a lot of Harry Truman.

They saw him across the street during the centennial of the old 1859 jail, its future looking squarely at a wrecking ball. Truman helped save the structure, raising money and getting the building on the National Register of Historic Places. That may not sound like much. But think of all the old jails and courthouses and town squares wrecked by reckless developers who didn't give a shit about history. If Harry were around, he'd give 'em hell.

The Independence jail appeared on the world stage at least once. Its most infamous inmate was so popular among townsfolk that the jailer never locked his cell. Wanted for robbery and murder, Frank James chose to turn himself in to Governor Thomas Crittenden at the state capitol in Jefferson City, and that odd couple rode the train west to Independence. The event was more like a homecoming than a surrender. For six months over the winter of 1882, inmate James came and went as he pleased, before he was shipped off to trial at Gallatin.

Frank was acquitted. He became a performer in traveling shows, reenacting his bank robbing days. When he died in 1915, Frank's story took an ironic twist. His wife, Ann Ralston James, kept his cremated remains in a bank safe deposit box until she died in 1944. Then both were interred at Hill Park Cemetery, a few blocks from the old Independence jail.

So Frank James became a bank deposit. And Harry Truman saved the old jail. And he saved the world. After he left the White House, locals saw Harry almost every day during his morning walks from his house. What a house. The fourteen-room Victorian home sits in an old neighborhood not far from the town square. Today it's preserved as a national monument. But in his retirement years, it was simply home.

Most of the Trumans' belongings still sit where Harry and Bess left them. Harry's hat, cane and overcoat adorn the hat tree in an alcove. In the parlor, Bess's official First Lady portrait watches over the Steinway baby grand piano. It's the only official first lady portrait missing from the White House. The story sheds light on Bess's backbone. When federal officials asked for the portrait to return to the White House, they promised a copy for the Truman home. Bess had another idea: She kept the original. The copy hangs in Washington.

Harry and Bess Truman's kitchen is farmhouse functional, opening onto a screened-in porch where two common aluminum lawn chairs with webbed seats sit lonely for their owners. It's only twenty paces to the garage, where Truman's last car sits, a lime green 1972 Chrysler Newport with the license number 5745. I wondered how the former leader of the free world could only get a four-digit license plate. Then I realized the significance of 5745: VE Day.

The warmest room in the house is the library, where Harry

surrounded his recliner with piles of books, themselves surrounded by shelves of books. Harry read them all.

He was famous for his daily walks through the neighborhood, cane in hand. A friend who used to deliver newspapers in the neighborhood recalls seeing Truman on one of his walks, as a Volkswagen beetle pulled up beside him. "Hello, Mr. Truman!" four high school students in the car greeted in unison. Truman walked to the curb, smacked his cane on the car's German fender and said, "You're not good Americans."

Local Truman stories abound. Dave Lineberry tells a gem: "I was born in Independence, and as a child, we took our evening walks a few blocks away and past Truman's home, where we saw him on many occasions.

"Between his home and the few blocks to downtown, there was then and remains now a gas station that at that time was a full-service mechanics shop as well.

"Several years ago, I was visiting with a professional acquaintance, Bob Watkins, retired longtime superintendent of schools in Independence. He patronized the mechanics at that station, and one day while having his car serviced, happened to ask if they had ever known or seen Truman.

"One mechanic responded brightly, and told him about how, after Truman's service as president, he would walk into the shop with a book under his arm, and say, 'Lift me up, boys!' And they would bring down the hydraulic hoist of whatever car they were working on. Truman would get in the car, close the door, and they would raise it back up again, where he would read for as long as they could justify keeping the car under work. Then, they'd lower him back down and he'd leave with a grin, claiming it was the only place he could get away from the press and Bess with no one being the wiser."

Crisscrossing downtown, we must've run a dozen stop signs, smiling broadly as we crossed each intersection. "The mules are immune" to things like stop signs and traffic tickets, my guide told me as he held the covered wagon's reins to Harry and Ed, named for two partners in a bygone local haberdashery.

Ralph Goldsmith was born for this job. He looks like he could be a member of the Cole Younger gang, whose ranks lived in this area, or maybe a wagon master among the millions of people who launched from here on the perilous journey to a new life on the western frontier. Ralph's been guiding this tour long enough that the mules probably could haul the wagon along his route without him, but it wouldn't be the same. Ralph delivers his lines with conviction, having cut his acting teeth at Silver Dollar City.

"You know my favorite Truman quote?" he asked. I didn't. "There's nothing new in this world, except the history that you don't know."

The thirty-minute wagon tour, a bargain at fifty cents a minute, set the scene for digging deeper into the many layers of history preserved in Independence. As Ralph talked about the pioneers and the Mormons and Truman and Frank James and the origin of Bill Hickok's wild nickname, we rode in the ruts—swales, they're called—formed by a hundred thousand wagons headed west. Deep swales, too, even tinhorns could see that.

Hickok? James Butler Hickok spent some quality time in Independence saloons, and on one visit, he broke up a fight by shooting a bully. When the bully's family showed up to lynch this unknown assailant, they cornered him outside a bar near the town square. He pulled his gun and urged them to back off. They didn't. Then a dance hall girl shouted from a second story window, "Shoot 'em all, Wild Bill Hickok!" The family realized they were face-to-face with a legendary gunslinger. They backed off. Hickok had a new nickname.

With a firm foundation of tales about the town, I thanked Ralph Goldsmith, and drove down the street to the great flyover's most intense museum. Well, one of 'em.

The Candy Bomber, Calvin Trillin and Sanctuary

It was the size of a baby's fist, but it stopped me in my tracks.

Inches from my face was a safety plug from the bomb dropped on Nagasaki. Suddenly the stark reality of war hit home. Pull the plug. Drop the bomb. End the war.

That action began a controversy that stirs emotional debate today.

The plug is only one startling display at the Truman Library, an unsettlingly stunning museum experience.

Nearby is a pocket-sized prayer book and a metal spoon, both pierced by the same bullet, both slowing that sniper's bullet from killing PFC George Farris.

A cold corridor recreates Berlin's postwar reality: refugees who didn't freeze to death had nothing to eat. Enter the Berlin Airlift. A photo captures the spirit of that humanitarian armada: an American plane flies one hundred feet over starving Berliners dropping candy to children.

The Truman Library is not for the faint-hearted. Harry saw to that, the way he made decisions, the way he lived his life. "I would much rather be an honorable public servant and known as such than to be the richest man in the world," he said.

Everybody talks Truman. Few *act* Truman.

We drove to the birthplace of Kansas City, Old Westport, the site of one of the five greatest restaurants in the world, according to food critic Calvin Trillin. Mario's Delicatessen makes the galaxy's greatest grinder, an Italian roll stuffed with meat, cheese and sauce, then toasted. Mario's superiority among grinders stems from a stubby little bread plug stuffed in the open end of the hollow loaf which seals the sizzling ingredients inside the sandwich like a ship in a bottle.

It was a sad return to Mario's. The sandwich was superb, tasty as ever. And the narrow passageways, rickety stairs and cramped ambiance of this ancient brick structure might as well be in Rome. The sad thing? Big cheesecake chains are rattling their forks, taking big bites out of Kansas City's historic epicurean skyline, and Mario's is closing, following the old Bristol Bar out of a once-unique neighborhood.

Some relics hang on.

That night I holed up in the Raphael Hotel. Since 1928 this nine story Italian Renaissance work of art has anchored Brush Creek, opposite Kansas City's Country Club Plaza, America's first shopping center. Back before online shopping drove a spike through America's gregarious heart, people would show up at malls and buy things in person from another person who may not like her job but now that online shopping ate her job she'd love to have it back. Until Amazon figures out how to deliver the Raphael Hotel to my house by drone, I guess I'll have to show up in Kansas City to check in to the Raphael, which got a makeover recently, and while the guest rooms got new upholstery and pillows and flat-screen TVs, they preserved the bathrooms with the postage stamp-sized white tile, and the boxy little elevator with the retractable scissor-gate door that yearns for its old friend the elevator operator who was last seen being carried by a drone to an island called Obsolescence where hope and dignity die.

Next morning I was running down Main Street when a fledgling robin flittered in front of me and hopped into the street. To save the little creature from oncoming rubberdeath, I stepped into the street to shoo the baby back into vegetation. Mother and father robin converged on us, flapping and squawking to divert my attention. The couple had come from Central America to assist in the harvest, to pick fruit in Missouri, and make naturalized American babies. The parents thought I meant harm to their child. "Be safe, young family," I spoke as the fledgling fluttered into a tree. "There are people here who don't care if you die."

I resumed my run.

Music wafted into my conscience from my left. Curious, I climbed the steep hill to find an exquisitely manicured lawn the size of an aircraft carrier, where 10,000 fans swayed to a blues concert fundraiser for Hurricane Katrina victims. Thousands of storm victims had moved to Missouri. Many needed a helping hand. This concert was a Kansas City welcome to these unfortunate refugees.

The hill offered the very best view of the Kansas City skyline. The grounds resemble the National Mall in Washington DC. And on this hill, America built its only national monument to the veterans who fought tyranny at Verdun and Chateau Thierry and the Maginot Line. Descendants of these brave soldiers named the conflict World War I.

It's unique in America that this Liberty Memorial stands in America's heartland, and not Washington DC. The Liberty Memorial watches over its public sister, Union Station, where millions of doughboys boarded trains, headed for war. Blackjack Pershing must've liked this spot for the memorial. He grew up a few miles east of here, and became General of the Armies over there. Pershing had a secret weapon: He knew the key to victory stood on four legs: The Missouri mule was the forerunner to the WWII jeep.

This monument's secret weapon is Holocaust Museum designer Ralph Applebaum, who performed a stunning museum makeover. Life-size trenches and chilling testimony bring the horrors of war to your senses.

Patriots and historians and international visitors flock to see this grand national treasure, pay their respects, and teach their children the lessons from the War to End All Wars. Are we listening?

Two giant sandstone sphinxes whispered to me as I left the museum. They wouldn't look at me. Both covered their eyes with their wings, but I heard their whispers. The sphinx named Memory shields its vision from the grisly battlefields of France. It whispered, "You helped the robins." The other sphinx, named Future, hides its eyes from the next atrocity. "We're all refugees," it sighed as the band played for Katrina's homeless children.

Back on the street the robin family prepared to return to Central America.

———— ∞ ————

After a cool immersion in the National Jazz Museum and its neighbor, the Negro Leagues Baseball Museum, I inhaled the planet's best burnt ends sandwich in the no-frills dining room at LC's Bar-B-Q, then retreated to Forest Hill Cemetery, burial site of Confederate General Joseph Shelby, Hallmark Cards founder Joyce Hall, and baseball Hall of Famers Satchel Paige and Zack Wheat. But I came to see my friend Buck. After a Hall of Fame life, John "Buck" O'Neil came to this peaceful spot. His stature on and off the baseball diamond equals the legendary Roberto Clemente. Buck played baseball in the Negro Leagues, and when Major League Baseball finally integrated, Buck was in the twilight of his career, so he never took an MLB pitch. He's a Negro Leagues Hall of Famer. But the Major League Baseball Hall of Fame never inducted this saint, to baseball's enduring shame. Oh, after he died at ninety-four, they erected a smiling statue of Buck at the entrance to the Cooperstown museum, so he's the first player to greet visitors. But he's not in their Hall of Fame. No matter. Buck was bigger than life, and his baseball prowess always played second to his kindness, humility, and ready smile. Beneath the inscription on his headstone, "A Life of Learning and Loving," his own words calm the controversy: "If I'm a Hall of Famer for you, that's all right with me. Just keep loving old Buck. Don't weep for Buck. No, man, be happy, be thankful."

Okay, Buck, my friend.

As Erifnus delivered me to dinner, weathercasters called for heavy thunderstorms later in the evening. The forecast didn't faze Erifnus Caitnop. She's built low to the ground so she cuts through the wind like a wedge, and under her hood she wields the power of a hundred mules.

She's saved her driver dozens of times when he pushed her through hailstorms and blizzards, and deep into wilderness ravines where her tires ached for firm pavement.

"We make a good team," I patted her dashboard as Erifnus pointed her hood ornament west on old Highway 24, an array of stoplights and junk, and proud old wayside inns that slid into new lives as apartments and turnkeys for flophouse flirts. On the bridge approach to the Missouri River, we crossed above two dozen railroad tracks feeding America's foremost stockyards. We waved at the bright lights of the old riverboat casinos, which really aren't riverboats at all. Ahead bright colored balloons painted on the giant Worlds of Fun water tower signaled that we were nearing one of the planet's top three fried chicken havens. I coaxed Erifnus to take the exit, and within minutes I sat in the homey ambience of an old farmhouse built in 1829. Stroud's Oak Ridge Manor has wowed food critics from *Gourmet Magazine, Bon Appetit, The New York Times, People Magazine, Conde Nast* and *Esquire*. Oh, and Calvin Trillin says it's one of the five greatest restaurants in the world. My window table looked out onto a scene from two centuries ago. A one room school house perched beside a lake where ducks and geese and swans mingled, oblivious to the interstate just over the hill.

Inside, the farmhouse décor sets a stage where friendly servers dote. Sarah the server served my meal family-style, even though I was a family of one on this trip. Homemade chicken noodle soup greased my gullet for four pieces of chicken, real mashed potatoes and gravy, and green beans seasoned with bacon and onions. Then Sarah tried to stop my heart with a giant gooey buttery cinnamon roll.

We motored back to the Raphael Hotel with enough leftovers to get my per-meal cost down to two bucks.

Pretzel Streets and the Elements of Sin

Erifnus likes river roads. She pointed to Highway 9, an obscure route that arises like a fuse from Kansas City's downtown crown. We alighted on it, following the Missouri River's north bank to a town that dodged the infestation of interstates. For all the conformist byproducts of our interstate culture—hypnotic concrete sameness, blue signs corralling our senses into boxes of corporate chain choices—the interstates have helped preserve the towns they don't touch. Clinging to the river, safe from the pace of modern highways, real America thrives.

We rounded a bend and fell into Parkville's charm.

Tuck a town into a river bluff, and nature bends the streets like pretzels. Houses and shops dig their heels into the hillside, hanging with one arm, while beckoning with the other.

Beneath a picturesque clock tower—which reminds visitors of a European setting—Parkville cradles an eclectic collection of shops and restaurants attracting Kansas Citians to this town like buffalo, to find some of the best funnery in this part of the Milky Way.

When national magazines discovered Parkville, they gushed headlines calling Parkville one of the ten coolest communities in America, and one of America's top ten commutable towns. But national spotlights couldn't ruin the town. There's only so much room in those rugged hills.

North America's first western highway keeps churning past here, making its own potholes, even though people don't travel on it much anymore. It was on this highway, the Missouri River, that the steamboat Arabia—packed with pioneers and supplies and one mule—passed within pissin' distance of Parkville when it hit a submerged walnut tree which punctured its hull. The steamer sank in minutes with no casualties except for the poor mule, tied to the railing and abandoned to drown.

Among 400 shipwrecks along this busy pioneer waterway, the Arabia—after 170 years preserved deep in mud—is one of the few to be resurrected.

The boat didn't make it to sin city. Just up the river, Weston is a port built on three major provisions for pioneers headed west: liquor, tobacco and hemp.

Years ago the river meandered more than a mile away from Weston, leaving the port high and dry. It's a metaphor for the town, which is still a conduit for booze and tobacco, the latter mostly of the chewing variety. They sell big bales of tobacco at auction in a huge warehouse in the town's bottoms near the old riverfront. It's called the Burley House—not because burly people brawl there, although they could, since its wooden floor is twice the size of a roller rink. Burley is a synonym for air-cured tobacco. And the whole region is dotted with burley barns.

Isolated from the river and major highways, the town remains blissfully mired in the past, much like a box of old postcards in your great aunt's attic.

In a litany of businesses that are the "oldest west of," Weston boasts McCormick Distillery, serving up whiskey and clear liquors since 1856. But if you want to get deep into your drinking, descend into O'Malley's Irish Pub. Back in 1842, a distillery dug storage caverns three levels deep beneath Weston. Somewhere along the way the caverns became barrooms, and their curved stone ceilings and tight passages and steep slopes that stop just short of Hell remind me of the ancient Roman catacombs, except O'Malley's occupants are still very much alive and in various stages of inebriation, some of them so drunk they can manage only to wander into a narrow catacomb passageway before they piss themselves. The old brewery site has served up suds longer than anybody west of the Hudson River, and traditional Irish music boils up like cabbage from those caverns, performed by the best Irish musicians in the world who play for drunks in cellars.

Weston's curse is also its charm: isolation. Main Street could be a Norman Rockwell painting. Or maybe it's a movie set that can dress the part of a dozen different decades. Up and down the street, old buildings shout history, while visitors scour the shops. Shopkeepers come and go, often lured at first by the town's charm. Some quickly realize that the town's refreshing isolation limits the customer traffic. It can be hard to compete with major shopping malls like Zona Rosa, a few miles away up on the interstate. But Weston's history survives in those protective bluffs along the river.

Under the only neon sign downtown is the venerable Sebus Hardware. Your parents remember hardware stores, before the advent of corporate chains. The Sebus claim that "if we don't have it, you don't need it" may not sound impressive until you see the store. At first glance the storefront doesn't look much bigger than the Weston port-o-potty. But send the friendly Sebus brothers on a search for that thingamadoodle you need to finish the job, and they disappear into a labyrinth of aisles and shelves, only to return with your item. It's a marvel, the Sebus fine art of having it all...and being able to find it.

Speaking of fine art, it was a short walk to the National Silk Art Museum containing the largest collection of silk tapestries in the world, more than 150 visuals the way people made pictures before Polaroid.

Westonites chuckle when architects flock downtown to get inspiration to create their big city malls. The townspeople gently remind the architects: Why build a replica when you can visit the real thing? Indeed, the real thing is on display at places like the Weston City Museum, telling tales you'd expect from a town steeped in stockpiles of liquor, tobacco and hemp.

I dropped in for a beer with Cloyd Louk. Cloyd looks like he played in the Allman Brothers Band. He's a perfect blend of Norse and South, fair complexion, slow drawl. He volunteers his butt off to help promote the town, when he isn't working his own business. He's a rare individual, one who can tolerate strong opinions, fervid arguments about an isolated town's road to success. I took a drink. He told me a Weston businessman was planning to climb onto a semi truck in a parking lot up the hill, "and he won't come down until the truck is full of holiday toys and food." His name was Tommie Jones, the owner of the Bunk House, a bar up on the highway. The Bunk House gets my vote for the most Deadwood-looking saloon this side of Dodge City. In the Bunk House parking lot, Tommie jumped atop an 18-wheeler to collect toys and food because "a lot of people are suffering," he said. "A little discomfort on my part is nothing."

That night I stayed in the old Saint George Hotel, a throwback to European elegance with its mansard roof and lovingly-preserved facade. Craftsmen carefully restored the hotel's historic 1845 charm.

Weston is the real deal. Sure, townspeople sometimes quarrel about how they want to portray themselves. But as shop keepers come and go, the strength of Weston is its history, proudly preserved, damn near pickled, and on display.

Erifnus was looking for a fight. Driving north of Weston we passed through Easton, and found a brick shithouse, a two-door outhouse made of bricks, strategically located near the confluence of two roads. It was built solid, but since the old wooden doors fell off, only exhibitionists stop. Rumors waft that Jesse James holed up there, and Bonnie and Clyde robbed it.

Up the road we found drama.

———— ⨳ ————

The arrow smashed into his jaw, knocking out five teeth. It was his second wound. He had jerked the first arrow out of his arm and kept riding. Now Pony Bob's mouth had an extra opening, and his shoulder was in pain. But he was young—a teenager—and his horse was fast. He rode for the Central Overland California and Pike's Peak Express Company, better known as the Pony Express, a venture that lasted only nineteen months but looms larger than life thanks to sixteen decades of glorification. Up close, this job wasn't as romantic as I thought. Cindy Daffron, curator of the Pony Express Museum in Saint Joseph, smiled as I shook my head. Probably couldn't find many people today who would work in those conditions.

I walked outside, and saluted an old friend, a neon rider clinging to a galloping horse stuck atop a ten-foot pole. A giant neon arrow underscores the horse's hooves and aims at the museum stables. This old Pony Express Motel neon survived the wrecking ball, and was transplanted to the museum's parking lot. It's the first sign that Saint Joseph is into its museums—more museums per capita than any other American city. Hell, the whole downtown is a museum, with damn near as many historic buildings as Rome. Many of these old buildings remain abandoned. A few get facelifts and they become museums. A doll museum. A fire museum. A military museum. An old Gilded Age mansion with parquet floors exhibits stories of Native Americans, westward expansion, and, of course, Jesse James's 2.2 billion exploits.

A historic hotel, the Patee House, is the second-best museum ever in a city with 77,777 residents. Surrounding the centerpiece 1860 Baldwin railroad locomotive, thousands of artifacts depict every aspect of life over the hotel's 151-year history. At the beginning of the Civil War, the Union charged the hotel's owner with treason, and convicted him. The trial was held in his own ballroom. Later, it was called the World Hotel and Epileptic Sanitarium when the widow of Jesse James was interviewed there, not far from the spot where Robert

Ford's bullet had killed her husband the previous day. Oh, and it was where the Pony Express was hatched, and served as its headquarters. The museum's police exhibit lines up a century's worth of murder weapons, including a drill with hair and skin still wrapped around it. Yikes.

The museums were warming me up for the big scare.

Erifnus rolled down Frederick Boulevard to another cluster of museums.

Inside the first building, a familiar face surprised me. Oh, I see him every time I fish a dollar from my pocket. But this time, big as life, he gazed at me from Rembrandt Peale's canvas, a copy of Gilbert Stuart's George Washington portrait. The father of our country sits in good company at the Albrecht-Kemper Museum, along with canvases by Mary Cassat, Albert Bierstadt and Wayne Thiebaud. Hopper. Stuart. Wyeth. In a front room, ink visages penned by Thomas Hart Benton peer from the walls. But in a side gallery I was greeted by a sight scarier than Hieronymus Bosch's *Last Judgment*. Glaring at me with the intensity of his vengeful God was John Brown, the stridently violent abolitionist. The tornadic portrait instilled a fear that would be overshadowed by a succession of exhibits at my next stop.

The Black Archives Museum displayed newspaper accounts and photos detailing the graphic horror of a lynching in downtown Saint Joseph. In 1933, a crowd of thousands watched as a mob laid siege to the jail for hours, finally dragging young Lloyd Warner out where they beat, hanged, and burned him. He had been accused of rape. Many people maintain his innocence. Regardless, it's a ghastly chapter in the town's history. The museum didn't whitewash the display. The presentation overwhelms other great exhibits at the Black Archives, like Mathew Brady's photographs of Abraham Lincoln and his generals on Civil War battlefields.

Next door in the Saint Joseph Museum, I was grateful to see the amazing sophistication of Native American cultures, but saddened that for the most part, native art and invention are relegated to displays from the past. What did I expect? The Fox and the Sac, the Algonquin and the Osage peoples no longer roam the Missouri prairies. For that matter the prairies have been uprooted, too.

No unsettling emotion compared to the final fright on my self-guided tour. The Glore Psychiatric Museum is America's most straightforward presentation of the relics of past treatment of the mentally ill. At once disturbing and enlightening, the museum probes the dark recesses of imagination. The first exhibit set the mood: 1,446 items swallowed by a patient: nails and screws, bolts and bobby pins and thimbles. Yes, the patient eventually died of his self-inflicted torment. Down the hall is a human treadmill resembling a giant gerbil wheel made of wood, with no windows. Near the straitjacket straps of the tranquilizer chair was a chair in a box that rotated one hundred revolutions per minute, causing anxiety and vertigo, not to mention release of bodily fluids. One after another, the displays showed evidence of mankind's inhumanity: a pillory, a contraption called Bedlam, and several coffin-like cages with names like the Utica crib and the lunatic box. There's even a boob tube version of a message in a bottle: 525 notes scribbled secretly and stuffed into the back of a television set by a resident who believed his mind was trapped in a pair of boxcars outside.

The Glore sits in a real-life setting, the former Saint Joseph Psychiatric Hospital. Its rooms are stark, cold and clinical, its doors reinforced, foreboding. The basement morgue peels away your defenses that this is just a representation. This shit is real.

I asked Kathy Reno about the future of the Glore. She's the public relations person for Saint Joseph Museums, Incorporated, the guts behind the Glore and three sister museums. "We've heard from several museum consultants," she said. "Some suggest cosmetic facelifts, like, 'Turn the entrance into a walk inside the brain.'" I sensed that she wasn't sold on the facelift idea. Me neither. Let these stark walls speak.

Then I asked her, "What's the most unique response you've heard from visitors to the Glore?"

She thought for a moment. "One lady said, 'Why didn't the doctors try these methods on themselves?'"

Erifnus made a run for it. We escaped along the cat roads, the same roads bank robbers drove to elude pursuit. In his 1981 book, *Run the Cat Roads*, Kansas Citian L.L. Edge describes how bank robbers in the 1930s made their getaways by zigzagging through a labyrinth of back roads. Cat roads. Folks romanticized bank robbers during the Great Depression, when dirt poor Midwesterners hit rock bottom hard times. Their hopelessness and despair helped them cheer for bank robbers and later, NASCAR. Of course, bootleggers get top billing as the romantic role models for racing cars. That's understandable, if you believe that whiskey is the motor oil for the soul.

Today, electronic tracking gadgetry erases the bandit's back road advantage. But those old cat roads remain, connected like capillaries, built atop their ancestors, Native America's earliest trails and trade routes.

We followed those cat roads, twisting through Agency and Gower, Grayson and Trimble, and passed the site of the Red Crown Tavern and Tourist Cabins. Inside one cabin on July 19, 1933, Bonnie and Clyde made a fatal mistake: they sent Blanche Barrow to order food next door. Her high boots and baggy whipcord riding trousers may have been the rage elsewhere, but in small-town America she stood out like a preacher in a speedo. Authorities closed in and the Red Crown shootout began. Buck Barrow was mortally wounded and Blanche lost sight in her left eye. The gang escaped, the dying Buck and blinded Blanche leaving a trail of blood and bandages as they passed through tiny Dearborn.

Recently the equivalent of one half ton of gold fell out of the sky on Dearborn when a resident won the Powerball jackpot. But poor Blanche had to rely on winning jackpots the old-fashioned way. Police eventually captured her in Iowa still wearing her riding outfit. If only she'd had a horse.

Our route twisted through Rochester and Helena, Clarksdale, Amity and Maysville. We passed a one-car carhenge, a '60s Cadillac, nose buried in the ground, tail lights poised to flash the heavens. Elvis wonders why.

Plattsburg sits pretty, with much of its old architecture intact. Main street bustles and the town is well manicured, featuring a row of delightful old homes, including Victorian gingerbread houses along the boulevard. The town's elegant demeanor is what you'd expect as the home of a former president of the United States. Well, sort of a president. David Rice Atchison was leader of the Senate back on March 4, 1849, when he stood in as president for a day, because it was Sunday, and Zachary Taylor would not conduct business, including taking the oath of office, until the next day. Missourians are proud of David Rice Atchison because of this little twist of fate.

As an attorney, he took up the cause to help some Mormons regain land seized by state authorities. But later he led the state militia to drive the Mormons from Missouri.

So Atchison had a side that was a little less gingerbread than his hometown. He was a slave owner, and wanted Kansas to be slave territory, too. He worked to import slave owners into Kansas, and even helped form a pro-slavery Kansas town that bears his name today. He even participated in the 1856 sacking and burning of Lawrence, Kansas—the first time Missourians burned Lawrence.

They were hiding back among some barns and sheds, another spot where a traveling carnival sleeps in the off-season. Only partially visible from the road, the unique shapes and garish colors jumped out from the octopus, with light bulbs for suckers on its arms folded into a truck. The tilt-a-whirl truck and the Ferris wheel truck sat beside trailers that morph into carny games of skill and chance. Mostly chance. It was hard to recognize some of the rides, packed tight as a Swiss army knife. Shake machines and simp heisters, maybe.

It seemed like a small group of trucks, as far as carnivals go, and would need to set up like a John Robinson, a carnival that arranges all the rigs and games end-to-end. Looks bigger. No matter the size, when the carny powers up, the show offers a thousand distractions in a dozen directions. The bright red Tilt-A-Whirl grinds out another batch of thrills, its halfapple carriages swinging around one foot bolted to the heaving floor. The hiss of compressed air signals the spookhouse floor has blown up another pretty print dress. The green and golden neon lights of the Rock-O-Plane flash lightning-like as it spins and dives across a starry black backdrop above the edge of towering pines.

At night, darkness surrounds the carnival's energy so completely that everyone who steps within its bounds becomes bonded to the lightbulbs. Crowds ebb and flow through the sights and sounds of heavy metal. Sideshow barkers process fresh meat every minute. The sideshows and game stands crowd along a narrow gauntlet, where grass gives up the fight to dirt and cigarette butts and cotton candy cones. Step carefully over thick black cables that keep the lightbulbs flashing in a movie marquee pattern.

But when we passed, the carny was at rest, silent, its barkers and babes scattered to the winds, hunting southern comfort and absorbing new tattoos.

Pioneers Need Pants

We passed the Hillbilly Grill in Lawson, just went right by it, even though that wasn't my natural instinct. I'll come back. Nowadays the traffic flows fast and furious through Lawson, a farm community that evolved into bedroom community, sitting on a busy feeder route that funnels country dwellers into the Kansas City workforce.

Just south of Lawson, in the pastoral countryside, a huge factory, built more than 150 years ago, made pants and sweaters. The factory may have sold pants and sweaters to Harry Truman, who sold pants and sweaters when he was a haberdasher. Of the nearly 900 textile mills in the Midwest during and after the Civil War, only Watkins Woolen Mill survives intact, sheltered in a giant brick building taller than the trees surrounding it. It's an unusual sight: Factories normally spring up in an urban scene, colored with soot. This mill is bathed in fresh air and undeterred sunshine, no city in sight, and more trees than people. The builder acted on one basic tenet: pioneers need pants.

The mill's power comes from a steam engine salvaged from an old steamboat. Walthus Watkins built the mill in 1860 near his home. He spared no expense, adding worker comforts including a six-stall privy a few yards away, with the women's stalls closest to the factory. A community built up around the mill to house the workers but dissolved back into rural bliss when the mill stopped producing sweaters. The mill is not far from the old James homestead, where Zerelda James raised her ornery younguns. I assume she got a good deal on pants and sweaters.

Imagine the scene: Zerelda picks out a couple of outfits for the boys, a dress for Susan, and brings her shopping home.

"Here, Jesse, try these on."

"Thanks, Ma."

"Hooey, Jesse, you look dandy!" Frank hooted.

"I'd rather be a dandy than a dingus, Frank."

Jesse called everybody dingus. He coined the word. Nobody—excepting Frank—ever called Jesse dingus to his face.

As we left the mill, I saw a canine kin to Jesse James—a coyote—cross the highway. Around the next bend, somebody with too much free time had hoisted a tractor twenty feet into the air and impaled it on a pole. I whispered a short orison to the tractor in the sky as we passed, and turned toward Richmond.

You can't get to Excelsior Springs by train anymore. That's the way Harry Truman liked to travel. But he arrived in town by auto the night he defeated Thomas Dewey to win reelection as president. It was in all the papers. Harry stayed at the Elms Hotel, a palace in its heyday, built above the therapeutic mineral springs that gave the town its name. I rolled into downtown, a precipitous dive down Route H into the valley of the springs, and the old hotel.

Erifnus came to rest in the hotel parking lot. When her engine switched off, the sound of live music filled the air. Across the street a blues band wailed at the Wabash BBQ & Blues Garden. Well, slap my grandma, there's bound to be a chair over there for my derrière.

The restaurant occupies a historic old train station, a spur to the Wabash main line. After only a six-year run Wabash stopped passenger service to Excelsior in 1933. But the brick mission-style station survives, smokin' meats and smokin' music.

Daylight had turned to dark when I finished my railroad rib dinner and checked into the Elms Hotel.

For decades the Elms Hotel stood simple and elegant. Plain might be a better word, in this age of glitz and glitter. Plain was just fine for Harry Truman.

But recently the Elms Hotel got a makeover. Stately elegance. Handsomely appointed guest rooms offer ultimate comfort.

Next morning the hotel's Grotto, inspired by Roman baths, lured me into the steam room, and then a cool-down in the European lap pool. After a whirlpool bath I sat in the sauna and sweated out stuff from college. A relaxed dinner at the hotel filled me with smoked wild salmon, shaved asparagus with pickled shallots and mustard mousse, and a succotash with vegetables and herbs harvested from The Elms's own raised-bed gardens.

I retired to a comfortable bed and dreamt that Jesse James defeated Dewey, and as president he tweeted a lot and robbed everybody.

Next day after scouring the art-deco Hall of Waters with its therapeutic springwater baths, I searched for lunch. It's hard to overlook Ray's Diner. On Broadway downtown, Ray's low-slung exterior shouts the name "Ray's Famous HamburgerS" stretched across the diner's brow in mismatched hand-lettered fonts over an awning that screams candy cane colors. Open the old-fashioned screen door with the Rainbo Bread handleplate, step onto the red and white checkered floor in the shadow of a hundred memorable logos from your childhood, and enter ninety years of fried or scrambled, white or wheat, ketchup and mustard, pickles and cheese, chili, fish & chips and homemade pies.

Sated, I resumed exploring downtown. Around the corner, the neon marquee on the Playhouse Theatre promised "Bathroom Humor." Theater plays a big role in the psyche of Excelsior Springs. This is the birthplace of Graftina Leabo, who, as actress Betty Joyce, starred as Jane in five Tarzan movies.

We left Excelsior behind and plunged into the deep woods, set on a path to rendezvous for dinner. Even as I glanced at my watch, I knew Cheryl, who has endured me for forty years, was already driving from two hours east. And friends were headed to our dinner spot from all points of the compass.

Deep Country Cuisine

Bela, an aging Great Pyrenees dog, greeted me in the yard with a friendly bark that said, "What took you so long?"

Bela had a point. It took us three years to get here for dinner. Mostly my fault. Procrastination. Missed signals. Several of our friends kept thinking about a rendezvous here, but nobody could agree on a good day to meet, until now. That's mainly because dinner at the Dancing Bear requires a commitment. And therein lies the charm. Not much more than an hour from Kansas City, we were in the sticks.

Erifnus felt her way from Independence toward Highway 13, and east of Higginsville, south through Corder, then down a gravel road sorely lacking signage. That doesn't deter Kansas Citians from venturing out to taste this hidden gem. Or me either, finally.

It was worth the trip.

I walked into a monument to comfort, country style. Soft yellow light from lamps with earthtone lampshades, and chairs that don't mind if they don't match the tables or each other, and a low ceiling, not so low that you bump your head on the turn-of-the-century rafter beams. If these old tile block walls could talk....

Already, several Kansas City residents were deep into dinner at a couple of the seven tables in this intimate setting.

I joined our dinner party, kissed and hugged Cheryl, and took my seat next to an old pump organ, as faint strains of John Hiatt's "Memphis" played from the kitchen. Ambiance. I looked around at the rugs and tablecloths and tapestries, working together to wrap the room in layers of comfort. Layers is the operative word, because this house, my friends, was built as a chicken house. The laying hens are long gone, of course, and the place has been scrubbed but not screwed up. Behind its overstuffed chairs and the warmth of a fire in the hearth, it's still an old chicken house, and that sets the stage for a gastric extravaganza.

The meals were lovingly created by Dancing Bear owner Katie Crutchfield, a west coast chef who transplanted here. Different pace. Her menu began with ginger butternut squash soup and a pair of home baked breads, and I proceeded through red hot shrimp and peppers sautéed in a spicy lemon and butter Tabasco gravy. I used every drop of the accompanying cream to tame the Tabasco. And through tears of joy I could've devoured the whole thing, if I wasn't forced to share. At our table, everybody traded food in a chicken ranch orgy: macadamia nut-crusted salmon, capiello chicken with prosciutto and a sauce with mushrooms and artichoke hearts, and tender corn cakes with roasted red pepper salsa, black beans and a cilantro lime crème fraiche. It was the best corn cake I ever stole off Cheryl's plate.

We ate like camels drink: deep. After all, it's a long way outta here.

We hugged goodbye in the parking lot and drove separate ways into the darkness. Tomorrow was a work day for our friends, and for Cheryl.

Dark and Stormy Night

As Erifnus rolled onto a dark country road, lightning flashed a warning. A thunderstorm was gnashing toward us. Luckily, my dining companions were driving away from the storm. Not me.

Erifnus took me north toward the riverport of Lexington to spend the night. A rising wind collected autumn leaves from the ditches and blew them across her headlights. Lightning flashed incessantly. Each strobe illuminated the rural countryside for a millisecond. Between strobes, the darkness surrounding rural Highway 13 got even blacker. Gusts of wind rocked Erifnus as the first fat raindrops hit her windshield.

I fumbled for the radio dial.

"Hello Kansas City, your temperature is 58."

There may not be a dozen people at Kansas City listening to KMZU Radio. That just proves it's Missouri's best radio station. At least it's best for me, as I drive these back roads. The station broadcasts from Carrollton, a center of agrarian commerce. Real live radio personalities mix cornball talk, country music and usable information. Real Americana. They bring out music that's past dusty, it's caked with auditory neglect. But the music is classic, underappreciated, like Roger Miller's "Do Wacka Do."

Hearing from an old dead friend like Roger Miller brings comfort, especially in this welling storm. "Do Wacka Do" is travelin' music. And when Roger finished his classic, he gave way to a live radio voice who told me where we would intersect a chain of blossoming thunderstorms. The announcer shouted out warnings to the townspeople of Coloma and Chula, Stet and Wakenda, whose combined population struggles to eclipse 400. The station really works to provide the region's best weather coverage, and on this night, it paid off. Every ten minutes, the announcer interrupted Roger Miller and Willie Nelson and Hank Williams to tell me the thunderstorm just pelted Ethel and was bearing down on Elmer. The tiny towns of Ethel and Elmer list less than a hundred residents each. But they all bond to the voice from Carrollton.

Lightning strobes in the darkness couldn't give me the whole picture of the storm movement. So the radio announcer helped us through the deluge.

Erifnus Caitnop and I have busted through hundreds of storms along our journey. As we approached this squall line, my mind replayed my father's voice: "You can do more things that don't make money," Dad chided me. Before he died, Dad made peace with my obsession to drive every mile of every road on my highway map. He knew I'd inherited his vagabond gene.

The storm crashed into Erifnus broadside. Her tires dug a death grip into the pavement. As we passed the old Confederate Cemetery at Higginsville her headlights caught a strange form that danced over the black road against the wind and disappeared into the woods. Smaller than a deer and whiter than an albino cat, it flashed across my eyes like a rolling wheel of bones. If it came from the old Confederate Cemetery, it might be the half-ghost of the king of the Bushwhackers.

Only five bones from William Quantrill's body are buried here. That's enough to make a ghost, according to Washington Irving. And Quantrill was a spirited individual.

Hunted like the Devil during the Civil War, Quantrill was shot to pieces in Kentucky, where he was buried. His mother asked that he be exhumed and re-interred in his home town of Dover, Ohio. Most of his body parts made it to Dover. But skullduggery diverted his head and five bones to a dank corner of a museum at the University of Kansas in Lawrence, a town Quantrill's raiders burned and pillaged in 1863. Those bones finally were liberated from Kansas in 1992 thanks to successful negotiations by Robert Hawkins and other Sons of the Confederate Veterans. All of Quantrill's bones would have been reunited, but Dover refused a Confederate burial ceremony, preferring to dodge controversy. When the dust settled, the skull was interred quietly at Dover, and the five bones were given a Confederate ceremony at their final resting spot here. The Sons of the Confederate Veterans poured a slab of concrete over the casket to keep it from wandering off. But ghosts can seep through caskets and concrete, right? Even half-ghosts.

Quantrill was the king of the bushwhackers, but he isn't the only bushwhacker buried along Highway 13.

A few miles west of us, somewhere under this violent storm, in a peaceful cemetery outside Waterloo lies a cutthroat who tortured victims and took scalps. He also led the first peacetime daylight bank robbery in America.

Popular lore credits the James Gang for the robbery. But the leader's name wasn't James. Fierce as a wolverine, Archie Clement stood only five feet tall. He cut his teeth with Quantrill and became chief scalper for Bloody Bill Anderson as they cut across Missouri's heart.

Little Archie Clement's post-war career was brief. On Saint Valentine's Eve, 1866, a howling blizzard provided cover as the Clement gang, including Frank James, robbed a Liberty, Missouri bank. Two robbers entered the Clay County Savings Association, took $60,000 from two employees and sealed them in the bank vault. The robbers forgot to spin the lock. No matter. Jumping on horseback the gang vanished into the blizzard, murdering an innocent college kid as they fled. A posse followed the gang's fading hoof prints through the snow to a ferry at the Missouri River. There, the trail turned cold. The ferry had reached the other side of the river.

Eight months later, on the day before Halloween, Clement's gang struck again, robbing $2,000 from the Alexander Mitchell & Company Bank at Lexington. By the end of that year, Clement was dead, killed in a shootout in Lexington, and buried in Arnold Cemetery, a lightning bolt away from Erifnus as her tires squeegeed heavy rainwater off Highway 13.

Five months after Archie Clement died, Frank and Jessie rode into Richmond with a gang that robbed $4,000 from the Hughes and Wasson Bank. They killed the town's mayor and two lawmen.

The James Gang legend didn't become famous until their chief cheerleader began telling their story. Buried a dozen miles east of our stormy path is the principal architect of the legend of Jesse James. Major John Newman Edwards lies in Dover Cemetery. He rode with Confederate General Joseph Shelby, and after the war he battled the harsh imposition of Reconstruction on southern sympathizers. He founded the *Kansas City Times* newspaper, from which he corresponded with Jesse James, and his stories about James elevated the outlaw to the status of an American Robin Hood.

When Robert Ford murdered Jesse James, Edwards wrote: "Tear the two bears from the flag of Missouri. Put thereon, in place of them, as more appropriate, a thief blowing out the brains of an unarmed victim, and a brazened harlot, naked to the waist and splashed to the brows in blood." The thief was Robert Ford. The harlot was Reconstruction.

We approached Lexington and the region's most prolific killer, the Missouri River. Like most killers, the river has no respect for the sanctity of humans. A 1993 flood scoured tiny Hardin Cemetery, four miles from the riverbank, washing nearly 900 bodies across flooded farm fields downriver with the flood. Concrete vaults, caskets and corpses floated among the flood debris. Recovery efforts found a few hundred bodies, identified a fraction of those. Most sailed away.

On the back end of the storm, a calm sky filled with stars. I put my faith in the message from my trusty radio friend:

"Hello Lexington. You're in for a beautiful starlit night."

The Dean of Tunes

Hemp is vital to civilization. Pioneers knew this. But a century ago, a movement resembling prohibition outlawed hemp, because it has a cousin that will get you high.

Until recently, growing hemp was illegal in Missouri. Even a few years ago, a Missouri senator tried to reverse the ban, realizing the economic value of hemp, and the fact that it grows wild and thick along almost every railroad ditch. "Missouri can corner the hemp market," he reasoned, "and produce everything from clothing to tires." The bill almost passed, except for the efforts of an unholy alliance. The state highway patrol testified that growing hemp would send the wrong signal to our youth, even though ditch weed lacks the ingredient that gets people stoned. NORML sided with the cops, for a different reason. The National Organization for the Reform of Marijuana Laws testified that their members didn't want this impotent hemp crop cross pollinating with their potent pot plants and dumbing them down.

It's not the first time folks in Missouri fought over hemp.

Real blood spilled along the Lexington riverfront at the Battle of the Hemp Bales. At the time of the Civil War, people weren't afraid of hemp. They made rope and clothing and just about everything else from the sinewy fiber. Early in the war, General Sterling Price led Confederate forces on a roll across Missouri. During a siege on Union fortifications atop a Lexington hill, Price used unique shields to advance up the hill under heavy fire. The rebels found giant round hemp bales on the wharf, waiting for a steamer to take them to a rope factory. The rebels soaked the bales with water, and arranged a hundred of them as a rolling breastworks, each pushed up the hill by three or four men. Union cannons poured hot shot into the wet bales, but couldn't get them to burn. The shields worked, and after almost 160 casualties, the Union troops surrendered.

The hemp battle isn't Lexington's most notable story.

Local historian Byron Nicodemus told me about Lexington's brightest star. Back in the silent movie days, a young organist named Carl Stalling wowed patrons at the local theaters. He was so good he gravitated to Kansas City, where an upstart cartoon animator named Disney heard Carl playing the score for a silent film and hired him as musical director at Disney's fledgling Laff-O-Gram Studios, the birthplace of Mickey Mouse. Moving west to Los Angeles with Walt, Carl later left Disney Studios—a move some people questioned at the time—to work for Warner Brothers. There, Carl Stalling became "the dean of tunes," the musical genius behind more than 700 cartoons that formed the wallpaper to your childhood.

He arranged a Dave Franklin song, "The Merry Go Round Broke Down," in a 1937 cartoon named *Rover's Rival*. The song became the theme for *Looney Tunes*. You've heard it as many times as you've sung "Happy Birthday." But that's not Carl's most important contribution to civilization. His most lasting legacy happens every time a child sees a Warner Brothers cartoon. Daffy Duck, Bugs Bunny...it doesn't matter. Behind every visual, a musical score introduces the viewer to the classics. His scores dig deeper than the obvious classical greatest hits, like "William Tell Overture." His work blends Brahms and Chopin and Mozart. It's a safe bet that if your next door neighbor whistles a classical tune while sweeping his driveway, he learned it after school watching Porky Pig.

There's little trace of Carl Stalling in Lexington, Missouri. It's a paradox: In a town with layers of rich history, a town boasting more historic homes per capita than anywhere, the fate of Carl's house remains unknown. My car didn't care. Erifnus Caitnop promised to shout Carl Stalling's arrangements from her cd player, while avoiding the fate of his last name.

So I slid back behind the wheel, and we headed north to the cadence of Wagner's "Kill the Wabbit."

———⚬⚬⚬———

We tried in vain to find the Bloody Bucket, a hoppin' little nightclub in its day. Better fortune smiled as we passed an old juke joint called the Mittieville Peckerwood Club. Woulda stopped but the place has been closed for years. Somebody said it may reopen. Hope so. The nightclub clings to an embankment like a ramshackle cabin from your grandpa's photos. Great old jukebox and dance floor. Mittieville really isn't a town. Birdie May and Oscar Mittie were the original owners, and liquor was the medium to grease the gullets of Kansas City mobsters who came here to meet and play and drink and eat boiled shrimp and fried catfish, and add to tall tales like the story about where the machine gunners hid after the Kansas City Massacre back in 1933.

The landscape along Highway 13 is splattered with notorious killers. For Erifnus the brush with death came around the next bend. Crossing north from Lexington was the scariest Missouri River bridge ever. Screeching brakes and a hard turn set us upon the old bridge, so narrow it was difficult to insert a dollar bill between passing vehicles.

Erifnus wasn't fazed. She was gliding up Highway 13 toward Richmond, and the graves of two of America's most infamous killers. They're buried within blocks of one another.

Murderous Row

"Hello, Bob."

It was the last thing Bob Ford heard. As he turned, two blasts from a shotgun tore through his throat, "carried his gold collar-button out through the back of his neck," said Cy Warman, editor of the Creede, Colorado *Daily Chronicle*.

Outlaw Robert Newton Ford never tried to duck his reputation. In fact, he profited by posing for photographs. He and brother Charlie reenacted the murder of the world's most famous outlaw in a stage play called *The Brother's Vow; or, the Bandit's Revenge*. The pair thought they would become rich. But the play soon fizzled. Bob migrated west to capitalize on the Colorado mining boom. When Bob's saloon in

Creede burned to the ground, he opened a tent saloon called the Leadville Dance Hall. On June 8, 1892, Edward O'Kelly entered the tent and killed him.

Ford was buried in Colorado, but his body later was moved home to Richmond Cemetery, where he lies under the epitaph, "The man who shot Jesse James."

Bob and brother Charlie—who rode with the James Gang during the Blue Cut train robbery—had been sentenced to hang for the murder of Jesse James. Both were pardoned by Governor Thomas Crittenden on the same day they were convicted and sentenced. Always on the run from vengeance, Charlie couldn't stand the shame, and soon after their play ended he committed suicide. He's buried in Richmond Cemetery too.

A few blocks away, Pioneer Cemetery holds the bones of Oliver Cowdery, the main scribe for the Book of Mormon, and one of three witnesses who said he saw the sacred gold plates an angel delivered to Joseph Smith, founder of the Mormon Church.

In the same Pioneer Cemetery lies the body of the Devil, or so thought Union sympathizers who were terrorized by Bill Anderson. "Bloody Bill" earned his nickname from a murderous rampage through Missouri during the Civil War, including a slaughter of Union forces called the Centralia Massacre. After Centralia, Union cavalry focused on finding Anderson. They tracked him down near Orrick, Missouri and killed him, paraded his body through Richmond, photographed his corpse, then buried him in a field. Nearly forty-five years later, retired outlaw Cole Younger reburied Anderson in Pioneer Cemetery in a Confederate military ceremony.

Cemetery searches make me hungry. We started combing the hillsides for some local fare. People in Richmond and Ray County are proud of the food that made them famous: a fungus that looks like a pointy sponge. Fifty billion morel mushrooms hid in plain sight in the warm damp hillsides around Ray county, but I'll be damned if I could find one, even though some sprout to the size of the Travelocity gnome. Plus, my shotgun kept jamming, so I'm not sure what I would've done had I seen one. They sure are good eatin', though. Better than steak. More expensive, too.

We gave up hunting and rolled back onto the highway. A tip from ROMEO (Retired Old Motorcyclists Eating Out) sent us sliding into the parking lot at Daddy's 10-13 Diner. ROMEO members ride their motorcycles for miles to sample diners and greasy spoons throughout the heartland, so it was a no-brainer to follow their lead. The group has no rules, no dues, no president or board of directors. They don't even ride together to their chosen destinations, posted online a few days ahead of the meal. They avoid interstates and big chain food outlets, preferring to drop into a mom 'n' pop shop for a home cooked meal and good vibes. My kind of travelers.

A cadre of servers at Daddy's welcomed me as I wandered to the end of the counter next to a unique piece of wall art. A few years back when new owners repainted the interior, they left one square foot of wall unpainted and framed behind glass. It's the spot where Daddy, the original owner, sat at the counter leaning against this wall for many of his eighty-nine years, leaving a worn spot on the wall, and smears of his DNA, I suppose. This strange shrine represents the essence of local diners: each diner becomes a unique thumbprint on the folds of your brain.

My hamburger steak and mashed potatoes were smothered in gravy. It's a genetic predilection inherited from my dad. Extra gravy.

We hit the road. Building on its reputation as the route through robbers and assassins, Highway 13 snaked through more turbulent history. Atrocity is Missouri's middle name, especially in this area... the Indian wars, the Border War, the Civil War. Layers of genocide mix deep in this soil. And the local fights over religion and territory, freedom and slavery made folk heroes of some unsavory characters: Archie Clement, William Quantrill, Bloody Bill Anderson and Jesse James.

Before those Civil War bushwhackers were buried along this route, another civil war raged here, turmoil over religion. And the earth still bears the scars and the blood stains from that ugly chapter in our history.

East of Eden

It's a pastoral drive into rural Caldwell County. Farmland drapes over rolling hills framed by forests, punctuated by old redwood barns. It's easy to imagine why folks of the Mormon faith—or any faith—settled in this beautiful area. The truth is less pastoral: Mormons in 1830s Missouri were relegated to this spot by neighborly intolerance, pushed from one county to the next.

Tensions turned into violence.

When the Mormons first came to Missouri, they settled in Jackson County near a spot where their Prophet Joseph Smith taught was the origin of mankind, the Garden of Eden. Local settlers had no tolerance for this unfamiliar religion; they expelled Smith and his followers. The Mormons moved a dozen miles north to Clay County. A few years later locals drove them out of Clay County, too. Moving east a few miles, they planned to build a temple in the tiny community of Far West. The town existed only for a few years before neighbors forced the Mormons to leave. The construction of the temple never advanced beyond a cornerstone. Today a shrine marks the spot, telling about the Mormon struggle in Missouri.

———— ∞∞∞ ————

From Far West we rolled through Kerr and Kidder, and Nettleton, first called Gomer, across Poor Tom Creek, named not for a man without money, but, according to local lore, for a child who ate too much honey. Down the road, New York is named for, well, New York. We crossed Panther Creek into Proctorville, down to Braymer and Black Oak, over Mud Creek to Easterville, named not for the religious observance but for a man named Easter, and past Mirabile, the Latin word for wonderful, over Goose Creek and Plum Creek, past the ghosts who lived in the shanties near Brushy Creek.

Driving this outback I'm amazed at the stories behind the names. Many of these stories would be lost were it not for Martha Ewing, who dutifully recorded these unique appellations and the tales of their creation. It must have been a tedious project, back in 1929. Why would anybody drive all these roads to uncover their stories?

Erifnus rolled up Highway 13 through Polo and tiny Kingston, second-smallest county seat in Missouri. At Shoal Creek we left the highway to view a monument to seventeen Mormon victims shot and hacked and dumped in a well by an angry militia led by the sheriff of neighboring Livingston County. The Haun's Mill Massacre happened on Halloween eve, 1838. Public sentiment against Mormons propelled these vigilantes. The attackers likely were unaware they had been granted permission to murder, by an "Extermination Order" issued a few days earlier by Missouri Governor Lilburn Boggs. The horrific massacre included killing two boys aged nine and ten. Defending the murder of children, one militia member said, "Nits will make lice…."

It was a vicious incident in the brutal history of the Mormon War in Missouri.

———— ⊗⊗⊗ ————

Approaching Hamilton, home of baseball Hall of Famer Zack Wheat, a road sign calls this stretch of pavement the Zack Wheat Memorial Highway. Hamilton also is J.C. Penney's birthplace. There is no J.C. Penney Memorial Highway. This oversight can be fixed: From the bottom of Erifnus Caitnop's coin bin I fished her good luck charm. It represents a solution to this snub of J.C. Penney: memorialize these two great men on one sign—the Wheat Penney Memorial Highway. Alas, this Wheat Penney will garner little interest.

We reached Gallatin and headed to jail. It's the most unique jail in America. Called a squirrel cage, the rotary jail features a circular cage divided into pie-shaped cells. To enter a cell, the jailer must rotate the entire structure to align with the outer door. Only three such jails remain anywhere on the planet. The citizens of Daviess County built the jail seven years after Frank James arrived here in 1883 to stand trial for the 1869 murder of local bank cashier John W. Sheets. Much of the trial focused on Jesse James; this was Jesse's first publicly identified bank heist. But fourteen years after the robbery, Jesse was dead. Frank was acquitted.

———— ⊗⊗⊗ ————

Driving north on Highway 13, we found the spot in the Grand River valley where Joseph Smith said Adam and Eve settled after they were expelled from the Garden of Eden.

At least fifteen million followers believe the second coming of Christ will begin at this tranquil valley just off the highway, a place Smith called Adam-ondi-Ahman, which has been translated several different ways, including "the land where Adam dwelt."

Mormons believe when the end is near, prophets and leaders of all time will gather, Adam will appear and turn the government of the human family over to Christ.

Needless to say, Mormons hold sacred these spots along Highway 13, as sacred as Jerusalem or Mecca, since they're the post-asp-and-apple home of Adam and Eve, and the launching pad to heaven.

Just north of Adam and Eve's pad we entered yet another war zone.

The Devil's Dirty Work

Missourians can't help it. They keep tearing Lawrence down.

Apologies to the good people of Lawrence, Kansas—both of them—but there's bad blood between them and us. In fact, the Civil War really began along the border between Missouri and Kansas, long before the first shots rang out at Fort Sumter.

The first time Lawrence got torched was in 1856 during the Bleeding Kansas conflict. Jesse James was only eight years old, so it's doubtful his mom let him make the trip. Seven years later, he likely missed the second burning of Lawrence, too. But brother Frank was there, along with William Quantrill, Bloody Bill Anderson, Archie Clement and a cadre of Bushwhackers.

Ang Lee's movie, *Ride with the Devil,* wasn't the first celluloid treatment of the 1863 burning of Lawrence. But he was the first to use an old abandoned Missouri town as the movie set. Lee found the perfect torchable town in Old Pattonsburg, Missouri, a town so ravaged by floods that the inhabitants moved out of the Grand River valley, up the hill and established a new Pattonsburg. Left behind, solid old brick buildings—a church, a post office, mercantile stores—stood empty along Old Pattonsburg's main street.

With Hollywood skill, Lee transformed the old ghost town, made it look like Lawrence, and torched it again. Ang Lee's circus of actors and technicians and trailers added a cash infusion to the local economy. Motel rooms sold out for weeks as movie crews spent money in local stores on food and booze and gas and stuff.

After Lee's movie, folks were excited that a burgeoning movie industry might take a foothold in this old ghost town, which could be dressed up to look like anytown main street from the 1850s to the 1950s.

With low overhead that would compete with the Canadian film industry, the town was poised to nickname itself Movie Set, Missouri. Instead, local authorities finished off what Bushwhacker actors had left standing. After Ang Lee's carnival left the old ghost town, bulldozers razed the solid old buildings on Main Street. They just tore them down. According to more than one source, the county couldn't afford liability insurance. Plus, law enforcement authorities worried that teens would party in the empty streets and buildings.

Legitimate concerns.

But with one big movie under its belt, Old Pattonsburg had street cred. It could have provided the small-town backdrop for movies about any era from Twain to Truman. Film a movie on the lot once every ten years, and you could reap enough income for liability insurance, two deputies to chase out the vagrants, and enough money left over to pay a few teacher salaries.

It was a forfeiture of forward thinking.

Kansans had the last laugh. They rebuilt Lawrence. Old Pattonsburg died.

But if there's ever a living testament to the phrase "Life goes on," it's new Pattonsburg.

When the citizens of Old Pattonsburg got tired of the floods and planned their new shining city on a hill, they designed a new school in the shape of a geodesic dome. They built a modern business district, with artifacts from Old Pattonsburg.

In new Pattonsburg's Old Memories Café I found the best blue plate special this side of the senior center. I had pork chops with dressing, and mashed potatoes and gravy, cottage cheese and a salad with bleu cheese chunks the size of the Hope Diamond. All for under $10. So they saved the Old Pattonsburg prices, along with the Old Pattonsburg recipes.

In that café I found something else: paintings on loan from artist Elanor McMahall commemorating *Ride with the Devil*. The scenes are vivid reminders of Old Pattonsburg's last days, when Ang Lee brought his Hollywood carnival to town, dressed her up like Lawrence and set her ablaze.

Rest in peace, Old Pattonsburg. You went out in a blaze of glory.

Murder and Rebirth on the Prairie

Highway 13 cuts through a rogue's gallery of America's most brazen killers. The most ruthless killer in this area was a government employee: General Philip Sheridan. A Union General during the Civil War, Sheridan led a mostly unsuccessful raid on Richmond, Virginia that "smacked of unnecessary showboating" according to historian Gordon C. Rhea. Later in the war he executed a scorched earth campaign in the Shenandoah Valley, burning crops to the ground and destroying railroads and factories, mills and barns. He left 400 square miles uninhabitable. The campaign was a preview of Sherman's March to the Sea [the wallpaper to *Gone with the Wind*].

After the war President Grant and General Sherman appointed Sheridan to command the Military Division of Missouri. His empire was vast, encompassing all the Great Plains. His goal was to uproot and move Native American tribes. Calling buffalo "the Indians' commissary," Sheridan employed professional hunters to trespass on Indian land and murder millions of buffalo. Similar to the scorched earth campaigns he waged against the South, Sheridan urged the hunters to "kill, skin and sell until the buffalo is exterminated." To punctuate Sheridan's deplorable attitude, he suggested the hunters should receive medals, engraved with a dead buffalo on one side and a dejected Indian on the other. Sheridan vehemently denied uttering the phrase "The only good Indian is a dead Indian." Still, popular culture credits him with the phrase.

Today only one percent of the thirteen million acres of Missouri prairie land remains. Along with the prairie, the bison herds were obliterated. But Sheridan couldn't render them extinct. Thanks to conservation efforts, Missouri prairies and buffalo are making a comeback.

So is a break dancing bird.

It was 5 a.m. when we entered the sanctuary of Dunn Ranch Prairie, too early to watch the bison, and well before the break dancers would hit this prairie stage at sunrise. We crept up to a bird blind and sneaked into the back door of the double-dumpster-sized structure to see the show.

We waited. And waited. The pre-dawn sun painted a curtain of clouds tomato soup red. We waited. One dancer appeared, spinning and flapping his wings. Another dancer staked out his ground at a respectful distance, and he spun and jumped ten feet in the air and fell to the ground in a frenetic swirl. He pumped his pumpkin-hued jowls to the size of a tennis ball, and made the booming noise that attracts chicks, or more precisely, hens. The boomers are prairie chickens, almost gone from the Earth, doomed to be remembered only in Native American dance ceremonies if these dancing birds don't get a boost. Thanks to Dunn Ranch Prairie and a coalition of public and private well-wishers, the bird and its passionate mating dance have a chance at survival.

Meanwhile, the bison came into view over the prairie horizon. They travel together and don't feel compelled to text, which is refreshing. Dunn Ranch Prairie reintroduced the buffalo to this area in 2011... now herds are thriving here and at Prairie State Park in southwest Missouri. Other preserves around the state raise buffalo for food. But these bison are wild.

The boomers and buffalo roam the 70,000-acre Grand River Grasslands, a tallgrass prairie restoration partnership between Missouri and Iowa, private landowners, and several conservation groups and agencies.

Smaller prairie restoration projects in Missouri stand against the tide of tillers and concrete. La Petite Gemme Prairie. Friendly Prairie. Drover's Prairie. Paint Brush Prairie.

It's a scary thought that wildfire is the prairie community's best friend. In a rejuvenating process, Mother Nature applies the burn with a lightning bolt. The wildfire scorches everything above ground, ridding non-prairie invasive species, most notably cedars. Prairie grasses burn to the ground but their roots are resilient, and beneath the ground surface, the wildflowers—with deep roots and long memories—survive the fire. After a burn, natural or man-made, the flowers will be popping.

Better for the prairie chicken, upland sandpiper, Henslow's sparrows and bob-o-links.

We left the prairie and the buffalo, and beat a path back to Saint Joseph, hometown of two of the world's greatest reporters: 1) Walter Cronkite, and 2) the young University of Missouri student who wrote this:

Saint Jo. Buchanan County,
Is leagues and leagues away,
And I sit in the gloom of this rented room
And pine to be there today.

Fresh out of Mizzou, nineteen-year-old Eugene Field wrote *Lover's Lane, Saint Jo* in a London hotel room.

Yes, with the London fog around me
And the bustling to and fro,
I am fretting to be across the sea
In Lover's Lane, Saint Jo.

And the girl should do the driving,
For a fellow can't, you know,
Unless he's neglectful of what's respectful
In Lover's Lane, Saint Jo.

Erifnus didn't drive to Lover's Lane, since I was by myself.

The World's Greatest Taco Stand

Driving the backroads between fields of corn, some folks think about ethanol. Not me. While Erifnus laps up a diet laced with corn liquor, I see the cornfields and think of their ancestors: maize, and its most cherished byproduct. Flat, fried, rolled, stuffed or buttered, the corn tortilla has tantalized taste buds for 12,000 years, dating back through the magnificent Aztec culture.

Erifnus never strays far from one of the 2.3 billion Mexican restaurants that sling salsa in the great flyover.

Mexican fare is thick around the stockyards of Saint Joseph, where generations of Mexican Americans have worked up an appetite to savor old family recipes at Barbosa's Castillo, a three-story century-old delight of a mansion, and Palma's and La Mesa. Down the road in Holt, near the big red Old Bill's Mill and Ben's Junky Pawn Shop, we learned the cantina El Guapo bit the dust. Ned Nederlander, Lucky Day and Dusty Bottoms would be perplexed.

But it wasn't yet 7 a.m. out here among the cornstalks, and five hours of pinball driving could deposit me for lunch just about anywhere in the state. In a rare fit of planning, I knew if Erifnus continued east along the blacktops bordering Highway 6—crooked sister to the Avenue of the Greats—I might find real authentic Mexican food. I followed my hunch for lunch, tacking back and forth along Highway 6 like a sailboat on the backroads, with an eye on the tiny farming community of Milan, more than a hundred miles away. There's a reason, I reasoned, why Milan would have the best Mexican food.

Like most sojourns, the adventure is getting there. And like all of my sojourns, driving lonely roads by myself, I had time to think. Today, my thoughts kept coming back to food.

When ethnic foods fall into the American melting pot, it's hard to preserve the essence of the old country. Nothing wrong with the melting pot. But in a world where big chains employ clowns and kings to spice up the sameness, the rugged individuality of the Mexican culinary art form engages all five senses. Ample artwork shouts from the walls, loud as Mariachi music. Even the presentation of food is fun. Sizzling fajitas announce that your olfactory will soon bathe in the aroma of roasted peppers.

Driving farther northeast into the Green Hills, we began squishing hundreds of apples strewn along the highway. Their distinct aroma rose ahead of Erifnus, and mashed by her tires, their bruised fruit smelled even more pungent in our wake. Road apples. They make the Green Hills green.

The advice of Harry Truman came to mind: "Never kick a fresh turd on a hot day."

Smashing through road apple country made me think of a vacation somewhere in time, when Cheryl and I stayed at the Grand Hotel on Mackinac Island. There are no cars on the island, only horse-drawn carriages. And the sweet smell of a billion blooming flowers mixes with the pungence of a flower's favorite food: road apples. Islanders scoop the poop and crumble it into flowerbeds. Grundy County residents do the same.

Turds turned the roads into an endless two-lane checkerboard. We kept our eyes peeled for a hockey wagon. Up the road, a dozen buggies parked outside a Jamesport produce market, clues to Amish culture. A giant four-horse draft team approached in the oncoming lane, its wagoneer headed to plow a field. We waved to each other, two drivers, each a foreign object to the other, with one common bond: friendly tolerance. It's refreshing to absorb elements of this passive community, even as an outsider looking in.

For anything smaller than a goat, this is free range country. There are free range chickens, and free range turtles, and free range turds. You can't dodge turds the way you dodge turtles. There are too many. We drove full steam ahead, breaking down the horse fodder so it could wash away more easily, and fertilize the ditch, which is dotted with chickens.

It's obvious that the predominant source of locomotion in the Jamesport area, at least among the good Amish people, is a vehicle with precisely one horsepower. It takes approximately 7,000 chickens to produce one horsepower. So Ben Hur didn't use chickens to pull his chariot. On Route WW, we drove through a flock of free range chickens crossing the road. I didn't ask why.

In Trenton, I stayed at the Hyde Mansion Bed and Breakfast, built for former Missouri Governor Arthur Hyde. Of course, it wasn't a bed and breakfast when it was built. And technically it wasn't built for Governor Hyde, since his widow built it after his death. But it honors his memory. Good enough for me. He's buried in the Odd Fellows Cemetery, and like too many of our ancestors, his memory gets boiled down to a few dates on a tombstone. And in Hyde's case, a bed and breakfast. Yet as governor during the early 1920s he presided over big changes. Missouri finally allowed women to hold state office, and developed its first plan to build roads—some of the same roads Erifnus drives today. Hyde was Herbert Hoover's secretary of agriculture when farm prices crashed, the stock market crashed and the Great Depression began. Ouch.

His lasting legacy is something you can touch. He launched our state parks system.

Erifnus rolled into Crowder State Park, to take a break from the road. I switched off her engine and instantly rhythms changed. The motor's sound, the radio chatter, the low roar of wind and the song of tires on pavement gave way to songbirds talking to each other, and the backbeat of water lapping against the lakeshore.

It was a chance to decompress, to think.

Why the hell am I driving these roads? There's no reward, other than knowledge. There's no pot 'o gold, other than experience. The cash I've paid for gasoline over thirteen years and 294,000 miles could have bought 8,000 lottery tickets. But lottery tickets never meant shit to me; I can count the lottery tickets I've bought on the fingers of one hand, with the middle finger left. Some folks might suggest I invest time with family. They're not wrong. The same suggestion confronted Magellan and Marco Polo and Lewis and Clark, and the guy who holds the Guinness World Record for hibernating. But retreating to a life of comfort and safety did not appeal to those intrepid explorers and hibernators. Or Erifnus. Our travels were worthless but valuable, expensive but edifying, time-consuming but time well spent.

At Crowder State Park, the owls and the red-tailed hawks and the wind and the waves breaking on the shore told me why we come here. Stress and deadlines and traffic and trucks fall off the edge of the earth.

Truckers never come here. At least, they don't drive their big rigs here. The truckships stay in deep water, interstates and commercial highways.

Long-haul truckers follow their purpose, hauling stuff. But under every trucker's hat dwells the spirit of a cowboy. They choose this life to feel the wind in their hair, figuratively. A healthy dose of lonesome suits them just fine. If they want companionship they break the silence on CB radio, or join a conversation over truck stop food. They're diesel cowboys who traded their factory jobs for extended cabs—trucker caves. A few drivers engage the brazen caste of independent entrepreneurs: lot lizards lurking like loreleis in the vast harbors where the truckships sleep.

On the busy interstates these truckships look down on Erifnus as a gnat. She sees herself as a pony. She always allows a truckship to cut in or change lanes. Or maybe she's a frigate, rolling in the shadows of those lumbering 18-wheelers, those Spanish galleons on concrete sea lanes. Her captain thinks he's a pirate, stealing stories from backwaters and bottoms, graveyards and greasy spoons. Each destination adds a chapter to the four dozen steno notebooks in her backseat, each notebook filled with random observations, half-stories and outright lies—some scribbled at 60 miles per hour.

We all choose a path. Mine has been random, which makes my anchors precious. Family. Friends. And Mexican food. I climbed back inside my friend Erifnus, and we left the peaceful park, circling through a worldly sounding list of tiny towns—Edinburgh, Melbourne, Modena.

Then came a disappointment that repeats itself along this endless journey. Almost 11,000 restaurants line our path, and we've passed a few of them in our haste to get somewhere else. Today we passed Spickard and the great country cookin' at Helen's Place. It must be great country cooking because a dozen cars filled its parking lot, impressive for sparsely-populated Spickard. It's fun to imagine the scene: We'd park at the edge of the lot. I'd enter the front door and absorb the wary stares of locals while Helen shouts a greeting as she scurries back to the kitchen. "Sit anywhere you like. Coffee?" Her rhythm comes from years of hosting diners, I suppose, because you don't name a restaurant after yourself unless you make great biscuits and gravy and serve homemade pies.

But I was on a mission for Mexican, and Erifnus passed Helen's again today. We'll come back someday.

As we meandered down the road, a car in a hurry swung out to pass me. Like a chariot he drew next to me and with his meanest bugger look he gave me the universal signal that he didn't appreciate my pace. He made certain I saw his finger stuck out of his fist, easily his most potent debate tool. I looked past his fist and into his glowering eyes, hateful bullets surrounded by a skinny ruddy face constipated by bad choices and bad luck and pent up rage from childhood beatings. I smiled the way I smile at scorpions, noted his Idaho license plate as he sped away from me. On cue, we crossed No Creek, a losing stream with a loser name.

Sad mileposts dot this backroad landscape, abandoned houses in various stages of decay. Proud old family farmhouses that felt the footsteps of generations now sag slowly back into the earth. There's a seed in every empty old house, in the dry rotted floorboards and the mildewy walls, in the moss on the roof where sunlight doesn't reach. The seed is in the windowsills, in the clawfoot tub with as many rings as Saturn, and rusty water stains around the drain. The seed hangs with the chains which used to hold the front porch swing. It's the seed of a Hawthorne or a Steinbeck, the kind that when nurtured and cultivated will bring to life vivid stories about the people who lived in the house, the old farmer who built the place, the mother who raised half a dozen children and watched helplessly as one of them died, and she cared for twenty grandkids and half again as many hens, and her ailing sister, too, and a succession of dogs and cats, each taking turn as the family favorite, each buried behind the barn in a shower of tears that didn't stop until well into the reign of the next favorite pet.

The seeds are there.

Yet the old abandoned farmhouses, thousands of them, stand silent, sad, starving for shingles and paint, hands and feet. And laughter. And love.

Each year brings more pain to these old houses, lined up as if the Grim Reaper had arranged them along my path. Their trusses and gables sag under the weight of neglect. Each house was a setting for celebration and despair and the rhythms of life. And each house thrived in our agrarian economy.

But during the 1980s family farms could not endure a deadly one-two punch. The first punch by itself was devastating for a small family farm. American farm policy changed from Depression Era price protections to wide open full-tilt production, a "get big or get out" policy of planting fencerow to fencerow which produced record yields but pushed prices so low that only big corporate farms could endure. The second punch happened at the same time: Inflation and interest rates soared into double digits. Small farmers couldn't repay ballooning loans, and farm families faced foreclosure. Family farms always had a tough row to hoe, facing harsh weather and uneven moisture, deadly disease, fickle markets and heartless bankers. Nonetheless, families always had the land, until corporate agriculture hit these families like a terminal illness, leaving a killing floor littered with abandoned family farms. The final nail in the farmhouse coffin happened when big hog nation moved next door. Family farm values plummeted. Over the past three decades thousands of farmers lost the battle to foreclosure. Big hog nation bought proud old farms for pennies on the dollar.

Left behind are the houses that raised generations, valuable only to nostalgia, still standing because it's a costly hassle to bulldoze them.

I breathed deep as we passed through the fresh air of Galt, then crossed a network of corporate hog barns. This beautiful countryside with its verdant rolling hills wrapped by thick hardwood forests could be mistaken for the English countryside. But my nose knows hog nation thrives in clusters of low metallic cellblocks. Each pig prison contains hundreds of prolific colons. A single corporate hog farm can have more colons than the nearest two towns. Big active colons.

The area struggles to survive other transplanted threats. Kudzu. Zebra mussels. But the most visible invader to the territory, corporate hog nation, ensures the area will remain underpopulated. By people, anyway. Big hog nation imposes its own double whammy: higher stink and lower property values.

Good fences make good neighbors. But no fence can stop the smell of megatons of manure, or breaches and spills from storage lagoons, contaminating our water.

And the families are gone.

It's a lonely drive through these beautiful rolling hills, punctuated by empty farmhouses and perfumed by the pungent poop of swine. Echoing in my mind are the corporate farm advocates: "Farms are supposed to smell like shit." But are they supposed to look like war zones, with gulags of live piglets and dead houses?

Around the bend Erifnus slowed, and we pulled to the shoulder. Mr. Fasty Pants, the angry Idaho driver who passed us had failed to make a tight curve and his car skidded into a ditch. He stood beside his car, cell phone in hand. He didn't seem so menacing standing next to a crumpled bumper sprouting ditch weed.

I got out and yelled, "You okay?"

"Yeah. Wrecker's comin'."

"You'll be alright 'til then?"

"I'm okay." He eyed me warily. Maybe he remembered passing Erifnus, flipping me off. Maybe I'm still his enemy. Maybe everybody is his enemy.

A farm truck approached from the opposite direction and stopped. A minute later a pickup pulled up behind me. Their occupants got out and yelled, "You okay?"

"Yeah."

"Is he hurt?" the pickup driver asked me.

"He says he's okay…wrecker's comin'."

"Did you see what happened?" the farm trucker asked.

"Nah. He passed me about thirty miles back, and I came up on the wreck a couple minutes ago."

Satisfied that Idaho was going to get good hospitality, I nodded to the local Samaritans, climbed back into Erifnus and headed east.

———— ∞∞∞ ————

An old drive-in theater screen greeted us at the outskirts of Milan. The aging screen was built to last, a towering wedge with a silvery face, willing to show the next feature, except for the mature tree growing in front of the screen. At the edge of the road, the theater's movie marquee stood blank, speechless.

Milan (MY lun) joins a platoon of Missouri towns mispronounced by locals. It's an art form, this stubborn adherence to nonconformist nomenclature. Locals must correct an outsider's mispronunciations of Hayti, New Madrid and Versailles, which are the right pronunciations everywhere else in the world, but not in Milan, New Madrid, and Versailles, Missouri.

Locals aren't concerned. They don't think twice about mispronouncing Nevada, La Plata, and Eldorado, all long As. The butchering of names is consistent, and rampant to the point it can be said the majority of Missourians are living a lie.

They don't care.

Erifnus rolled into Milan in the shadow of a big Cargill plant. Throughout this tiny hub of agri-commerce were signals Milan has morphed from Anglo to Hispanic. Church and restaurant signs speak Spanish.

In the midst of all this remarkable change, in this remote town of less than 2,000 people, with its burgeoning Hispanic population, I found my Coronado. Downtown on the square across from the plain walls of the county courthouse sits Flor de Mexico, a one-stop Mexican grocery store and restaurant. This far north, it's as authentic as a roadside restaurante on the Baja, right down to the pico de gallo on the table. The servers spoke halting English. I ordered in halting Spanish. My table faced a picture window framing the ugliest courthouse in America, a gray stone box built in 1938 during the WPA. The spirits of Chief Pontiac and Tatschaga and Black Dog joined my table. Pontiac pointed to a spot where a previous courthouse unearthed a Native American burial mound, using burial stones to build the first jail. My ghostly Native American companions nodded in silent approval of my meal: soft corn tortillas gently grilled, overflowing with cactus and tripe, onions and cilantro, and salsa verde to whet the eyeballs. It's much closer to their diet than burgers and fries.

Milan's new slice of Old Mexico suggests a growing portal for Mexican food lovers in Missouri. As the Hispanic population increases in both urban and rural Missouri, there's a corresponding healthy growth in the number of authentic Mexican restaurants. Erifnus lets me seek them all.

My search began in college. Manny's in Kansas City. Maria's in Santa Fe. But the Holy Grail of Mexican food sits beside the Fort Worth stockyards, in a little white frame house. In the 1970s, diners entered Joe T. Garcia's through the kitchen, passing Mama Garcia stirring a washtub-sized vat of refried beans. Joe T's menu offered only one item: a multi-dish family style presentation that remains the standard by which all Mexican fiestas are measured. I've sampled Mexican food from San Antonio to San Jose, from Los Angeles to La Paz, even Manhattan (decent), Detroit (fabulous) and London (don't bother).

Hundreds of Mexican restaurants dot the landscape like culinary cacti, none better than Flor de Mexico in Milan.

Filled to my *globos oculares* with Old Mexico's finest, we headed north to give those eyeballs a treat: At Boynton, Erifnus swerved to miss the town water pump. There's not enough traffic through Boynton to justify removing the water pump standing smack-dab in the middle of Route N, protected by heavy gauge railings and reflecting signs. It raises a question: Which came first, the highway or the well?

Harvard, Hunger and Howard Hughes

Day faded fast on these backroads, and out of the darkness we saw an industry at work. As a kid when I visited my grandparents' farm near here, the sunset would chase us from the fields into the safety of the porch light. Not now. Farming extends deep into the night. As we entered the beautiful Chariton River valley we passed dairy barns lit up like Dairy Queens and tractors crawling the fields. Monstrous harvesters with headlights five across mowed through fields chomping corn and soybeans and kicking up chaff and dust reflected in the lights like a low storm.

As the city lights of Novinger came into view we passed Billy Creek Coal Mine, Missouri's last deep shaft coal mine, shut down a half century ago. Locals recreated this deep shaft at the Coal Miners Museum in Novinger, quite an undertaking for a town with less than 500 residents. For a buck you can enter the replica mine and a blacksmith shop and learn about the immigrants who came here to plunge a thousand feet belowground to hack fuel.

In the darkness we crossed from the countryside with its fertile fields to a city known for its fertile minds.

It has been called the Harvard of the Midwest. Although a dozen larger universities may dispute the claim, none can match Truman State University as the best value for a five-star blue chip education. College is only part of the candlepower in this town of 17,000 souls. Kirksville is the birthplace of Geraldine Page and osteopathic medicine, not necessarily in that order.

Geraldine Page worked with Lee Strasberg and received four Tony Award nominations over a lifetime on Broadway, and was nominated eight times for an Academy Award, winning her last nomination for *A Trip to Bountiful.*

And medicine?

Geraldine's dad was a professor at A.T. Still College of Osteopathy and Surgery, now Kirksville College of Medicine (KCOM). Back then osteopaths struggled for respect among the traditional medical community. Today the stigma is mostly gone.

Osteopaths can be eccentric:

He stood out from the crowd even in the melting pot of our local grocery store, an elderly man with long gray hair under a Mad Hatter hat. He walked with a cane. As we passed and exchanged nods he spoke: "Guess it's old hippie day at the supermarket." I laughed, realizing we bonded because of our uncommon commonality: old age and long hair. We met again in the next aisle, and he stopped to show me his cane, a five-foot wooden stalk with two dozen stubs where branches used to be. "Look at this!" He offered the cane for me to hold. It was laminated, sturdy as steel.

"What kind of wood?" I asked.

"Hemp!" his eyes shone. "I've had this cane since '68." We laughed about the foolishness of outlawing Missouri's historic cash crop. He kept talking. "Practiced medicine for fifty years until I retired a couple years ago. Taught for a while at KCOM. My wife and I have been together sixty years." She rolled her shopping cart up beside him. We smiled and laughed and exchanged stories about the good old days.

I couldn't resist a parting jibe: "I hope your bedside manner is half as good as your bullshit."

"Better!"

It was reassuring to talk to a physician who believes laughter and hemp are beneficial.

Becoming horizontal in my Super 8 Motel bed, I grabbed mankind's most overused appendage—the TV remote. Minutes into some forgettable TV show, sleep won the ratings battle.

Next day brought a dining reminder: Students complain about food, even at diners they frequent. When it's midnight and Kirksville students are hungry, chances are they'll end up at "shitty's."

Students are like that. They attach affectionate names to their favorite places. So a decent diner with the utilitarian name Pancake City ends up with a caca caricature. Not because the food is bad. Quite the contrary, it's satisfying, especially for college students who've been partying into the wee hours and find sobering solace in this all-night diner with menu delights like the Nova Slinger. The shitty nickname may have more to do with the faces of the late night drunken diners. But Pancake City is more than collegial scatology. Choose from a pancake menu that includes Reese's Cupcakes, chocolate chip cakes and Georgia peach cakes. Breakfast be damned, they serve something called Bob's Belly Buster, and you can get it with Garbage Fries.

Like the menu, the place itself is a melting pot of cultures and comestibles. The décor is '60s prefab, with a big picture window view of the Northtown Shopping Center across the highway. The diner's promo says it's imbued "with the desire to provide an any time, every day, any thing you want kind of place for the every man. Look around you now and you are likely to see students, farmers, truck drivers, business men and women, factory workers and families—that is the kind of place Pancake City is." I looked around, scratched two of those likelies off the list and ordered Big Bob's Belly Buster, a nearly foot-long fish sandwich that set me up for our next stop.

Driving north we descended into Hungry Hollow. There must be a story about Hungry Hollow. My guess is somebody got hungry. Today it's the fish, because Hungry Hollow is the site of Hazel Creek Lake which offers a 530-acre habitat for the elusive Muskellunge. Muskies are fast swimmers. They grow to fifty pounds on a diet of ducks and muskrats, which they prefer to crankbait. They shy away from fishing lines and human smell and boat motors, so it's difficult to sneak up on them. Unlike the big blue catfish, which are disappearing, the big muskies appear to be thriving, increasing in number, thanks to restored habitat, and anglers dedicated to the catch-and-release method of live and let live. The waters of Hazel Creek Lake calmed my soul, reminding me not all battles are cataclysmic. Still, my restlessness didn't subside completely, standing at a spot both hungry and hollow.

Coasting into Greentop, we almost bypassed the world's greatest purveyor of smoked meats in a big red building. But Sam Western had stuck his barbecue smoker in the parking lot of Western's Smokehouse, just inches from the roadside, and sweet hickory smoke wafted over the highway, compelling me to slam on the brakes and hit reverse in a manner that annoyed Erifnus Caitnop. Minutes later I was surrounded by brats and jalapeno sausage and elk snack sticks and restructured jerky, a hall of fame in processed meats, a small-town success story that's achieved scores of awards and thousands of loyal customers worldwide. They're even a hit in Frankfurt. And you know how discerning Frankfurters are. I almost signed up for Western's Meat of the Month Club, because you "Get a free meat stick with every order," but resisted the temptation to shop hungry. Instead, I chowed through a plate of barbecued beef and pork. Then I fed Erifnus a meal laced with corn liquor, and we motored north.

Up the road is a connection to the gulf oil disaster. Well, that's a stretch. More precisely, Lancaster is the birthplace of Howard Hughes's dad, Howard Robard Hughes Senior, whose tool company invented the two-cone rotary drill bit, which revolutionized oil drilling, so it became easier to reach into faraway places. Howard's drill bit invention led to a fortune for Hughes Tool Company. His son Howard Hughes Junior transformed the fortune into gushers of fame. Movie stars. The world's largest airplane. And Trans World Airlines, until it got swallowed by a whale. I could uncover no evidence that junior, the daredevil flyboy, ever touched down in Lancaster. Regardless, the Hughes family has its roots here, including young Howard's uncle Rupert Hughes, Academy Award-winning screenwriter and novelist who published his first poem as a kid in Lancaster.

The Hughes family had the Midas touch. Erifnus wasn't much impressed, turning south toward the town of silver.

There's Silver in Those Rails

A solitary figure sat trackside on a bench outside the La Plata train depot. Approaching him I noticed he held a portable two-way radio.

"Train on time?" I asked.

"Three hours behind," he said in halting speech. He didn't seem concerned. "They'll make up some time."

His name was Dan, retired from the railroad. He told me he's had some health issues, suffered a series of strokes, but he still shows up every day to greet the train, answer queries from passengers, help out where he can.

Since 1926 the Santa Fe Chief has been stopping in La Plata. Nowadays the station has no personnel, no ticket master, no station master. It's just a whistle stop. "Most of the passengers who get off here are college students going to Kirksville," Dan said. Now the train is called the Southwest Chief, Amtrak's version of this historic ride from Chicago through Kansas City to Los Angeles.

Dan told me La Plata's oldest industry—the railroad—is its newest industry. The whole town has embraced its railroad heritage and turned it into a tourist attraction.

La Plata is the Spanish word for silver. With two hours to kill before the Chief arrived, I walked into La Plata to check out the town's new shine.

You can walk anywhere in La Plata, population barely into four digits. The downtown looks largely vacant, left barren by the Walmartization of rural America. Yet something big is happening here. I walked to the Depot Inn and Suites. Somewhere in the world, there may be a hotel more dedicated to the history of train travel, but I haven't found it. Sure, every town with a caboose in its park has a railroad museum of sorts. But the Depot Inn is a railfan's dream: a railroad museum with a hotel built around it. People come from all over the nation—by train—to stay here. I passed a pair of retired Amtrak mail cars packed with railroad displays, and a handcar near the entrance to the inn. The front desk looks like a train depot ticket counter, the lobby is a waiting room. Throughout the hotel, railroad memorabilia hang everywhere, even in the indoor pool area. But don't assume the décor is all track and no treat. The suites are damn near luxurious. Hundreds of visitors from every corner of the world roll out of La Plata impressed with this little gem in the middle of America. There's even a Train Watching Lookout Cabin, a covered shelter overlooking the railroad tracks, where folks listen to a radio scanner broadcasting conversations from approaching trains. Hotel guests can tune to the local railcam on their room's cable TV. They never wait long, since the rails feel the rush of eighty trains per day.

La Plata rides the crest of its newfound rail resurgence. Downtown, the American Passenger Rail Heritage Foundation operates the Silver Rails Memorial Library and the Silver Rails Gallery, focusing exclusively on railroad art and photography.

Returning to the old railroad station, I stood among a throng of anxious boarders, mostly students from Truman State University. The train arrived, and deposited a few riders, including a seasoned Chicago couple traveling the Southwest Chief to see the real America.

We traded stories.

They told me about this area's connection to the Saint Valentine's Day massacre. Historians whisper that Al Capone sent his assassins here on this train to hide out until the coast was clear. One of the suspected triggermen, Fred "Killer" Burke, cut his criminal teeth in the Cuckoos and Egan's Rats gangs in Saint Louis. His long trail of crime took him from Saint Louis to Detroit to Chicago, and ended when he was arrested in his hideout just off Highway 63, at the home of his in-laws, a small frame farmhouse outside Green City, where he was living under an assumed name. Authorities were pursuing him for an unrelated murder of a Michigan patrol officer. Burke's new bride said she married a man who called himself Richard White, and she had no idea about his past. Police determined that Burke's tommy guns were used as the Saint Valentine's Day murder weapons.

Awaiting extradition, Burke had a choice. According to an issue of *Time* magazine dated April 6, 1931, Missouri Governor Henry Caulfield said, "Fred, Chicago wants you, Michigan wants you. Where do you want to go?"

"That matter is out of my hands," Burke responded. He went to the Michigan State Penitentiary, happy he wasn't snuffed by his Chicago gang cronies who suspected he might kiss and tell about Saint Valentine. He died nine years later of a massive failure of his valentine muscle.

Burke picked a great place to hide. Law enforcement's first problem was finding it. Green City sits near Green Castle, Greentop and Queen City. The farm house still exists although there's no guided tour, no bed and breakfast. I was impressed that this Chicago couple knew so much about rural Missouri's connection to Capone.

I bade farewell to the solitary man with the halting speech on the bench with the two-way radio. "Good to see you're keeping things moving, Dan!" I offered cheerfully. He struggled to smile. Later I learned he lost his battle to the strokes. Local folks and die-hard railfans will miss him. The thousands of people who make the pilgrimage to La Plata to see eighty trains per day will never realize they have one less set of ears to the tracks.

Erifnus took me away from the trains. Her path randomly coursed the backroads, zigzagging and doubling back, past abandoned homesteads and forgotten places like Bee Ridge, Buzzard's Glory and Buttermilk, where passing Santa Fe Railroad crews tasted its namesake. We crossed the Salt River at Feltz's Bridge. The old bridge is crumbling from decades of weather and salt. Probably needs replacing. The original Feltz's Bridge was built in 1845 when ten-year-old Sam Clemens roamed the rivers just downstream. We passed Democrat Creek and skirted Little Troublesome Creek, which young Clemens might assume would lead to Big Troublesome Creek, but not in this case. We traversed the Lord's Bottom into Edina, skittered through Novelty, named for the first store on the site, and crossed the uninspiringly-named North River. Don't blame Zebulon Pike. He named this river the Geffreon after a local French trapper he met around La Grange. The name didn't stick. Pike's map editors complained that his names for anything seemed inconsistent, and he never seemed to spell a name the same way twice.

This area "was settled with startling rapidity, owing to its well-watered, undulating prairie, with its luxuriant growth of grass and ready supply of timber, its water courses ranging from only four to six miles apart," according to Katherine Elliott, who in 1938 wrote her master's thesis at Mizzou on *Place Names of Six Northeast Counties of Missouri.*

Thanks, Katherine.

Speaking of namesakes, people used to respect Thomas Jefferson and his ideas. They named Lewis County after Jefferson's personal secretary, and named the county seat after Jefferson's house. Back then the town was growing. Today as Monticello's population dips close to one hundred, it may be the world's smallest town with a bank, a jail, a courthouse and an airport. You can thank local resident Norman Merrell for the airport. He was a powerful state senator, helped my father establish Missouri's vocational schools. He was a pilot, so he built an airport nearby to fly to the capital city.

Canton lured me for an overnight, where I attended a free show at Culver Stockton College. A young comedian mesmerized the crowd with juggling and jokes, then the juggler asked the young lady sitting next to me to assist him onstage. He asked her where she was from. "Vietnam," she replied, in perfect English. When she sat back down, I asked her home town. "Ho Chi Minh City," she said cheerfully, matter-of-factly. I smiled, hoping some healing has happened in this country, at least among our youth.

Next morning we caromed across Lyon Township, named for the first Union general killed in the Civil War, at Wilson's Creek. We passed Neeper, and the hill where the old Cracker-Neck School stood, and the site of an old place called A Bit Nation because the soil was so poor the government sold the land for a bit: 12.5 cents an acre. We circled through Anson, also known as Greasy Point for a greasy spoon restaurant that used to do business there, and crossed the Fox River, first called Stinking Creek back in pioneer days, until a mapper tried unsuccessfully to change the name to Aromatic Creek. I didn't notice any smell, not even hog shit.

Anywhere you go in this region, you'll likely cross the Fabius River. There are three of them, paralleling Troublesome Creek as they eventually join together and empty into the Mississippi. Some say these Fabius rivers are named for a French pioneer. Others say the rivers are named for the Roman leader Fabius Maximus Verrucosus. His strategy of delaying the invader Hannibal instead of confronting him earned the scorn of Romans, who called Fabius "wart lip" (Verrucosus). But his guerilla tactics and scorched earth strategy probably saved Rome. Most other Roman generals who confronted Hannibal got their ass handed to them.

On cue we rolled into Hannibal, home of great voices from your childhood. Like this one:

Next time you sit down with the kids to watch Disney's *Pinocchio*, listen to the cricket. He was born here. At least, his voice was born here. When that loveable bug sings "When You Wish Upon a Star," the voice of Jiminy Cricket is a Hannibalian named Cliff Edwards.

Never heard of him?

One fan believes a curtain call is long overdue for Mr. Edwards. Stephen Andsager isn't from Hannibal. He's from Columbia. But Steve has something in common with Edwards: They're troubadours whose instrument is a ukulele.

Steve stays busy as a bandleader, dusting off tasty ballads and toe tappers from America's obscure musical archives. Years ago I played with Steve in the Mudbugs, a band with a honky swamp swing style and a sidebar campaign to make the mudbug (crawfish) the state crustacean. The Missouri legislature didn't share our zeal.

Steve is on a mission to reintroduce Americans to Cliff Edwards. When you look at his body of work, you'll realize Cliff is a familiar friend.

You've heard his voice as a dying Confederate soldier in *Gone with the Wind*. You've heard him sing "When I See an Elephant Fly" in *Dumbo*. His hit records include "California Here I Come," "It's Only a Paper Moon," and "Singin' in the Rain," which was a chart-topper *before* the Gene Kelly movie.

Clifton Avon Edwards was born in Hannibal in 1895. He later moved to Saint Louis and Saint Charles, and eventually Hollywood. He was a fixture on the vaudeville circuit, and the Ziegfeld Follies. He appeared in movies starring Buster Keaton, Joan Crawford and Tim

Conway. Along the way, he became Ukulele Ike, and appeared on *The Mickey Mouse Club.*

"He should be in the Hall of Famous Missourians," Steve told me the other day.

"Good luck with that," I cautioned him. One person—a politician—picks inductees into the Missouri Capitol's Hall of Famous Missourians. The waiting list is long, and choices by the Speaker of the Missouri House of Representatives are cluttered with too many politicians, in my opinion.

Steve makes a compelling case. "Who is the King of Rock 'n' Roll?" he asks. "That's easy: Elvis. But who is the King of Ukulele?"

Not Tiny Tim. Not Don Ho or Arthur Godfrey. It's Ukulele Ike.

"His achievements include nine Broadway productions," Steve said. "He had his own radio and TV shows. He sold seventy-four million records and performed in more than a hundred films.

"Long before the guitar was the must-have instrument, all the cool kids played ukulele," Steve said. "Just about everyone knows someone who plays a uke these days, but the instrument's first wave of popularity began before World War II. Ukulele Ike was the inspiration for millions of budding musicians.

"Despite his career success," Steve told me, "Cliff's personal life was problematic. Like most entertainers, his brand went out of style and the popular culture of the sixties left him behind. He died penniless in a nursing home with no family and no one to claim his body.

"Ukuleles are everywhere lately," Steve said. "But nowhere is there a memorial for Ukulele Ike. He was a great American entertainer who lacks the recognition he deserves. At the very least, there should be a memorial bust in his birthplace of Hannibal MO."

There are traces of Ukulele Ike in Hannibal. You can find his story in the Hannibal Museum downtown. But no statue. Underappreciating Ike can be forgiven of a town so immersed in Mark Twain.

But when you wish upon a star, what do you sing?

Chemicals, Court and Calder

Driving south from Hannibal, we entered a chemical town. Literally. Named by chemist L.P. Sprout, Ilasco is an acronym for the ingredients in cement: iron, lime, aluminum, silica, calcium and oxygen. The Atlas Cement Company built a plant just south of Mark Twain Cave in 1903, and soon the area became a melting pot of immigrant workers from Romania, Slovakia, Hungary, Italy and Poland. They worked at the new cement plant, and lived in the new town, which grew to 3,000 residents. These workers made the cement for the Panama Canal, the Empire State Building and Hoover Dam. The plant shut down fifty years ago, and Ilasco is damn near a ghost town now, having survived barely sixty years. Among the few remnants is an old jail and a monument to the immigrant workers who settled here.

Erifnus appreciates cement if it's road worthy, and she took a series of concrete ribbons to New London where she let me out to roam the Ralls County Courthouse. Built in 1861, these courthouse walls have witnessed thousands of tragedies and comedies, in character with its Greek temple look adapted from the Virginia State Capitol, designed by Thomas Jefferson. The courthouse cupola copied the belfry on Carpenters' Hall in Philadelphia. Designers fashioned the courthouse as a union between ancient Greek and fledgling American democracies.

The building's native limestone was quarried long before Atlas Cement showed up to ship 4.5 million barrels of cement to the Panama Canal. Builders sealed the cornerstone of the courthouse annex with mortar fortified with sand from the Nile River in Egypt. The courtroom has the best acoustics of any court in Missouri, thanks to sawdust insulation packed into the walls and floor. If the curved back wall of the courtroom could talk, lurid tales of murder and frontier justice would fill the room.

Two lurid tales crossed my mind.

From these courthouse steps my great grandfather met his grisly fate. He had helped convict a horse thief and was leaving the courtroom. The thief's brothers kidnapped my great grandfather and tied him to railroad tracks. He was killed by the train he rode each day into Hannibal to drink whiskey. It was a horrific end to a wild life. He had been a Catholic priest in Ireland until he fell in love with a young monastery maid. To wrest him from the maid, the church imprisoned him. He escaped, killing a guard. The church sought him for murder. He found the young maid, married her and they escaped to America. They had six children. And when he died beneath the wheels of a train, his family gathered the fragments of his body and paid a fat ransom to the Church to bury his excommunicated body in consecrated ground.

The other tale? A few years back the old courthouse got a facelift. Renovators uncovered an interior wall where the original stone masons and carpenters, architects and laborers signed their names. The renovators painted over the signatures. [Slap forehead]

Erifnus followed the flow of the Mississippi River, along scenic Highway 79, topping bluffs with panoramic views, past Big Dead Slough and Blackbird Island where wild rice attracts huge flocks, past Busch, a whistle-stop on the railroad where Anheuser Busch Company hired daredevils to cut ice from the Mississippi and haul it by train to Saint Louis.

We rolled into Louisiana, named in 1818 for a girl, Louisiana Bayse, born in 1804. She was named for the Louisiana Purchase. The town shouts history from its antebellum homes and historic downtown, adjacent to the Champ Clark Bridge over the Mississippi. It's a butt-clenching ride across this narrow span. Built ninety years ago, the bridge itself has lived longer than Champ Clark did. A replacement Champ Clark Bridge will unclench a lot of butts, too late for the poor souls who died in wrecks on this bridge, like the thirty-four-year-old man who was crushed when logging equipment fell off an oncoming truck.

Champ Clark's impact reverberated through the early 1900s. He was Speaker of the U.S. House of Representatives from 1911 to 1919, and was the leading candidate for president in 1912, until Woodrow Wilson upset him. Shortly before Clark took the gavel as speaker, in a hotly-debated trade agreement between the U.S. and Canada, he shocked the world with this remark: "I look forward to the time when the American flag will fly over every square foot of British North America, up to the North Pole." My grandfather Edward Greene Robinson, a Clark campaign aide, was aghast at that remark, and worked to control the damage from such a careless comment. Lucky there was no Twitter back then. Surely no American leader says such bombastic things any more.

Erifnus took me twenty minutes west to Honeyshuck, named for the locust tree seed pods in the yard of Champ Clark's home in

Bowling Green. It was a treat to see the parlor where my grandfather told Champ to shut up about annexing Canada.

Heading south we passed Buffalo Knob, the site of old Buffalo Fort, Buffalo Creek and Buffalo Springs, Buffalo Church and Buffalo School and another Buffalo Knob for good measure, lest we forget bison once roamed here.

Driving this outback with its strange nomenclature, the stories behind the names get covered by time. Many of these stories would be lost, were it not for Esther Leech, who dutifully recorded these unique appellations and the tales of their creation. It must have been a tedious project, back in 1933. I can't imagine anybody driving all of these roads to uncover their stories.

Erifnus cruised through Hutt's Tollgate without stopping, since the tollgate hasn't been there since the 1800s when tolls enabled Pike County to maintain roads superior to most rural counties.

We drove through Old Monroe past a battle site where the great Sac and Fox warrior chief Blackhawk ambushed a group of Missouri Rangers during the War of 1812. The war had ended three months earlier, but Blackhawk either didn't know or didn't care. Blackhawk's men ambushed the rangers in the Sink Hole, a depression near the Cuivre River. They killed seven rangers, losing one warrior. Today Blackhawk's namesakes strap on skates and carry sticks to battle the New York Rangers for a hard rubber puck. Ah, tribalism.

In Moscow Mills, Erifnus stopped at the Moscow Grocery. Two seasoned ladies behind the counter shook their heads when I asked how a red blooded American town got a name with Moscow in it. They looked at me like I was speaking a foreign language. Were they holding out on me?

Downtown Moscow Mills needs only one intersection. The grande dame of the block is the Shapely Ross House, a stunning stone structure which has seen two centuries. She knows how Moscow Mills got its name. But Shapely Ross wasn't talking. Neither were the dearly departed who passed through the McCoy Blossom Funeral Home across the street. Out of respect I didn't stop to offer McCoy Blossom my suggestion for a green burial campaign: "Bloom where you're planted."

Down the road, Chubby's Restaurant promotes its home cooking with the catch phrase, "Come catch a hot roll." A friendly server says they still toss rolls, but Chubby's was crowded so I didn't stick around to play with my food.

—————∞∞∞—————

We drove into countryside, passing history buried in names no longer used. The town Confusion got its name from the postal service because other names were too dull. Contention School arose out of a fight over its location. Best Bottom was a low spot named for a settler named Best. Dishwater Branch. Lost Knob. Loutre Lick. No Man's Land. Prohibition.

Along our homeward journey somebody adorned I-70 with Calderesque roadside art: three miles of beer cans capping small trees, bushes and tall grasses. Somebody went to great trouble to walk the ditch, pick up these cans and place them on sticks and stalks. Daily, 70,000 people zoom past this art. Maybe seven of them noticed. Maybe seventy threw more cans in the ditch.

Chance Encounters

We followed Route B toward Centralia. Since 1864, modern road-building techniques have changed the road, but not the route. My Pontiac melded into the queue and we drove north. This ribbon of asphalt and concrete brought a steady stream of oncoming commuters headed to work in Columbia's factories and schools, hospitals and insurance companies.

The heavy traffic along Route B has brought change to its way stations. Hallsville recently got a stoplight. It's a rite of passage for small communities when they install their first stop 'n go signal, and graduate to the gridlock of modern electronic gadgets.

Idling at the Hallsville stoplight, I recalled my first visit to Centralia. As a student in a career pursuit now defined by *Mad Men*, I enrolled in a journalism course called "Ad Campaigns." While other student teams built balloony promotions for Worlds of Fun, my advertising team tackled the industrial-strength challenge of promoting the 125 Kv Connector.

Unless you're intimate with a utility truck, there's no practical reason you'd know about the 125 Kv Connector, or its maker, the A.B. Chance Company of Centralia. They don't advertise on TV. You don't buy their products at the Spiffy Mart. But you depend on them. The Chance company makes connectors for America's electric grid. They've made 'em since shortly after Albert Bishop Chance founded the company back in 1912. Thanks to such heavy gauge electric connectors, small towns can erect pretty stoplights.

It was nearly forty years ago when our student team was invited to the inner sanctum of A.B. Chance. There, I learned a valuable lesson. As a fledgling presenter with split ends that hadn't felt shears for years, I entered a roomful of crewcuts. This was during the turmoil of the early '70s, when long hair caused Communism, and crew cuts guaranteed conservatism. Despite appearances, Chance bought our idea.

Looks can be deceiving. Even though the Chance factory and distribution depot sprawl along the confluence of three railroads, Centralia is much more than a company town. Away from the industry, Centralia looks like a thousand other comfortable rural communities. Modest homes sit behind giant oaks and maples lining broad, sleepy streets, some paved with curbs and sidewalks, some not.

Approaching downtown, Erifnus passed a vacant lot on a street corner that offers a clear view of an old brick building off the town square. The building is unremarkable, similar to a thousand others of its Depression-era vintage. But it wears a unique tattoo on its flank. The Prairie Queen mural on the side wall shows highlights of the town's history, including the old railroad station, the scene of a slaughter.

———— ◈◈◈ ————

The congressman survived.

Headed north out of Columbia the old stagecoach from Jefferson City to Paris nearly reached Centralia when robbers stopped its progress. The robbers, a band of bushwhackers, would have murdered at least two passengers, had they known the true identities of Boone County Sheriff James Waugh and Congressman James S. Rollins. But even as the congressman and sheriff were lying to save their skin, they were saved by the bell...or more precisely, the whistle.

When Bloody Bill Anderson's robbers heard an approaching train whistle, they galloped to Centralia to intercept it. Stagecoach robberies and farmhouse raids were sidebar windfalls for this gang. Their real purpose focused on wreaking guerilla mayhem on Union forces. The Centralia Massacre—two acts of cold-blooded carnage—is a Civil War story so dramatic it begs for a movie script.

On September 27, 1864, Bloody Bill Anderson's guerilla gang—including a young recruit named Jesse James—had come to town to disrupt the North Missouri Railroad, a supply route for the Union prosecution of the Civil War. Many gang members wore blue uniforms, disguised as Union troops. A train carrying furloughed Union soldiers rolled up to a blockade at the rail station. Anderson's men boarded the train and robbed civilians of their watches and jewelry, then forced the unarmed soldiers and passengers off the train. They made the engineer set the train's throttle at full speed, sending the empty train hurtling down the tracks to crash a few miles out of town. The marauders ordered the soldiers to strip down, and twenty-four unarmed federals—on furlough after months of fighting—were executed in cold blood.

Anderson was just warming up to the carnage.

The highways leading out of Centralia quickly find rural farmland and forests, just as they did during the Civil War. In a field off Route Z, things are peaceful now, interrupted only by the occasional train whistle from the three modern railroads that intersect in town. But in the moments following the massacre, with black smoke pluming into the clear sky, Union Major Andrew Vern Emen Johnston, known to his troops as Ave, got wind of the massacre. Enraged, he led 155 mounted soldiers into town. On the outskirts, three bushwhackers thumbed their noses at Johnston and his men, enticing the Union cavalry to pursue them into a box ambush in a farm field. Firing from forest on three sides, Bloody Bill's bushwhackers killed 123 federals, and according to accounts, Jesse James shot and killed their commander. It took 142 years to mark this spot with a monument.

That monument happened by chance. Jack Chance. Jack's slight frame and thinning hair betray his retirement stage of life. I don't know if he's retired. But I know his passion. With his family's fortune, Jack Chance could accomplish anything he wanted. What he wanted was a commemoration of this battle on the field where it happened. The monument is a reality, with help from allies, including a pair of influential writers who bought their ink by the barrel: *Columbia*

Daily Tribune former publisher Hank Waters and former managing editor Jim Robertson. On the day the monument was dedicated we joined a thousand onlookers at the wooded edges of the killing field as reenactors demonstrated what happened here five generations ago.

Missouri saw more Civil War battles than any other state besides Virginia and Tennessee. Thanks to Jack and Jim and Hank and a battalion of Civil War enthusiasts, more and more Civil War battle sites in this state are telling their stories. I waved to the reenactors in blue and gray, and drove north.

Not two minutes out of town, Erifnus was into the countryside again. Along our travels, we've passed all kinds of yard decorations, some cluttery, some trashy, some art. The latter is on display on Route T, where Larry Vennard shows off his ironclad animals. A self-described construction gypsy who's lived in forty-three states, Larry now lives among his lifelike iron sculptures, welded into dinosaurs and birds and bugs. Unlike real fauna, these ferrous critters will stand the test of time.

Turning west, Erifnus passed a homemade city limit sign announcing Little City. At 60 miles per hour, I took a visual census of the town: a mobile home park with four or five dwellings and a couple of outbuildings. I didn't see a post office or a fire truck, no gas station convenience store. An American flag keeps company with the city sign. Little City may not have a mayor, but rest assured: somewhere in those trailers there's a city manager.

Raised on railroads, Moberly is a hub in an archipelago of attractions, a launching point to visit nearby birthplaces of great American generals Blackjack Pershing, Sterling Price and local hero Omar Bradley.

Tom Waits knows Moberly. He sings about a lady with Moberly connections—"Black Market Baby," *a diamond that wants to stay coal.* Erifnus knows Moberly, too, and she took me across railroad tracks and entered an old neighborhood on the fringe of downtown. Most of the houses, once proud diamonds, sag with the weight of time and weather. But they remember when they were fresh and young and smelled like pine and paint mixed with the aroma of creosote and burning coal from the railroads that built this town. Today the neighborhood raises blue-collar families whose breadwinners work for the hospital or the prison.

This old blue-collar neighborhood hides what some folks swear is the best tavern in the world. We pulled up to Lula's, an aging white frame building with no fancy marquee. Entering this unremarkable building my eyes adjusted from five o'clock sun to dive bar dusk. A row of old depression era movie theater seats offered me one empty spot to wait the customary hour to get a table. For me, waiting for food is like sitting through a sermon or an Amway spiel. Finally a cheerful server led me through an old hallway past an open sink to a back room, once segregated for blacks only. Nowadays chatty servers treat all maws and tastebuds the same.

Lula's limited menu matches the dive bar décor. But to paraphrase the Bard, the food's the thing. Depending on the source, rave reviews tout baked potatoes the size of your head, the best burger anywhere, crab legs and boiled shrimp that put you seaside, and ribeyes good as any hifalutin' steakhouse.

It's a good bet hometown hero Omar Bradley ate here after he returned to Moberly for a victory lap after the war. Bradley, General Eisenhower's right-hand man during World War II, is Moberly's favorite son. He said, "...freedom demands as much respect for the other fellow's ideas as he gives to yours. Let each man be able to choose what he studies and decides, what form of government he lives by, and what God he will worship."

Bradley stands among the world's greatest generals ever. That this gentle soul competes with other Missouri generals for that distinction—Pershing, Price, Grant and Sherman—is a testament to his insight.

Boonslick

Back before steamboats, in a giant Missouri River wilderness from which a dozen counties would be carved, trappers and traders and pioneers called the area Boonslick, named for a thriving salt business developed by Daniel Boone's sons.

The Boone family established a lasting legacy. Boonville. Boonesboro. Boone County. But before all the Boonity, Lewis and Clark noted several salt water springs in the area. On the frontier, salt was a valuable commodity needed to cure meat and tan hides. The

Boones capitalized on Lewis and Clark's discovery; a year later, the new family business was boiling salt water in big iron kettles, evaporating the water, and collecting the salt brine at the bottom, which they sent downriver on keelboats to Saint Louis.

At Boonsboro, nothing much remains. It's a state historic site, protected from development, which really isn't a pressing issue in this remote spot along the Missouri River. Nature has reclaimed the land from the salt merchants, and today only a single iron kettle and one saltwater pool remain in the narrow ravine that channels the trickling saltwater springs.

Beside a small parking lot next to a picnic pavilion, a kiosk explains the salt operation, and shows a picture of Nathan Boone, who looks a lot like Johnny Cash. The kiosk explains the salt operation's demise, shortly after an operator's son fell into a boiling kettle and was scalded to death. With only one futile attempt to revive the business years later, the land sat dormant. It's a lonely state historic site. Sparse visits don't justify a full-time attendant. I had the site to myself on this Monday morning, and left Erifnus alone in the parking lot, only slightly apprehensive she'd be molested by a drive-by vandal, or I'd be the first victim of a serial killer who would become known as the State Park Slasher. A gentle mist enlivened the green moss on the railroad tie steps as I slipped and slid down the steep trail to the ruins. If I fell and broke my back, the next visitor might not show up for days.

For decades commerce flourished in Greater Boonslick. History drips off the bluffs and buildings. From Boonville and Franklin and Rocheport, this was the launching point for pioneers. Now, most of the descendants of the farriers and fur traders, the provisioners and trail guides have moved away.

But history remains. Names like Hungry Mother Creek and Tickridge School make me wonder what young schoolchildren endured.

Paved roads make it easier today to travel from Boonslick to Franklin, although not much of Franklin remains. It's a multiple-ghost town. Ghost number one is a man named Carson who was killed by a falling tree. His widow raised fifteen children by herself. Their eleventh child, a kid named Kit, worked in the town's saddle shop, where he heard tales from the Santa Fe Trail, which began at the shop's front door. By the time Kit Carson was sixteen, he had left to work on the trail. Unlike his dad, Kit's ghost spends most of his time around his Taos, New Mexico home among wealthy Hollywood types.

Franklin devolved into a ghost town in stages. After the Kit Carson era, the town withered when the wagon trains subsided. It surged with the rise of riverboats, and prospered from the railroad. It shrank again when the old Katy roundhouse closed shop. Finally, a flood wiped out the rest of the town and residents moved uphill.

Fayette teems with aging elegance, from the old homes along the boulevard leading to Central Methodist University, to the town square around the stately old courthouse. Even vacant old structures cling to life like stubborn teeth in an aging jaw. The town's history-minded stewards work tirelessly to preserve these gems. Scaffolding rose beside one brick wall where an unfinished mural took shape. On this Monday morning in the mist, the scaffold was empty, no artist in sight. The mural caused controversy. The state highway department thinks the scenes are nothing but billboards for local businesses. Indeed, most of the scenes include business names and telephone numbers, tastefully incorporated into the mural. The highway department looks at the mural and sees a rule infraction: illegal unlicensed roadside advertising sitting too close to a state-maintained road.

On the town square Emmett's Kitchen & Tap pumped out the aromas of Angry Shrimp and Heaven & Hell Pasta. It's refreshing to find savory Louisiana cooking this far north. After an oyster po'boy and jambalaya, I left Fayette on an upbeat, belching shrimp, driving headlong into a musical mystery.

Up the hill, New Franklin is a tidy little town, proud of producing a local composer who got little credit for his most famous song.

The Graveyard Waltz

Kit Carson never met Jelly Settle, victim in one of the most baffling tales since Mozart met Salieri. Around these parts, anyway. Some folks shout that Jelly was robbed.

In Jelly's hometown, I stopped at the Franklin School to ask a school receptionist, "You know the cemetery where the guy who wrote 'The Missouri Waltz' is buried?"

"Not familiar with that," she said, "but there's a cemetery about two miles up Highway 5 toward Boonsboro. Mount Pleasant."

Sure enough, Highway 5 led me to the sign:

Mount Pleasant Cemetery
Burial Site of J. Edgar "Jelly" Settle
Composer of "The Missouri Waltz"

A short drive down a gravel road led to the cemetery, a beautiful spot on a sloping hilltop framed by forest land, overlooking undulating hills packed with mature cornstalks, holding their ears like pistols, patiently awaiting the reaper. I parked Erifnus and waded into the rows of tombstones, all shapes and sizes. My eye kept landing on the bigger monuments, expecting to see the name Settle. I finally stumbled onto a modest stone about collie-high, with the inscription:

Lee Edgar "Jelly" Settle
1882-1949
Composer of "The Missouri Waltz" melody

J. Edgar on the sign had become Lee Edgar on the tombstone, just another inconsistency in a neglected life story. At least at this peaceful spot Jelly gets credit, posthumously.

Jelly was born in New Franklin, died in New Franklin, and somewhere in between, he wrote a tune called "Graveyard Waltz." His friends say other musicians showed interest in the tune, and matched the melody to words that eventually became the Missouri state song.

But Jelly Settle didn't get credit.

Nobody cared, even Jelly, because the song wasn't popular until Harry Truman played it, three decades after Jelly wrote the tune.

"To this day it remains unclear who exactly composed the melody for 'The Missouri Waltz,'" ragtime historian Bill Edwards notes, "but there is enough evidence to suggest that Lee Edgar Settle had a significant role in shaping the piece into something appealing—at least to the point of making it a viable property for theft."

Jelly's brother J.B. Settle, publisher of the *New Franklin News*, wrote this blunt statement in Jelly's obituary: "…the John Valentine Eppel orchestra of Iowa came to Moberly for two dance engagements and it was at that time, while Edgar was visiting the orchestra at the Merchant's Hotel, that the melody was stolen."

Jelly and Eppel were friends, J.B. explained. "Their paths would cross from time to time," he said. Jelly was playing the piano one night before dinner at the Merchant's Hotel when Eppel, in town with his band, complimented Jelly's waltz. "That's a catchy tune... Where'd you get it?" Jelly said the tune was his, and he had been playing it for years. Eppel asked Jelly if he would play it for "the boys in the band."

Jelly agreed. While he played, he noticed Eppel's musicians writing notes on their cuffs. Jelly "didn't think a thing about it 'til many years later" so "he knows how the air of the thing got away from him."

Eppel never denied he got the tune from Jelly. And there are theories that Jelly actually learned the melody from African American musicians.

Originally titled "Hush a Bye My Baby," lyricist J.R. Shannon's words were changed before it became Missouri's state song.

Edwards says, "The irony of all this is that Harry was not particularly fond of 'The Missouri Waltz.' As it turns out, he objected more to Shannon's lyrics, which included some racial references, than any other part of it."

After Truman made the song popular, reporters asked him if it was his favorite song. The White House published Truman's reply: "President's attitude towards the song? He can take it or leave it. Is it really his favorite? No. Does he play it often? No. Is Margaret ever heard singing it? No. What is the President's reaction to song's adoption by Missouri as state song? See answer to first question."

Truman was equally blunt in a television interview: "If you let me say what I think, I don't give a damn about it, but I can't say it out loud because it's the song of Missouri. It's as bad as 'The Star-Spangled Banner' as far as music is concerned."

Rest in peace, Jelly Settle. Wherever the song emanated, you played it well.

Party Time

There's always a party in Rocheport. Even back in 1840, when Tyler Party Whigs convened their state political convention in June, a young artist named George Caleb Bingham showed up to sketch the speakers, who included, according to professor Lew Larkin, "A tall,

Ichabod-like thirty-one year old named Abraham Lincoln." For several days Bingham sketched characters in the crowd, in various stages of speechifying and drunkenness. He would use many of these characters in unflattering poses during later genre paintings on politics. Lincoln doesn't seem to appear in any of Bingham's paintings, maybe because Abe was decades away from greatness.

There are three ways to reach Rocheport: by river, by auto, or on the Katy Trail. Trail traffic helped launch a resurgence in Rocheport, anchored by the School House Bed and Breakfast for the sleeper set, and the Rocheport General Store for revelers. The general store purveys fun and food, and some of the best blues music on the river.

Next door I crossed through an 1800s glass storefront past seven tables set in a row stretching to the back of the narrow room. Susan and Todd named this restaurant for their daughter Abigail, and all three scurried through the shotgun interior, doting on guests. They stage their cooking in plain view on one side of the room, separated by an island of display cases that don't match, their glass shelves showcasing rhubarb pie and nut toffee tortes tantalizingly close to diners. The place defines the Rocheport style: These are river folk, who serve in shorts and sandals, as you sit at tables draped in linen, then covered with butcher paper and crayons. I joined friends at the back table and the server brought our menu, a giant blackboard on an easel. From the blackboard beginning to the torte finale, this is the dining experience as it should be: relaxed atmosphere, rich delicacies, rewarding company.

A few years ago, some revelers came to town under the pretense of business. Well, it was business for the lobbyists who staged the event, aimed at filling the bellies and cranial caverns of a few legislators. They gathered at another local restaurant known for good food and charm, accented by nifty knickknack table settings, including a dazzling collection of rare salt and pepper shakers. The shakers were porcelain works of art in an array of shapes and themes, figurines and still life actors. As the night grew wee, and eyelids drooped around bloodshot peepers, somebody started pilfering. Two by two, the salt and pepper shakers disappeared from the tables. Next day, the proprietor of the Word of Mouth Café put the restaurant's name to work, starting a campaign that sent shock waves through the state capitol. "Bring back my salt and pepper shakers," said the owner. No response, as the looters laid low, hoping Shakergate would blow over. No such luck. No amount of money or apology would take the place of the owner's purloined condiment containers. "Bring back my salt and pepper shakers." Four shaker sets made it back to her. A fifth set, a $40 pair featuring the man in the moon, remained in outer space. In the annals of history, Shakergate will struggle to be a footnote. But it's a reminder that little things will bring down great empires. One legislator at the dinner offered a unique defense: "I don't even use salt." But pinching a little salt ended at least one legislative career when one lawmaker pled guilty to the theft of four pairs of salt-and-pepper shakers. She contends she doesn't know how they got into her purse. Damn poltergeists are always hiding in wine bottles. And the man in the moon is still on the loose.

Honest Abe was right. You can't fool all of the people all of the time.

———— ∞∞∞ ————

From its beginnings, Boonville has traded in sin. The town was founded as a convenient Missouri River port, to ship local products like tobacco and hemp. And slaves. For much of Boonville's early history, folks arrived in town by packet steamer. For decades during America's westward expansion, Boonville outfitted pioneers with shoes and candles and buttons and lard and beans before they jumped off civilization's roadmap into the unknown. More recently, people seek Boonville for fame and fortune. Fame is fleeting. But fortune seekers flock to the Isle of Capri Casino, a conflagration of noise and lights, and an endless roundabout of slot machines and blackjack tables.

Sin is back in Boonville.

Walter Williams is back too, as a bronze bust in Morgan Street Park. Williams was a journalist with ethics, at a time when yellow journalism stunk up society. He built the world's first school of journalism down the road in Columbia. The bronze of Williams joins great company, with busts of other nationally prominent figures who left their marks on Boonville: artist George Caleb Bingham, "Mother of the Boonslick" Hannah Cole, abolitionist James Milton Turner and educator Frederick T. Kemper, who in 1845 established the precursor to Kemper Military Academy. The academy has been closed for a few years now, but the ghosts haven't moved out. Locals swear the school is home to the ghost of a Civil War veteran, and the ghost of a student who died in a hazing incident. That reputation only helps the school in its new role as a movie set.

For a town with no movie theaters, Boonville is all about theater.

Thespian Hall is the oldest functioning theater west of the Allegheny Mountains. Built in 1855, the Classic Greek Revival structure served as a hospital and morgue during the Civil War, in the bloody second Battle of Boonville.

Boonville's newest historic icon is the Hotel Frederick, sitting atop a bluff on the corner of Highway 5 and the Missouri River. It could be a movie set, refurbished now as a boutique hotel catering to high rollers. For years it was a nursing home, a warehouse for the parents and grandparents of folks too busy to take care of grandma. I suspect more than a few elders died of heartbreak in the old hotel.

The historic Frederick stood vacant for years, falling into disrepair, awaiting the wrecking ball. But the Frederick is back, a five-star masterpiece. Loving hands not only restored the structure, the rooms have been furnished with the world's finest accoutrements, and retrofitted with bathrooms encased in clear plexiglass, for a better view, inside and out.

For a while the Frederick's aromatic anchor was Glenn's Café, born as a roadside greasy spoon along Columbia's Highway 40, resurrected on this bluff overlooking the Boonville Bridge. Glenn's served the best Cajun dishes this side of the Mason-Dixon line.

Good Cajun restaurants follow two rules: 1) Burn the roux, the greasy flour base for gumbo and étouffée, and 2) Don't throw food away. Throw it in the gumbo, the answer to leftover crawfish and shrimp and oysters and okra and just about anything else that might spoil. Mixing these ingredients together in gumbo adds another week of life to the sum of its parts, and the taste reaches its zenith after three days.

My fondest memory of Boonville happened when I left Glenn's Café after slurping oysters, and walked down the street into a surreal scene.

"We're rolling!" The sound tech yelled. "Quiet on the set!"

"We're rolling!" A half dozen film crew members repeated the chant as they tended to their duties in the yard outside a grand old building. "Quiet on the set!"

The set for this movie, *Saving Grace*, was inside the building. But the crew outside could hear the director's commands.

"Action!" Her voice spilled through open windows and crackled from a half dozen tiny walkie-talkie speakers strapped to crew belts.

"Do the scene again," the director implored her actors, "and *slam* the door this time."

The director was no stranger to a movie set. Her name is Connie Stevens. For most of her life she was in front of the camera, singing, acting. Today, she commanded the actors, and the sound tech, and the crew of this feature length movie filmed in Boonville. Beyond her role as writer and director, Connie has a personal connection to the movie. It recounts events that happened after young Connie, born Concetta Rosalie Ann Ingoglia, witnessed a murder in her hometown Brooklyn and was sent to stay with relatives in Boonville during the 1951 flood.

Boonville is no stranger to a movie set. In fact, this set location, the campus of the former Kemper Military Academy, hosted Chucky in *Child's Play 3*, and George Clooney in the 1986 TV movie *Combat High*. Still, the carnival atmosphere of a Hollywood production is a rarity in a quiet river town. Drawn by the allure of this makeshift Hollywood outpost, gawkers drove up the narrow street, between the trailers and trucks, to catch a glimpse of the activity in the yard, and maybe spot actors Michael Biehn, Piper Laurie or Tatum O'Neal. More likely, they only saw behind-the-scenes activity as the property master, the transportation coordinator and the special effects coordinator scurried between assistants and interns, and extras waiting for their big debut.

Fred Early, the sound tech, muttered as another pickup truck buzzed past. The pickup's motor bled through his headphones, and if he can hear it, so will viewers of the finished movie. Fred is affable, but he's also passionate about his work, a perfectionist. Stray sounds grate on his nerves. More than that, he explained, if the sound has to be overdubbed in Hollywood, the cost goes up.

It's a compromise, trading the controlled atmosphere—and the price tag—of a Hollywood back lot for the real-life location.

Walking out of the building's side door into the yard, Cat

Cacciatore wore a *Killer Diller* T-shirt. She was the property master for the blues drama *Killer Diller*, filmed in central Missouri. And she was the property master for this movie, too. Cat has a reputation in the movie industry as one of the most resourceful property masters around. Her handiwork has adorned dozens of actors with rings, necklaces, even a tobacco pouch. She gets a lot of her items on E Bay, or at local stores. Her latest search was for a nurse's bag. After a pair of futile calls to medical suppliers, she went shopping. She found a suitable bag at a local discount store, but the bag was pink. A can of black spray paint later, she produced the perfect prop.

Mike Strain, the special effects coordinator, borrowed a wrench from the Boonville Fire Department, and prepared a fire hydrant to supply water for an upcoming scene that called for rain. David Houlle, the gaffer, repeatedly traced and monitored the electric cables flowing out the door from the movie set to the sound cart and the equipment trucks.

"Somebody turn that motor off!" Fred barked. The director was ready to shoot another scene, and Fred wanted quiet. An assistant obliged, rushing over to turn off an air conditioner cooling a makeup trailer parked on the street. The trailer was from Saint Joseph, and its owner, Grace Klein, the transportation coordinator, owns most of the trailers along the street. "Three actor trailers, makeup trailers, stake bed trucks, and the honey wagon," she reported. The crew likens a honey wagon to a glorified outhouse on wheels. Grace got into the business twenty years ago, when Paul Newman suggested she capitalize on her family's business. With her husband, Grace owns a recreational vehicle dealership in Saint Joseph, so they have much of the rolling stock necessary to supply the needs of a remote shoot. Her competition is scarce. "There are zero transportation coordinators in Saint Louis, zero in Kansas City," she reported. Her next gig might take her caravan to a movie set in Omaha or Denver, she's not sure yet.

Grace likes to see the movie business come to her home state. But she's quick to point out that Missouri needs to stay competitive with tax credits for movie production. Missouri was the first state to offer tax credits to entice movie producers to choose Missouri film locations, back in the early 1990's. Since then, most states have capitalized on the idea, and surpassed Missouri's restrictive credit offer limits.

Fred agreed. "I have $80,000 invested in this sound cart, right here on the sidewalk," he said. "It's supporting a couple of families."

Eschewing movies seems to be a fundamental maxim among Missouri's traditional "bricks and mortar" economic developers. They don't see the value of investing in a temporary production. Don't tell that to Sarah Gallagher, one of Boonville's biggest promoters. She pointed out that over the two-month production, the people of Boonville saw a tremendous economic infusion from this $3 million movie budget. Hotel rooms. Meals. Paychecks. And *status*.

It's a sin that two of those three movies trashing Missouri—*Ozark* and *Three Billboards outside Ebbing Missouri*—were filmed in other states. Another uniquely Missouri story, *The Assassination of Jesse James by the Coward Robert Ford*, was filmed in Canada. Pitiful.

In the yard outside the movie set, Missouri Film Office chief Jerry Jones laughed as he recounted the tale of his "one day intern." Jerry hired Matt, a young Saint Louisan, to get some experience in the film office. On the intern's first day, Jerry sent Matt to the set of a real motion picture production...the set of *Saving Grace* in Boonville. Executives hired him on the spot to help with craft services, a euphemism for slinging chow for the crew. His foot was firmly planted in the doorway to a career in film.

Matt hustled through the yard, from the snack table to the old Kemper chapel, which served as the dining hall for cast and crew. He passed a trio of locals in bath robes waiting for the call to shoot a mental hospital scene. Susan Douglas admitted this was her first foray into the heady world of acting. She loved the experience. "I was sitting on the couch last night," she recalled, "with a pensive look on my face. My husband asked me what was on my mind. I said I was just wondering who my agent will be."

That attitude was infectious. Handyman Sonny Daniels, known to Boonville neighbors as Mr. Fix It, wanted to rent a limo to arrive on the set for his scene. But with a day's wages amounting to $65, he already was taking a pay cut for the experience. Nobody complained about the wages. "It's a story I can tell my grandchildren," Susan said.

The movie has engendered a mutual admiration society. Jim Simone, the movie's second assistant director, said, "I've just fallen in love with Boonville." He made no secret he'd like to move here, buy a house.

"Everybody's so nice," Susan gushed, referring to the Hollywood crew. "They just don't seem like what you hear about Hollywood people. And Connie Stevens is just wonderful. She's so down to earth."

"She's like your next-door neighbor," Sonny added.

On the movie's last day in town, the folks from Boonville threw a wrap party for the crew. Connie was there, along with childhood friends Arlene Hostetler and Carol Strick. "From the time Connie called early last spring," Arlene recalled, "the whole thing was surreal." At Connie's personal request, Arlene helped find locations and materials for the movie.

What did Connie Stevens think? "I live in a town that's so fast-paced. Boonville is such a quiet, elegant life." Cinematographer Denis Maloney and producer Ralph Singleton (*Because of Winn Dixie*) agreed Boonville had been wonderful. "We got some extraordinary footage," Denis beamed.

"The other night," Connie said, "we were sitting in the lobby of the Frederick Hotel, and we were saying how much we're going to miss this place."

Arlene gushed, "We had so much fun, I miss her all over again. We made a lot of new memories."

Old memories are thick in Boonville. Down the street, giant concrete dogs guard the middle school on the main drag downtown. The dogs were a gift to local families from Jay Gould, who built a railroad through town. Mark Twain had an opinion about Jay Gould: "The multimillionaire disciples of Jay Gould—that man who in his brief life rotted the commercial morals of this nation and left them stinking when he died—have quite completely transformed our people from a nation with pretty high and respectable ideals to just the opposite of that…."

For a region that saw several Civil War battles, it's amazing that an estimated 2,000 buildings in the Boonslick region are eligible for the National Register of Historic Places. Folklore credits city officials during the Civil War: any time they saw soldiers coming toward Boonville, they went out immediately and surrendered the city. Those far-sighted decisions probably saved homes and businesses from destruction. It seems in this case, "Discretion *was* the better part of valor."

An amazing number of Boonville buildings have been restored, like the Old Cooper County Hanging Barn, which staged its last public hanging in 1930. Lawrence Mabry, nineteen years old, was convicted of robbery and murder in neighboring Pettis County and hanged here. The jail, used until 1979, still has remnant iron rings bolted to the walls, to shackle slaves before auction on Main Street.

Heading south on Route 5 a stop at Ravenswood Plantation opened my eyes to beautiful antebellum grandeur...and the ugly institution of slavery. Behind the house on a gravel road, four old log cabins sit in a row. They're still occupied, at least a couple of them, by descendants of slaves who lived in these quarters when they had no choice about location. Now, the descendants have a choice, just not much opportunity.

On a spring morning a few years ago, I climbed into a van with a platoon of the area's strongest promoters. In a whirlwind look at greater Boonslick, we drove through thirteen communities. I heard a library of stories.

The group feels the frustration of trying to get a dozen tiny communities to join together to market this historic area. Oh, they all want to promote their towns. They just don't have the money, or the marketing skills. They may get a boost from Tom Hanks. Maybe.

Larry McMurtry wrote a novel called *Boone's Lick*, based here, and rumors rise and fade that Barry Levinson is directing the movie, starring Hanks and Julianne Moore. It couldn't happen to a better lick, if it happens, before civilization ends.

Name Calling in Jug Town

Jug Town is just a nickname. Years ago a jug factory flourished here.

The jugs are gone, replaced by horsepower, as we discovered. At Calhoun—population 500 if you count dogs and cats—we ran onto a parade, effectively blocking the highway for a short duration. Erifnus rolled up behind a long string of proud old cars—'57 Chevys and Little Deuce Coupes—part of the Calhoun Colt Show parade. For an instant on that highway Erifnus idled as the parade line turned a corner onto the highway in front of her. She's a proud old pony, too, and almost joined in line. But Erifnus hates parades. Hurts her motor to go so slow, her temperature gauge flares rebellion.

I glanced down at the passenger floorboard where an old unmailed letter had settled, yellowed by the sun. It was a pitch to the Pontiac division of General Motors to feature Erifnus Caitnop as a symbol of reliability and endurance. Alas, before I mailed off the letter, the news came that after an eighty-five-year run, the Pontiac brand crashed.

Sad day.

Pontiacs carried names like Chieftan and Star Chief, a nod to the car company's namesake, the intrepid leader of the Ottawa nation who led a rebellion against the British, and was assassinated in 1769. Some people say Chief Pontiac's bones lie buried beneath the old Southern Hotel in Saint Louis.

Now tens of thousands of old Pontiacs lie rusting in auto graveyards throughout the world.

Pontiac made muscular studs: Grand Prix and Trans Am and GTO, nicknamed Goat. The company built its reputation for excitement, helped along by legendary designer John DeLorean.

Pontiac's muscle cars showed up on the silver screen, in *Smoky and the Bandit, Hooper,* and *Cannonball Run.* James Garner drove a Firebird in *The Rockford Files,* and who can forget the Monkee Mobile, or *Knight Rider,* even if you try? The brand is immortalized in songs by Lyle Lovett and Sammy Hagar, Tom Waits, J.J. Cale and Sonny Boy Williamson, Jan and Dean, Ronny and the Daytonas. The brand even made the country western charts with a tearjerker called "That's Why I Hate Pontiacs."

When he heard the sad news, auto inamorato Jay Leno eulogized Pontiac.

The death of a car company is nothing new. The roadsides are littered with the carcasses of once-mighty brands. Packard. Hudson. Studebaker.

Some extinct cars carried historic names, like DeSoto and Pierce-Arrow, or became historic names in themselves, like Edsel. Long before Star Trek, the Vulcan roamed the streets. Even a hundred years ago, there were electric cars and aqua-powered cars like the Stanley Steamer, and the Water Car.

Crosley. Soules. Nash. Gone, gone, gone.

There was even a car called the Saint Louis. The Saint Louis Motor Carriage Company produced cars for eight years at the turn of the century.

All told, North America has produced about 750 auto brands. Worldwide, the number is staggering.

Even though the Pontiac factories are gone, thousands of their progeny still roam the earth, including mine.

———— ∞∞∞ ————

Meanwhile at the Colt Show, Calhoun's tiny population had swelled to thousands, rallying around the old town square to soak themselves in the loftier rungs of Maslow's Hierarchy of Needs: car show, pet parade, baby contest, karaoke competition, horseshoe pitching.

We stopped to savor the flavor of this small town reveling in itself, in the shadow of its notable skyline: one towering wooden grain elevator, a relic from the past, painted red. Calhoun's Colt Show began a hundred years ago when two breeders argued over who had the best colt.

Crowds flowed past the booths, and brave kids waited for a turn on two vintage rides that looked like they'd seen ten thousand carnivals. I bought a chance for a quilt, knowing I wouldn't be around to win it. The Henry County Cattlemen sold me a giant smoked brisket sandwich, which I smothered in home-grown tomatoes. Five bucks. I took a seat in the beer garden, waving the country flies away from my food, waiting for the band to begin, listening to the conversation among locals gathered around the long folding tables.

The word jumped at me from the end of the table. A man firmly attached to his beer pitcher called out a small-town white trash racial slur about a neighborhood where African Americans live. He spoke the word jovially, confident, as if his brazen utterance would heal four hundred years of old wounds and dissolve the stigma of the term. He was emboldened, with help from his Belgian brew. The man sitting across from me was black.

"Even the deputies call it that. Isn't that right, Emmett?" the white man said to the black man facing me. Others nodded and laughed. I kept my face buried in my brisket and tomatoes. Instead of rising indignant, Emmett responded. "You call the fire department and tell them your house is burning down. 'Where at?' they ask. 'Washington Street.' Silence. Then you say that word. Pretty soon, you hear the siren." The white people around Emmett chuckled and nodded knowingly.

In fairness to the people of Jugtown, there is no Washington Street in Calhoun. So the racist folks at this table were from out of town.

Along my journey, I've seen beauty and inspiration. I've witnessed faith, hope and love. But I also keep colliding with the unholy trinity: Poverty. Prejudice. Ignorance. The greatest of these is ignorance.

Emmett kept his cool, and maybe he had no choice in the beer garden. At the Colt Show, Emmett was outnumbered a thousand to one. The folks around him seemed to like Emmett, racist comments notwithstanding. I wonder if they like him only if he stays where they want him to stay. It's hard to accept the idea that people think that way. In the beer garden at the Colt Show, the table talk says we have a long way to go.

I finished my sandwich and wandered out of the beer garden toward the security of an old red Pontiac in the shadow of an old red grain elevator.

As we drove east into the countryside, another beer garden conversation came to mind. One guy called his Amish neighbors termites, because the Amish hire out to tear down barns. It was an ugly slur. And why the hell are the people in this area tearing down barns?

I'll wager a white-faced colt the Amish can dismantle a barn and rebuild it before bigmouth lets go of his pitcher.

Oh, and the Amish recycle everything.

Intermission: Stubby

Erifnus rolled into her familiar spot in front of the sidewalk that leads to the familiar steps, up to the familiar door with the familiar lock that opens into the kind of well-worn comfort that welcomes me perfectly, because I helped arrange it and decorate it with furniture and art, with Cheryl's supervision. Instantly I felt soothing contentment, surrounded by my own stuff: My own hearth with fire-tested pokers and tools I can wield with the confidence of a Samurai. My own woodpile waits out by the back fence, wood split and seasoned and stacked, waiting patiently for autumn's first Alberta clipper to chill our bones so we can set a blaze in the hearth, and send a smoke signal to the neighborhood that we're ready for the cold with our own overstuffed living room chairs and a TV remote I can navigate without looking at its keypad, and next to the chair, my old floor lamp, the kind with an arm that swings the lampshade behind my shoulder, closer to my ear to illuminate the pages of the book that will slip from my hands as I nod off to sleep and the book will fall off my lap onto a hardwood floor, the floor we rescued from under a smothering carpet.

The comfort of home makes me want to stay home.

I don't want to leave my own bed or my own refrigerator, or the peace lilies who love the dining room window, or the plants in the sunroom who await my voice, at least I think so; or the giant trees in my back yard, one a sappy elm, the other a towering apartment house for several families of squirrels.

I never want to leave the squirrels.

Home offered me the opportunity to review the trio of movies trashing Missouri. *Winter's Bone* is a depressing peek into poor white trash. Set in the rugged Ozark hills near Branson, it dips deep into meth and death and depravity. *Three Billboards Outside Ebbing, Missouri* treats depravity and death with dark humor. The scenery is beautiful, filmed in North Carolina. Damn. The series called *Ozark* is a tale of greed infesting Missouri's Lake of the Ozarks. The scenery is beautiful, filmed in Georgia. Son of a bitch.

I forced myself off the couch and out into the back yard.

The ancient ash tree in our back yard reaches halfway to Orion, where its loftiest branches fork and fork again to throw new shoots toward the sun. Tucked into those soaring ash cradles—not big enough yet to make Louisville Sluggers, but the perfect size for slingshots—a trio of squirrel nests ride out the seasons and the storms, safe from most predators, safe from me.

As springtime yields to summer, and my young tomato plants push out of the soil to bask in the warmth of the sun, a menace gnaws at the back of my mind.

Squirrels are thoughtless thieves. They rob indiscriminately. Bird feeders. Dog dishes. They don't care. Worse, they don't remember. You can scare a squirrel by beating a galvanized pail with a crowbar, and in the time it takes your bartender to mix a mind eraser, the squirrel will return to tip the pail and check for birdseed. But the squirrel's biggest fault, its most unforgivable transgression, is lack of attention to detail.

Stubby is different.

The other squirrels in our backyard have no ethics. They're worse than robbers. Worse than pirates and land sharks and extortionists and pick-pockets. Worse than marauders and picaroons, smugglers and swindlers and poachers. Well, maybe poachers are worse. But few filchers and pilferers do a sloppier job of destruction than squirrels.

Stubby is none of those things.

He's instantly recognizable because he has a fuzzy stub where a flowing tail should twitch.

Not sure how he lost his tail. It might be a birth defect. Maybe a dog bit it off. He might've skittered too close under the wheels of an oncoming car.

Stubby is a loner.

Other squirrels seem to have mates, or friends. Stubby appears to be an outcast from squirrel society where a bushy tail is prized for balance and warmth.

No matter. Stubby persists. And he's learned to hang around Cheryl and me on our back deck, where we fatten him with walnuts and pecans. So despite being shunned by other squirrels, he eats well.

We're orphans, Cheryl and I, Since Baskin Robinson and Queenie Beanie departed. We opted to stay petless for a while, since our vagabond schedules would annoy any self-respecting territorial terrier.

So Stubby fills a void.

We believe Stubby is smarter than the average squirrel, to quote Bullwinkle, pal and confidant to the legendary Rocket J. Squirrel. Of course Rocky the Squirrel can fly and make witty conversation. Stubby is light on chatter, and carries an extra layer of fat, thank you very much. Yet somewhere in his walnut brain, he has recalculated his ability to leap—without a tail—from roof to tree.

Springtime triggers Stubby's curiosity. He begins to eye the vigorous tomato plants. And we welcome him to taste the fruit when I transplant the tomato vines into the garden. When Stubby takes a tomato, he eats the whole thing. Not the other squirrels.

We believe Stubby is crafty and cunning, wily and sly, stemming from his close encounters with grim reapers. He'd be a dashing mate for one of the other squirrels, if only they could see his good side. Alas, the squirrel kingdom is unforgiving.

But we'll keep favoring Stubby.

If you think obsession with a rodent is stupid, don't take your kids to Disneyland.

III: Drive-By Elvis

Rising Above It All

Dunklin is Missouri's tallest county, standing almost forty-four miles from its sole to its crown, and shaped like the left side of an hourglass, stuffed with cotton, mostly. We scratched a little deeper to learn its unique culture.

The Missouri map dangles a strange appendage that looks like a Bootheel, or a hatchet in the forehead of Arkansas. The area is definitely a member in good standing of the Old South, and its people, for the most part, feel alienated from politics in Missouri's capitol, five hours away.

I formed a plan to crisscross these roads and peel back the cotton curtain to reveal real life.

In this part of the world, it's common to find two communities side-by-side: one black, one white. Historically, African Americans didn't live in Wardell, they lived in North Wardell. They didn't live in Hayti, they lived in neighboring Hayti Heights. A local newspaperman told me a story about a truck driver back in the '50s who serviced the region with dry goods. He drove from Holcomb to Hayti, from Portageville to Gideon, and everywhere in between. At the end of his day, when he reached Wardell, he'd park his truck on the white side of the road, pull out his guitar, and sing to the black folks on the North Wardell side. Elvis could energize a crowd, and soon, blacks and whites alike were dancing like crazy. But not together. Young truck drivin' Elvis saw that everywhere he went.

———— ✺ ————

Erifnus rolled into the shade of beech trees and cherry bark oaks in Morris State Park, straddling Crowley's Ridge, a geologic backbone that juts diagonally across the Bootheel. In pioneer days when this area's vast swampland was a roadblock to a pilgrim's progress, Crowley's Ridge offered safe passage across the swamps for settlers headed to Texas.

Peach orchards surround the park, their sappy aroma suggesting healthy food choices. But in this neck of the woods, my culinary antennae point to smoky Memphis-style barbecue, my chance to load up on some of the best dry rub ribs in the world. Today, we drove south toward the tiny waistline of this corseted county where Strawberry's Bar-B-Que awaited.

Finding Strawberry's for the first time was a barbeque epiphany. Years ago, just outside Puxico at the Mingo National Wildlife Refuge welcome center, a crowd had assembled to discuss agritourism. When it was my turn to speak, I tried to flatter the locals. "When Americans talk about barbecue, they mention Kansas City," I offered. "But I know where to find the best barbecue in Missouri. It's right here in Stoddard County, down the road in Dexter." As soon as I mentioned two of my longtime favorite Southeast Missouri barbecue stops—The Hickory Log and Dexter Bar-B-Que—folks started squirming and shaking their heads. In a flash, members of the crowd drew strength from each other, and the mob began flailing their arms and shouting "Strawberry's!" I was puzzled, not knowing what strawberries had to do with barbecue. The crowd kept chanting, "Strawberry's! Strawberry's!"

I bit. "Strawberries?"

"In Holcomb! In Holcomb!" they shouted. Next day was my first Strawberry's, a dark cozy corner of rustic where the table tops double as yellow pages, with ads for car parts, funeral homes, bail bonds and real estate laminated into each table surface. That was just window dressing. When the server brought my slab of ribs I never read another word. Indeed, the slabs at Strawberry's are so tender, the meat falls off the bone from the vibrations of your voice.

Locals love Strawberry's pork steaks. Only a half slab of Americans outside the Midwest ever heard of a pork steak. Missourians take for granted that the world enjoys them. Coastal meat cutters might respond if you asked for "sliced pork shoulder." But pork steaks draw blank stares.

Barbecue is a way of life. It's the perfect marriage of sloppy and civil. It blurs the line between humans and sharks. It's the foundation of our culture and will singlehandedly see us through tough economic times. There should be a mutual fund specializing in barbecue business: sauces, grills, utensils, clothing and tailgating.

Not long ago, Bodean's Kansas City-style BBQ in London hosted a dozen literary giants. Well, they were travel writers. I offered them food for thought. "A few years ago a London newspaper surveyed its readers, asking one question: Who is your favorite American? The top four vote getters were Mark Twain, Jesse James, Harry Truman and Mickey Mouse. All Missourians." Okay, I lied. Harry wasn't in the top four. But giving these writers a taste of Harry's hometown barbecue convinced them that Missouri should be a destination.

Counting backyards, more than two million barbecue pits saturate Missouri. Who has the best? Everybody. Just ask them. Each has a story to tell. But act fast. Barbecue shacks appear and disappear like mushrooms.

Like pork steaks, barbecue is a regional specialty. Everybody south of the Mason Dixon line believes they have the best barbecue. Carolina. Georgia. Tennessee. Texans, bless 'em, are no different, just more obnoxious about it. They think they originated barbecue.

Let 'em think what they want. Pass the Strawberry's.

Birthright

To get to Strawberry's, Erifnus descended deeper into the Bootheel. Along the way we stopped at Campbell to solve a mystery. Campbell is famous among peach lovers. You've heard about Georgia peaches. Campbell peaches are just as sweet, an indication of the demeanor of the locals who built a tourism industry around their fuzzy fruit. But the area hasn't always been sweet for everybody.

I searched for the Birthright house. The Birthrights were an uncommon couple for the Missouri Bootheel after the Civil War. Charles and Bettie Birthright were born into slavery on different plantations, and they had to ask permission from their owners to marry. A barber and a seamstress, Charles and Bettie later became bankers and philanthropists.

They used their financial power and influence for the greater good, helping educate black children in the Bootheel. Later they bequeathed much of their fortune to Stillman College in Tuscaloosa, Alabama. A friend told me that the Birthright homestead still exists on the outskirts of Campbell. So I stopped at a convenience store in town to find directions. I wasn't prepared for the answer. "Are you sure they were from here?" one lady asked. She gave me a look that told me there were no African Americans in Campbell back then. Another lady chimed in, "Maybe they were from Clarkton, up the road. There's a black population up there."

The folks at the convenience store, customers and clerks alike, were very polite to me. But the message was clear.

I drove down to the local restaurant to make sure there was no Birthright in Campbell. On the door, the sign said No Smoking Vandy's Daisy Hut Country Home Cooking. I walked into Vandy's, a pleasant place with a great aroma. A young woman brought a carafe of coffee from behind the counter. "Welcome!" she said cheerfully, as she whisked past me to attend to an octogenarian couple by the window. She poured coffee into two cups clutched in grateful hands.

"What's the special?" I asked.

"Chicken and egg noodles with three sides!" she chirped. But it was 10 a.m., and I was there for another purpose.

"Ever hear of the Birthright house?" Blank stares, even from the elderly couple attached to their coffee cups. I explained what I knew about the Birthrights.

"They wouldn't have been from around here." The group looked at me not so much with suspicion as pity, for being an outsider who didn't really understand where he was. I tipped my cap and left.

Four miles from Campbell as the crow flies, in the small farming community of Clarkton I found the house where Charles and Bettie Birthright lived out their days.

Their story is a study in perseverance. Charles was born into slavery in Virginia to Petram and Hunnie Birthright, who instilled in him a sense of duty and purpose. The slaveowner, Jack Birthright—who gave Charles his name—moved west to Madrid Bend, Tennessee, where Charles met Bettie Scott. She had moved there from Roanoke with her owners, and eventually to Beach Grove, the "metropolis of Dunklin County," thanks to a plank road that crossed the swamp, connecting the town to the Mississippi River. The plank road opened commerce to the area, but locals didn't care much for the ride, referring to the rough wooden planks as the Devil's washboard.

Beach Grove became Clarkton, named for one of the builders of the plank road. Charles, a fiddle-playing barber, eventually proposed to Bettie. Permission would be necessary from not only Bettie's owners, but Bettie's family back in Virginia, who hoped to buy her out of slavery and reunite their family. Permission granted, the couple married, yet saw little of one another, owned by families who lived twenty miles apart. They saw each other on weekends until the Civil War, when Charles was taken to Arkansas to serve "Marse Jack," a major in the Confederate Seventh Missouri Regimental Cavalry. During this period Bettie gave birth to the couple's only child, who died in infancy. The child's name was Sterling Price Birthright, a strong clue that owner Jack influenced that name, too.

Emancipation brought freedom for Charles and Bettie, free at last to go wherever they wanted. But they stayed in Clarkton, in demand for their skills, he as a barber and musician, she as a cook and seamstress. They prospered in business, barbering and stitching and catering, including Bettie's famous forty-egg wedding cakes, and farming land that eventually sprawled over 500 acres. They even held shares in the local bank and made loans to white people. They invested in the local rail line, which helped revive the town after the plank road was destroyed during the war.

Bettie Birthright helped Charles build the frame house with a long porch in 1872. She continued to work as a seamstress, he a barber. The Birthrights not only prospered, they gave back to the community, helping build two schools. At the turn of the twentieth century, the *Dunklin Democrat,* a local newspaper with a stalwart statewide reputation, lauded Charles for "contributing to Dunklin County's greatness," although when Charles died, that same newspaper noted his passing with a telling remark about "the always popular old colored man, of Clarkton." The newspaper said the Birthright home was a central gathering place for the whole community, "as popular as if its master had been of purest Caucasian blood." Next to the Birthright obituary was a story about a lynching of a black man in Oklahoma. The lives of the Birthrights are remarkable during a time of apartheid and adherence to "social Darwinism." They not only prospered, they left a lasting legacy in a white-dominated environment. Well, at least folks in Clarkton remember them. I couldn't find anybody in Campbell who knew about this legendary couple. Harry Truman's words hit me: "There's nothing new in the world except the history you don't know."

The odds are stacked against any old clapboard house surviving 140 years. But loving hands from the community and the Clarkton

Historical Society—and a grateful Stillman College—helped keep the Birthright house intact. Recently, the home was added to the National Register of Historic Places, to offer an extra layer of perpetual protection.

Buster Brown

Bill's Real Pit BBQ in Kennett checks all the boxes for great barbecue: It's a local favorite hangout, not much bigger than a shack, soaked in smoke. Bill's deals in two types of tender: ribs and cash. The place hadn't had a makeover since your grandfather ate here back in 1947. But four days before Christmas, 2012, Bill's burned down. Undaunted, Bill's reopened nearby. At the counter, Dennis waited for my order.

"What's your specialty?" I asked.

"Ribs, pork steaks, pulled pork..." He stopped talking and pointed to the menu board behind him. "Just about anything." Dennis stood at the counter and waited patiently while I studied the menu on the wall behind him.

I chose a pulled pork sandwich and picked a spot by a window.

Fresh on my mind was a blog post from a local man who had won a million-dollar lottery. In this region, millionaire land barons seem to be doing fine. But driving the Bootheel backroads, we pass poverty, punctuated by an archipelago of empty shoe factories. Making shoes once was the economic backbone of this entire region before Brown Shoe Company closed the factories during the '80s and took the jobs overseas. International Shoe Company did the same. Like dominoes, the factories shut down. Malden. Ironton. Charleston. Sikeston. Fredericktown. Piedmont. Steelville. Saint Clair. Perryville. Cape Girardeau. Jackson. Caruthersville. In many towns the factories sit like giant ghosts. And whole families lost jobs.

Now a systematic drive through the Bootheel reveals two things: Rich farmland and abject poverty. Haves and have nots.

The land has changed radically over the past two centuries. Earthquakes rearranged the topography. But man has put an equally dramatic stamp on the land, draining the swamps with a system of canals, and planting row crops everywhere.

To say this is rich farmland meant little to me until I learned that Dunklin County sent a forty-six-pound cucumber to the 1893 World's Fair in Chicago.

Interrupting the flat land are rare mounds, sacred burial mounds of native tribes who lived here long before the first white settlers arrived. According to Mary Smyth-Davis, in her 1895 *History of Dunklin County,* "Among the Indian chiefs whom the first settlers of this county came in contact with were Chilletacaux, Senaca, Kinamore, John Big Knife, Corn Meal, John Ease, Moonshine, Buck-Eye and Chickolee. Chilletacaux near Kennett was the principal Indian village; the Indian chief of the same name lived there in a small log hut, the cracks of which were sufficiently large for his many cats to go in and out at will. Even after the county had a considerable number of white settlers the Indians came back in summer to their old camp grounds. The squaws tended a common corn-patch, from which each one received her portion. They also made beaded moccasins and ornaments. The men hunted and fished. The Chickasaw Indians are said to have been lost during the earthquakes at Cuckle-Burr Slough, between Buffalo Creek and Big Lake. The Indians were all peaceable and kind when treated so by the whites."

Buffalo Township is named for the wooly bulls that used to roam these parts. The buffalo are gone. Gone too are the native tribes.

We passed the Hollywood Church of Christ and drove through Nesbit, nicknamed Need More by early residents who wanted a better selection from the general store. Need More could be a nickname for the panorama, too, unless, of course, you look past the flat.

We drove down to tag the very bottom of Missouri, paralleling the Pole Cat Slough past Senath, through Bucoda and Europa, a town built for the purpose of selling whiskey, and down to Red Onion, Missouri. We've reached the low point in this story, which is two miles west of Red Onion, where the land is a mere 205 feet above sea level.

Near the Arkansas border is an unusual sight, at once startling and familiar. Outside Hornersville down a dirt road, a cemetery holds the remains of Buster Brown. Most kids who grew up wearing Buster Brown shoes probably thought Buster was a kid. Not so. He was born Major Ray back at the beginning of the Civil War, and he stopped growing when he reached 44 inches tall. He performed with the Sells Brothers Circus along with his wife Jennie, 37 inches tall. They were heralded as the World's Smallest Couple. They retired to Hornersville and opened a general store. Always the salesman, he not only sold Buster Brown shoes, in 1900 he sold an idea to the Brown Shoe Company: make him the spokesman for the brand. At forty years old, Major Ray became Buster Brown. He died in 1936, and sometime thereafter, folks erected a tombstone with his likeness, dressed as Buster Brown.

He's a memory now, same as the empty shoe factories that dot the Bootheel landscape.

The road swerved through Hayti, pronounced HEY tie. On a dusty corner, Jiffy Jim's Grocery reveals a sense of community. People were everywhere, walking, visiting, out and about. It was a welcome sight in this vast cotton veneer, where too many towns struggle to rebound from long-abandoned shoe factories. But Hayti shows promise.

Today Hayti and Hayti Heights are less segregated. At the park in the white part of town, a black family reunion sprawled over the grounds, and several dozen family members walked the two blocks between the park and Jiffy Jim's.

Driving north past Limbaugh's Creek into the Saint Francois Mountains, we passed tiny burgs: Floyd. Latty. Ebo and Aptus. We drove through Old Mines and Mud Town and Happy Hollow and Shibboleth, through Cadet and French Town, to reach an international destination known by everybody who ever dived for sunken treasure.

Bonne Terre Mine looks innocent on the surface. The entrance is underwhelming for the world class destination it has become. It sits in the middle of town, yet it's easy to miss; the mine's surface footprint is less than a block square. Years ago, the mine was abandoned, and when they turned off the last bilge pump, the miles of tunnels quickly filled with water. The immense finger lakes lurk beneath the surface like a reticular iceberg.

Most folks don't know much about the mine, unless they're scuba divers. Entering Bonne Terre Mine, divers have a multi-layer labyrinth to explore. Miles of well-lighted underground tunnels and channels lead to sunken treasures: mining equipment, a steam locomotive. The water is crystal clear. Consequently, divers flock here from all over the world.

While they're in the area, they see the old ghost plant. The long-shuttered Saint Joe lead smelter just south of the mine spreads over several acres, sitting like a big scab on Mother Earth's skin. Even from a distance, its steel superstructure sprawls over the landscape like an aircraft carrier. This vast industrial shell is now a museum with spooky relics from the early mining days...lamps and lanterns, giant tractors, drills and shovels and a monument to miners who lost their lives in Missouri's lead mines. Further south is an abandoned lead mine transformed into a state park for all-terrain vehicles, because the land is useless for anything else. Ominous signs on the property warn about contamination from the lead tailings throughout the area: Wash your hands before you eat. Don't expose young children.

I got outta there, and saw what seemed to be another ominous sign: The next couple of miles of highway were adopted by the Church Army Lead Belt. Sounds militant. But this army is a positive force, helping drug addicts get clean. When the old lead smelters shut down, communities were hit by a double-whammy: 1) Families lost jobs and poverty skyrocketed; and 2) huge piles and ponds containing an estimated 250 million tons of lead-contaminated tailings dotted the rugged countryside, free to leach contaminants into the air and water. Lead levels in children soared. As cleanup efforts continue, the area is still gripped by poverty, drug and alcohol addiction.

First impressions may be damning—like those three foreboding movies about Missouri's seamy underbelly—but Church Army Lead Belt and other Samaritans are working to rehabilitate the area's most needy people, and restore its land.

We drove through the guts of the Ozarks.

Twist and Shout

Cresting a hill we began our descent, curving and swerving downhill, face to face with vistas through the tall pines. To the left a deep valley the size of a thousand football stadiums packed a standing-room-only sea of hardwoods dressed in their fall colors.

The golly views repeated a hundred times in a drive on the twistiest turns this side of San Francisco's Lombard Street.

We drove into the heart of the Ozarks, where nature—with a little help from the highway department—lays down a series of thrilling roller coaster tracks along a driving loop called the Ozark Hellbender, named for the forearm-sized salamander that hides under rocks in Ozark streams. This endangered species lends the perfect name for the route. A few years ago MoDOT planned to straighten Highway 19 deep in its Ozark run. Planners had purchased extended right-of-way but locals joined to defeat the improvement and keep the gnarly highway. Sometimes it's better to leave old isolated trails alone. And in this neck of the woods, most locals want to be left alone. Many Ozark natives maintain a deep distrust of outsiders.

So Mother Nature and MoDOT maintain some of the best roller coasters in the world, a fact not lost on Alan Peters.

Alan loves to ride motorcycles. He has driven loops through the Arkansas Ozarks and the Rockies. And he knows that Missouri's Ozark blacktops take a back seat to nobody.

When Alan describes the rides through Missouri's Ozarks, he uses motorcycle terms like twisties and sweepers. Instead of tracking miles per gallon, he charts curves per mile. He's one of southern Missouri's foremost authorities on driving through this mountainous outback.

When Alan identified a half dozen driving loops, bobbing and weaving through great Ozark scenery, motorcyclists took note.

So did we.

Of course, Erifnus drives the loops using four wheels instead of two. Regardless of the number of wheels under your heels, these roads sing to your senses.

Alan didn't build these roads, any more than Magellan built Cape Horn. But like Magellan, Alan found some hair-raising passages.

These loops have personalities. Alan named them. Waterfall Wonderland. Big Spring Sidewinder. Elephant Rock and Roll. And the Jesse James Getaway.

Jesse James again?

Yep. The James Gang used a hideout at Maggard's Cabin on the Current River. Hard turns through the Jesse James Getaway loosely follow the escape route after the James Gang robbed a train at Gads Hill, Missouri in 1874. They got a sixty-mile head start on their pursuers and headed west on fast horses running along beautiful Logan Creek and Sinking Creek, over the hills and through the woods to Maggard's Cabin. The old cabin has been restored, accessible by water and by land.

These driving loops are great any time of year. Winter offers the most spectacular views, when the hardwoods have dropped their leaves. But take Mark Twain's advice: "If you want to see Missouri at her best, see her in October."

We drove the twisting roads deep into the Ozarks, and when the sun set over the mountains, we headed back to the comfort of our cabin at the Rivers Edge Resort next to the spring-fed Jacks Fork River, where Scenic Highways 19 and 106 cross paths in the town of Eminence. The Great Flood of 2017—ten feet higher than any previous recorded flood—loosed several of the resort's cabins and sent them downriver along with everything else in the floodplain: campground toilets and picnic tables, farm machinery and sheds, stables, cars, junk, trash, cattle, wild animals and a billion trees. Downriver, the flood wiped out downtown Van Buren. Van Buren built back, stronger, higher, smarter. Same for River's Edge Resort.

Upriver somebody reopened the tiki bar that hangs over the river. In summer the noise matches the bare flesh soaked in tattoos and baby oil. I worry for river travelers beneath the tiki bar, where young revelers can projectile vomit into the stream. My canoeing buddy Dave Johnston calls this river stretch the Key West of Shannon County.

Next day Erifnus and I made our own trail names: The Ozark Tilt-A-Whirl. Stills, Hills and Roadkills. The Texter Smasher.

Around here most texter drivers are dead, or soon will be. It's even hard to read billboards while driving. By the way, there are no billboards outside Ebbing, Missouri, because there's no Ebbing, Missouri. But we passed Many Springs, Missouri, whose two city limit signs stood back-to-back on the same post. Many Springs, one pole.

Andrew Jackson's Chief Justice

Driving west we hit the twistiest roads of all. We muscled through Ozark County along stomach-flipping slalom courses that make pretzels look straight, through tight curves where Erifnus could see her own back bumper.

Headed toward Branson we hit the Taney County line. Taney County was named for Andrew Jackson's Chief Justice of the United States Supreme Court, Roger B. Taney, who married the sister of "Star-Spangled Banner" author Francis Scott Key. Taney later delivered the 1857 Supreme Court majority opinion declaring Dred Scott was not a U.S. citizen, and therefore could not sue for his freedom. Taney County also is the backdrop for the movie *Winter's Bone*, the chilling tale of meth and death.

We drove circles around beautiful rural Taney County, passing the ghost of Who'd a Tho't It School near ProTem. We sought Coffin Spring and Dewey Bald, and the tall pine Signal Tree used by Bald Knobbers in Harold Bell Wright's novel *Shepherd of the Hills*. We passed Mud Socket and Murder Rock, Trigger Creek and Three Johns School, where there's no waiting. We found Gobbler's Knob and looked for Free Jack Spring, named for a freed slave who lived there, and Peg Leg Hollow, named for a Civil War captain's wooden leg. We searched for Lottie Lawless Hollow, named for a woman who hanged herself there, and Possum Trot—mentioned by Granny Clampett—and Granny Hole on Turkey Creek. No relation.

Driving all of this outback, the stories behind this strange nomenclature would be lost, were it not for Margaret E. Bell, who dutifully recorded these unique appellations and the tales of their creation. It must have been a tedious project, back in 1933. I can't imagine anybody driving all of these roads to uncover their stories.

Wrapped in remote obscurity until it reaches Branson, Highway 76 becomes Country 76 Boulevard, the aorta through Branson's theaters, restaurants, museums, T-shirt shops and go kart tracks. The pressure of eight million tourists on a town of 12,000 made Highway 76 the single most continuous traffic jam this side of LA's Carmageddon, finally forcing the highway department to perform bypass surgery. If you're in a hurry to traverse Branson, run the cat roads, the backroad shortcuts. These roads slice through the urban sprawl like slashes from Zorro's sword. The shortcuts don't seem to ease the pressure along Country 76 Boulevard.

In this rhinestone capital, unruly behavior is legendary. Even the name Branson was changed in 1902 to Lucia, because folks didn't like its namesake, early postmaster and reputed Bald Knobber Rube Branson. But the name changed back to Branson in 1908.

The Bald Knobbers, a loose association of unbridled vigilantes, applied a lynch mob brand of justice to accused wrongdoers. In the void of civility after the Civil War, vigilante groups including the Sons of Honor brought accused miscreants to justice. In doing so, they used their own brand of terrorism. "String 'em up!" the vigilantes yelled. "Right back at you," Missouri's militia chief George Caleb Bingham said, applying his own brand of terrorism to the Sons of Honor. Proving he was as creative with a Constitution as he was with a paintbrush, Bingham threatened to restore order by bringing in the state militia. The Bald Knobbers ignored Bingham's threat, until neighbors found out the militia's cost would be borne by local taxpayers. The angry taxpayers ran the vigilantes out of the county, thus avoiding a tax hike.

West of Branson, Stone County's history takes travelers back in time, past Medical Springs Hollow and Naked Joe Mountain, and Fox Hunter's Paradise, later named Fairy Cave, and Fractional School, where integers were a minority. We skirted Radical, named in 1870 for the post-war Radical Republicans who lived there.

Galena, named for valuable ore found in the region, was the site of America's last public hanging. More than 400 invited guests crammed into a temporary stockade on May 21, 1937 to watch Roscoe "Red" Jackson drop eleven feet to his death. He'd killed a traveling salesman near Branson, after the salesman bought him dinner. Nice tip.

Crossing the James River from Galena, motorists used to come to a fork in the road while still on the bridge. A new traditional two-lane bridge replaced the old y-bridge, now closed to all but foot traffic, so there's plenty of time to decide which way to go.

Route 413 undulates through ruggedness along Raily Creek between Galena and Elsey. Ancient guardrails use wood from trees planted by Moses, I suspect. A heavy wire threads through rounded wooden posts, squatty, silver, fat and unyielding. The guardrails guide the old roads through knobby beauty, cliffs and precipices, punctuated by intriguing names like Secret Valley, Hooten Town, and my favorite school, Blue Eye High. These roads also reveal a disparity between wealthy gentry and some of the poorest folks this side of the delta.

The old hills, scarred by human termiting, still serve up beauty. The picturesque Lorene Dairy Farm sits on sloping hills, surrounded by immaculate white fences. In their off time, dairy cows seek relief in ponds, reminding me that two weeks ago my glass of milk was cooled by pond water.

Running the Table

"Historic?" The chamber of commerce lady didn't buy my logic.

I persisted. Rock Lane Lodge already was historic when our family stayed there thirty years ago. I wanted to see how the old property had survived the ravages of time.

"It's near the end of the road." She motioned down the narrow peninsula called Indian Point. The chamber lady's response seemed more an invitation for me to get out of her office.

Even though Missouri is landlocked, the state has more peninsulas than Florida, thanks to a dozen lakes that look like dragons on the map. Indian Point is among the longest of those peninsulas. Looking at the anatomy of our nation, Homer Simpson calls Florida "America's wang." Indian Point is its appendix.

The native stone cabins of Rock Lane Lodge hold special memories for my family. Our daughters grew up drinking from big yellow plastic cups with colorful Rock Lane Lodge logos emblazoned on the sides, functional mementos of a fun family vacation. But over time, things change. The logos wore off the cups, victims of abusive dishwashing. The lodge still stands, but with modernization and facelifts, it has grown into the sprawling Rock Lane Resort and Marina, and bears scant resemblance to my memory. Ah, progress.

Erifnus backtracked up the slim peninsula, crept past the parking lots for Silver Dollar City, the Ozarks-themed shopping center with amusement rides perched atop Marble Cave, named by Captain Freeman Bowell. Careless pronunciation gradually morphed the name into Marvel Cave. More than a century ago, while the Prince of Darkness reveled in his namesakes along the spines and bowels of Missouri's karst topography, another prince first surveyed Marvel Cave. Fred Prince identified this cave as a great source of bat guano, prized as fertilizer. Beauty is in the eye of the beholder. Fred, a prolific writer and illustrator, spent two years studying the cave. "We put up a tent in the Cathedral Room," Fred wrote, "and even built a stone fireplace, and lived down there for a week, or even a month at a time!" Fred was fearless. "In the deeper and more remote places, I would often, when tired, simply stretch out where I was and rest—and then go on with the work; there was no change, just even darkness, even, unchanging temperature and moisture, and a blessed stillness!" He once escorted a gold prospector into the cavern. Finding no gold the prospector "flew into a rage, drew a gun on me, and threatened to shoot me if I did not tell him at once where it was. I laughed at him. 'And how will you get out without me,' I said, and blew out our candles! I slipped into a side crevice, and waited (until) he had relighted his candle, and seeing nothing of me, was getting properly scared.

"I let him worry awhile, then came into the passage with him. 'You are a fool,' I said. 'I'm not afraid of your gun.'" Fred led the man out of the cave, and the goldless digger ran off, grateful to be unearthed.

Later a couple bought the cave with an idea to make money. They took visitors on guided tours through the cave. Eventually they built a replica pioneer settlement at the cave entrance. Today, Silver Dollar City is part of an empire featuring Dollywood and several other family entertainment outposts scattered across the great flyover.

In this ruggedly beautiful part of America's oldest mountain chain, the landscape has been splattered by development projects that dot the hills like smoldering chards from the exploding skyrocket called Branson. Two by two, the old fishing cabins along these spring-fed rivers gave up the ghost to hotels and time-share condos. Folks flock to this area and fill the condos so they can partake in clean Ozark Mountain living. It's a paradox: all this development is making the Ozarks less clean, less Ozark. That's the price for success, and Greater Branson has been successful luring tourists. A group of concerned locals formed the Upper White River Basin Foundation to monitor the progress of removing septic tanks from the watershed and report environmental stories through its newsletter. The foundation's board includes members from Wal Mart, Cargill, Tyson, Bass Pro and Silver Dollar City. I hope they're committed to drinking local tap water.

Highway 13 takes a modernized slice through Branson West before it regains its twisty two-lane temperament. We stumbled upon a worldly sculpture: A life-sized copper hot air balloon looks like it fell out of *Around the World in 80 Days* into a cluttery roadside business district. The balloon stands tall as a giraffe, its skin a copper cutout depicting the globe's seven copper continents. Cocked sideways, the balloon appears to be sailing with the wind through a parking lot. The art is brazen because it's vulnerable. Copper thieves haven't figured out how to load this monstrosity onto their pickup truck and drive it under the power lines hanging over Highway 13.

Erifnus turned down Route RB, letters that signify a recreational boating access somewhere along this road. Sure enough, the end of this road found a Corps of Engineers waterfront park. Unfortunately, relentless rains and flooding had pushed the waterfront to the wrong side of the park, so the shelter and the playground sat underwater. A fisherman forty yards offshore stood in his bass boat smoking a cigarette, casting for crappie hiding under a picnic bench.

We retreated from the water's edge and headed back to Highway 13, to a handsome little log cabin called Jill's Ozark BBQ. My stomach said yes, so I took it in with me and sat down in an alcove at the world's coziest two-top booth, a chess match-sized wooden table framed by two pine benches with room for only one skinny butt apiece. Jill's specialty is baby back ribs. So I had a pork sandwich with butt fries. Jill offered a dozen different hot sauces, including Jill's Pig Out Hot Sauce and Liquid Stupid. I shunned Liquid Stupid...don't need no help. As we left, I noticed the picnic tables shrouded by Jill's stand-alone outdoor pig out station, screened-in to keep people from harming the bugs.

Rolling south, travelers enter the realm of the Lampe Litter Lifters, according to the Adopt-A-Highway sign. Some people believe we don't need Adopt-A-Highway signs because the signs encourage folks to throw litter along the roadside. Don't look now, but ignorant people will throw trash anyway. And they don't read. So the litter lifters perform a valuable service, teaching intelligent youngsters not to litter, and offering them an opportunity to pick up after their dullard schoolmates. The People Against Everything remain mute on this issue, since this government program is financed, in large part, by the private sector.

There are thousands of Adopt-A-Highway signs along these roads, and even though some purists protest the signs themselves are eyesores, the Adopt-A-Highway program is better than waiting for moonrakers to pick up the trash.

Ha Bob's One Stop hails at the corner of Highway 13 and Route H, which leads past Bread Tray Mountain to Table Rock Lake. Erifnus stopped and I stuck my head through the entrance and yelled, "Ha,

Bob!" If the folks at Ha Bob's get tired of idiots like me who stop to say ha, they didn't show it.

Deeper into the woods, Table Rock Lake's most romantic spot lured me in and kissed me. Like most of the rustic palaces in this area, White River Lodge hides off the beaten path, a picture postcard of alpine purity, situated in a stand of pines on the lake north of Blue Eye. The lodge is hewn from giant pine logs. The great room has a huge stone fireplace. Bedrooms named Couple's Cove and Foggy River Room beckon you to hand-crafted log beds. From the lodge's ample back balconies, the lake view opens the windows to your soul for a good pine scrubbing.

In a race across the western Ozarks, Routes 76 and 86 both try to lose. Each was built back in the days when highways followed the contours of the land, rather than blast through the hills.

On the drive down Highway 86, billboards dot the roadside waving and shouting to travelers about Dogwood Canyon. It's a canyon all right, but erase those mental images of Grand Canyon or Bryce Canyon or the Snake River. This canyon is more intimate, and more achievable in one session, spectacular in its own right, a rugged gash in the Ozark skin. In spots, the park seems manicured by man. They stock the stream with trout as long as your forearm. Remarkably, Texas longhorn steers made it all the way to this remote canyon. What the hell, the resident landscape architects apparently wanted to improve the natural beauty spawned by the Great Cosmic Architect, at least the parts bordering the tram routes. And the trams help sell tickets to visitors, since most visitors get here by car, and prefer to remain in a seated position.

Enhancement engineering aside, kudos to the canyon's operators, who realize this is the closest most visitors will get to an Ozarks ecosystem. For those who remain extra-ambulatory, the park goes the extra mile, sponsoring a 50k run through the Mark Twain National Forest.

Erifnus rollercoastered back to Highway 13, and we rounded the horn at the southern end of Table Rock Lake, on the approach to Big Cedar Lodge. In Missouri only a handful of spots lure megawealthy world travelers. This is one of them.

Big Cedar Lodge is legendary. The property is charmingly rugged and woodsy. The cabins exude rustic opulence. Big fireplaces. Showers with multiple nozzles resembling a balneal firing squad. The staff makes the difference, attending to every whim. Cookies delivered to your cabin. Firewood at your door every morning. Truthfully, Big Cedar is grand, but I'd be content with Medium Cedar. Cheryl loved it. I was slightly annoyed by timeshare salespeople ushering prospects past the swimming pool.

Driving past the ghosts of the O.K. School, Spooky Hollow and Tan Yard Hollow, the hills are pretty. Spectacular ranches sprawl next to the Elk River, first called the Cowskin River, named when a settler skinned dead cattle and dried them on the riverbank. Nowadays cowskins on the Elk have been replaced by human skins, totally naked, nurtured with alcohol and other brain exfoliants.

Long Metal Chicken Burritos

"Why did the chicken cross the rainbow bridge?"

Just past the Golden Church of God, we left Golden for the earthtones of Route J, a remote road down a remote peninsula on Table Rock Lake. It's a fishing paradise in the American outback. The anglers get their supplies from Viney Creek Store, where Margaret is content to let her dog lie on the counter while she sells necessities. The old vine-covered shack is a relic, providing supplies and cigarettes and night crawlers to locals since 1937. She's way off the beaten path, yet Margaret does a brisk business. One beer truck driver unloaded several cases of his product to the back of the room where thirsty coolers awaited, while another distributor squared up with Margaret.

Her dog didn't seem to mind, sprawled sleepy on the counter. The store would fit inside a Casey's convenience store, but the Viney store holds just as much stuff, packed to the rafters. Beer and bait, tobacco, Slim Jims...everything a fisherman needs. At the end of the peninsula is Viney Creek Campground, everything a sleeper needs, as long as you have liquor, bait, tobacco, Slim Jims and bug repellent.

Next day we dipped deep into southern Barry County and followed a blacktop road tracing the route where Union troops busted through Blockade Hollow and caught up with General Sterling Price's army just over the state line at Pea Ridge, Arkansas. At the state line a monument the size of a gas pump marks the point where the battle began.

This part of the world is rapidly deteriorating into a new civil war. People are choosing sides and getting testy. Some locals fret about an influx of workers whose Spanish is overtaking English as the predominant language. The slaughterhouses ask, "Who will rend a billion chickens?" Environmentalists worry too many chickens sit too close to the drinking water supply. They warn that when Mother Nature concentrates a downpour on a particular area, the resultant flood can wash any exposed feces into the karst topography to dissolve into our tap water.

The war is isolated, tucked into the folding hills, out of view of the rest of the world. Along the eight-mile road between Wheaton and Butterfield, I counted forty chicken barns. These aren't the quaint old barns from a Norman Rockwell painting. They're factories, converting chicken feed into Sunday dinners. In a way, the barns are living casseroles, long metal chicken burritos. Giant ventilator fans stand in the low walls of these sheds, cooling the concentrated bird flesh.

Big corporations contract with local farm factories to raise these animals inside the long low-slung chicken burritos, called confined animal feeding operations (CAFOs). A chicken CAFO can house as many as 65,000 birds. In such close confinement, dead birds happen. But with controlled conditions—temperature, diet, plenty of water—the mortality usually can be kept relatively low. If chickens die before slaughter, the local farmer must pluck the dead animals out of the barn and dispose of the carcasses. But the big mortality risk comes from disease. Living in such close quarters, if chickens or hogs get a virus—bird flu or swine flu—the end is near, not only for the animals, but for profits. So generations of these animals have received antibiotics to keep them from getting sick. Over time the viruses developed resistance to the antibiotics. Now disease-resistant superbugs can affect whole populations of birds and hogs...and people. In our hospitals an increase of deadly methicillin-resistant Staphylococcus aureus (MRSA) suggests the bugs are evolving fast.

This chicken culture shows up in American songs. Big Smith, an amalgam of brothers, uncles and cousins who portray vivid musical peeks into Ozark life, sings a woeful love ballad about running over a dead chicken in the road between Arkansas and Springfield, Missouri.

The highways are choking with chicken trucks. They're everywhere, emanating from a gulag of chicken factories, each flatbed stacked high and deep with bird cages, rolling stock riding to the reaper. The chickens welcome a cool breeze, and birds with a window seat get a nice view, an avian Bridge of Sighs. When chicken trucks reach the slaughterhouse, they wait in line to unload, parked along a gauntlet of giant fans to cool the birds and keep them alive long enough to kill them. The prevailing odor is foul.

Even on their final ride, the cluckers in the upper cages rain feces onto their cousins in the bottom cages. Shittin' rain sounds a lot like a song written nearly a half-century ago by a man named Cash and recorded by The Ozark Mountain Daredevils, a band just up the road in Springfield. "Chicken Train" became a hit among folks who like to stomp their feet. The song may be an omen. Hillbilly Orwell. "Chicken train take your chickens away."

Some people plead for more humane treatment. They say birds have feelings. But we all know that when you bite a fried chicken thigh, it doesn't feel a thing.

It began to rain.

Falling onto the Ozark Mountains, rainwater percolates into the ground entering America's most elaborate underground hydraulic network, coursing through total darkness…braiding through karst caverns—formed by millions of years of water erosion through massive limestone formations. Deep underground the water pushes through this Swiss cheese limestone until it springs from ancient caverns. One of those springs bursts out from under a bluff to become Roaring River.

We descended into Roaring River State Park, and checked into the park lodge, a modern facility catering to fishing enthusiasts and tourists. I couldn't wait to jog down the steep hill to the stream, its banks and waters dotted with fly fishers in chest-high waders. At the spring, in nut-shriveling cold water, the state conservation department makes trout. Millions of them. And some neighbors are angry. They say all this trout shit in the water is unnatural.

Wow. This war between neighbors will worsen as we raise our food in concentration camps.

Next day we entered Cassville, past the Seven Valleys Motel, an old '50s-style motor court, abandoned but salvageable. With a little spiffing, fishermen would flock to its overnight accommodations.

A chicken truck and I pulled over to pay our respects to a passing funeral cortege as it left Fohn Funeral Home. The chickens in their cages behaved themselves as the dead birdeater passed. I thought about stopping into the funeral home and offering my services as a sloganeer: "When you die, it's Fohn." I kept driving.

Returning to Cassville for my evening meal, a web recommendation cinched my restaurant choice: "Your clothes smell like fajitas when you leave." Good thing. I just couldn't bring myself to order a chicken burrito.

Liquor and Gambling and Fredville

Just a bunt from the Oklahoma border, State Line Liquors in Seneca is a jewel in the archipelago of liquor stores stretching across Missouri's southwest border, strategically positioned to take advantage of stringent liquor laws in neighboring states. Latching on the rim of these battle lines of sin, capitalism takes root. Booze boosts the bottom line on the Missouri side of the border, while the Oklahoma side— which lately has relaxed liquor laws—serves up blackjack and roulette, slots and craps.

Spilling from this battlefront is the story of a kid who turned whiskey bottles into bass boats. Brown Derby began as a chain of liquor stores. Along the way it became the daddy of a ubiquitous brand that has nothing to do with liquor, everything to do with worms. Half a century ago, the owner's kid wanted to sell bait at his dad's Springfield Brown Derby liquor store. Dad apparently thought the idea was cute, in a lemonade stand sort of way. In this instance, the apple didn't fall far from the tree, and the worms from that apple grew into an empire. The kid demonstrated keen business acumen, and the bait business grew, garnering a corner in every Brown Derby store throughout the territory. As his worm business evolved, the kid developed his own stores, and today they're called Bass Pro Shops. At a music show in Branson a few years back, I sat next to Johnny Morris, the bait boy turned big businessman. Shrewd guy, worth millions. But at his core, he remains a humble Ozark bait merchant.

The stately residences of Seneca sit just minutes from the state line. On the Oklahoma side Bordertown Bingo is a casino operated by the Eastern Shawnee Tribe. Hosting bingo, blackjack and Texas hold 'em among the one-armed bandits, the casino cranks seven days a week. Best I can tell, it's the closest casino to Branson.

So far, Branson has kept gambling at bay.

A few years ago, big gambling promoters outspent Branson ten to one on a ballot issue to bring slots and blackjack tables to Branson's sleepy little neighbor, Rockaway Beach. Rockaway Beach once boasted great resorts along the White River, which became Lake Taneycomo. But the town fell on hard times after a notorious incident that still echoes as a war cry for the righteous. It was the Fourth of July, 1965, when motorcycle gangs and thousands of college students converged on the town. The party turned into a drunken riot, and local lawmen surrounded the party animals. Cops trucked students away by the hundreds to area jails. The town never recovered from the stigma, and it slowly shriveled by the lake as vacationers bypassed it on their way to Branson.

So with a new gambling scenario, casinos promised big things for little Rockaway Beach. To the surprise of everyone except folks who believe God roots for the Dallas Cowboys, the gambling proposal failed at the ballot box, and Bransonites slayed Goliath. Truth is, they won because the gambling proposal shared the ballot with a proposal to legalize same sex marriage in Missouri. Every breathing opponent of same sex marriage voted. As a byproduct, they killed the gambling proposal.

Pressing on past the casino, Erifnus drove north, skirting Loma Linda, and turned toward Racine, past the Half Ass Mule Ranch, a name that's genetically precise. Just a bit further down the road than a mule can kick a football sits the Heavenly Dream Alpaca Farm, the pride of Fredville. For an outsider like me to find Fredville, I had to know the story. Fredville doesn't exist. But then again, it does, and everybody in Neosho knows about Fredville. Historian Wes Franklin explained the story in the *Neosho Daily News*. Years ago, when Highway 71 came through town, Fred Stacell was forced to move his house back from the road construction to save it. He wasn't happy. In defiance Fred stuck a hand lettered sign beside the new highway proclaiming the spot Fredville. The Missouri State Highway Department apparently replaced Fred's homemade sign with an official sign, even though

Fredville wasn't incorporated. Anyway, Fred owned a convenience store at Fredville for years, and everybody in Neosho knows where Fredville is, even though there's no Fredville highway sign anymore. Blame vandals. Maybe a half dozen Freds in the general vicinity have a Fredville sign on a bedroom wall. Technically they stole signs from something that doesn't exist.

We passed through Aroma and Beef Creek, Mud Prairie and Hell's Neck, named for rowdy miners, but changed to Neck City in 1899 when the postal service balked at opening a branch with such a profane name. We danced with the ghosts of Number One School and Coon Foot School, Pepsin and Tripoli, named because of the high quality magnesian limestone quarried here, same as the limestone imported from Libya. We drove through Blend City, named for the blend of ores found in southwest Joplin. All these old names might be lost, were they not dutifully recorded by Robert Lee Meyers. It must have been a tedious project back in 1930. I can't imagine anybody driving all these backroads to uncover their stories.

Jollification to Joplin

The band of bushwhackers rode into the tiny town of Jollification, in no mood for frivolity. They burned the village to the ground, with one exception: They spared the whiskey maker. Jolly Mill began as Isbell's Distillery back in 1848 to supply whiskey to locals and wagon trains moving west. After the attack, Jollification never got very big, but the mill kept providing spirits to locals and pioneers until the Great Depression, when the mill eventually switched from making whiskey to grinding flour, and operated until 1973. The mill was powered by Capps Creek, now home to trout stocked and managed by the Missouri Department of Conservation.

We rolled up Walleye Road to Jolly Mill Park on the banks of Capps Creek. In the middle of nowhere, along this little tributary, trout outnumber humans, even when the park hosts a concert or reunion.

"Hold it! I Think You're Gonna Like This Picture." If you remember that phrase, you watched too much TV in the '50s. Back then, *The Bob Cummings Show* featured a trendy photographer who flew an airplane that readily converted into a car. Cummings played a stranger from a strange land, a Hollywood playboy from the Bible Belt.

The show never makes anybody's "Top Ten World-Changing Theatrical Productions." But this story of a modern-day Casanova became a fountain of success for one local screenwriter who produced a gusher of subsequent hits. The scripts came from the fertile mind of Paul Henning, born and raised up the road in Independence. Harry Truman advised young Paul to become a lawyer. Henning rejected Harry's advice, instead choosing a life built around the boob tube. He created *The Beverly Hillbillies, Petticoat Junction* and *Green Acres*. Oh, and *The Bob Cummings Show*, aka *Love That Bob*...with its roots in Joplin, Missouri.

Joplin's other big TV star, Dennis Weaver, leapt onto history's stage as the gait-challenged Chester on *Gunsmoke*. My car warms up to him because he became the preeminent recycler of his time, building a Colorado Earthship home fashioned from old tires and beer cans, tastefully obscured within tons of adobe.

Most everybody can sing a phrase or two along with Nat King Cole as he covers Bobby Troup's song about Joplin, Missouri. And Joplin's frontage along Route 66 remains preserved forever in reels of celluloid. But some of Joplin's pictures took a little longer to develop. Shortly after the turn of the last century, a kid migrated to Joplin to find work around the booming lead mines. By his own admission, young Thomas Hart Benton came of age among the bawdy houses that flourished around the mines. A lifetime later, he immortalized those early days in a mural that watches over the grand room at Joplin City Hall. Typical of Benton, his characters in Joplin at the Turn of the Century—busty and bustling and busting rocks—jump from the wall. Now, the mural is joined by a companion piece, a '50s view down Route 66, completed by Benton's grandson, Anthony Benton Gude, a Kansan, but otherwise a good fellow by all appearances. Gude's canvas captures the essence of his grandfather's style, a style scorned by snooty art critics of his grandfather's day, praised by everybody else.

Beneath the mural sits a mother lode of Benton's drawings and studies of mural subjects, and letters of negotiation between a proud city and the world-famous artist. The exhibit adds a reminder that there's much more beneath the surface of this man and his work.

Much more beneath the surface. It's a metaphor for the whole town. Joplin straddles two counties, and the area offers a dizzying array of murals—train wrecks and telephones and teepees, fireworks and flowers, lizards and herons, conflagrations and inventions.

And mining.

Of all the Joplin icons—Langston Hughes, Bonnie and Clyde, Route 66—I never put mining on the list. But that's how Joplin got its start back in 1873.

I sought to uncover the boomtown you won't see from the interstate, the boomtown that two horrific tornadoes could not defeat. To do that, I offered my car as collateral for a canoe, put in at Shoal Creek, just a stone's throw from the birthplace of my hero George Washington Carver, and floated into town.

Guiding my canoe through vigorous riffles along Shoal Creek, I crossed under Highway 71 and floated to the edge of Grand Falls, a drop that stopped my forward progress. Beaching my canoe, I crossed Wildcat Glades to the Audubon center, where I met a collared lizard and a bluntfaced shiner.

Within the hour, I too had become a bluntfaced shiner, donning a miner's helmet to spelunk the Everett J. Ritchie Tri-State Mineral Museum. Yeah, the name's a billboard buster, but it honors a guy who assembled a bunch of ore specimens into stunning displays. Seriously, the presentation of lead hasn't been this tasteful since the Romans used plumbum for platters.

Helmets aren't required for the tour. I wore one anyway, this headgear as proud as any cardboard crown at Burger King.

I kept stumbling onto bonus displays, like photos of Bonnie and Clyde snapped near their Joplin hideout, and Bonnie's costume jewelry she left behind when they shot their way out of town.

But the icing on the cake came when I stepped into a small room called the National Cookie Cutter Historical Museum. In this big wide world, there are museums for everything. Tokyo's Parasite Museum. The Icelandic Phallological Museum in Husavik. The Cockroach Hall of Fame in Plano, Texas. Oh, and Leila's Hair Museum in Independence. In this little corner of collectordom, the cookie cutter exhibit reminds me what happens when you cross a color wheel with a geometry book, and add dough. A whole family can see this entire museum complex for the cost of a package of Oreos.

Heading east we passed Plu and Rescue and Roper. We glided through Albatross, named for a bus line, and approached Aurora, named for the Roman goddess of the dawn.

Aurora is a town of deep contrasts. It sits along the summit of the Ozark highlands, but much of its history lies below the surface. Like many westward towns, Aurora grew up around the railroad. But it struck pay dirt when some well diggers discovered galena, a rich ore loaded with lead and zinc. Almost overnight, the digging began. The mines popped up—or down—before the advent of mining permits, and soon shallow tunnels ran beneath the ground in almost every direction. When the mines closed people did their dead level best to fill these holes. For some time after the holes were closed and filled, the fill would occasionally settle and a house would tip into the chasm. Nobody knew where all the holes were, or where they led, because the area's first mines were mom and pop operations. Nobody kept complete records. Over time, some spots above the mines became contaminated with lead tailings and lead dust. The area became a Superfund site, and the healing began.

I approached the town square, showing the stress that comes with the sad faces of too many empty storefronts. But peeking around town, deeper into its fabric, I found rebirth.

Bootlegger's Restaurant & Brewery used to be a bank. Indeed, in its new incarnation, somebody invested a mint—and a lot of creativity—into the décor, right down to the bank teller's cage turned *maitre d's* stand, and bank vault turned brewery. A sandwich called The Heart Attack surrounds a half-pound burger with bacon, barbecued ham, cheddar and Monterey Jack cheese, topped with lettuce, tomato, onion, and barbecue sauce. Holy hamburger, somebody press the bank alarm.

Ballhagen's, Barrels & Boats

Sleeper, Missouri, hides some big stories. Years ago two trains collided in Sleeper. The trains piled up like accordions, and only a jigsaw puzzle master could put them together again. Appropriate, as I approached Nancy Ballhagen's Puzzles, a major distributor of jigsaw puzzles worldwide.

The store sat in plain sight of I-44, yet you'd probably overlook the long one-story metal building. Its dull shell belied its contents.

Inside, crammed to the rafters were tens of thousands of beautiful pictures on boxtops, each containing the elements of a jigsaw puzzle. Ballhagen's was the only store in Sleeper, and since Sleeper lost its post office, the store didn't even carry a Sleeper address. Looking for that Jean Guichard Lighthouse puzzle? Or maybe you're after the Hiroo Isono Ceono Emerald Dreams puzzle. Nancy had it. She could deliver a Jackson Pollack puzzle for the masochist, or Hieronymus Bosch's *The Last Judgment* to scare you silly, because, by all the signs, the end is near. As it turns out, the end came for Ballhagen's Puzzles store. Damn. Not sure what happened to all those puzzles. Hope they're out there somewhere, frustrating somebody.

—————◦∞∞◦—————

Clueless, we zigged and zagged into Lebanon, a town of many contrasts.

One of the biggest industries in town is the white oak barrel factory. Chances are good the whiskey you drank for breakfast was aged in a cask made in Lebanon. Wine barrels and whiskey barrels— all made here in one of the biggest cooperages in the world—get filled with liquid gold.

Thinking about all that sweet nectar made me break into song. I ran through all the verses of "I'll Fly Away" and "Turn your Radio On," at least the words I could remember. Yeah, I know it may border on blasphemy to pair gospel music with whiskey barrels, but hey, this is Lebanon, able to embrace both whiskey barrels and fellow Missourian Albert E. Brumley, who wrote those songs. Although Brumley lived southwest of here, down in Powell, people still gather in Lebanon to sing this whitewashed brand of music with its roots in the chants of slaves. I often marvel at the two very different interpretations of the root music that brought us gospel, one a drips-with-soul black, the other a save-your-soul white.

Harold Bell Wright wrote a novel based on people he knew in Lebanon, and although he changed the names, some of his characters had obvious connections to specific townspeople. At least the specific townspeople thought so. The characterizations were less than flattering. *The Calling of Dan Matthews* so angered locals when it was published, they effectively banned the book in Lebanon. But it sold like hotcakes in the rest of the country.

Lebanon may sell more boats than hotcakes. It's a bit of a surprise that Lebanon ranks with Baltimore and Philadelphia and New Orleans as one of the nation's leading boatbuilders. Granted, Lebanon's boats are of the pontoon and bass boat class, but they're boats nonetheless. Several manufacturers crank out thousands of watercraft each year. Not bad for a landlocked town a dozen miles from the nearest navigable waterway.

That waterway is the Niangua River.

The biggest lure on the Niangua is fishing, as it should be. Been that way since the 1920s when conservation officials dumped 40,000 trout into the cold waters below Bennett Spring, or as Native Americans call the spring, the Eye of the Sacred One. Since then, people have flocked to the spring to cast a fly for rainbow and brown trout. The Civilian Conservation Corps built the stone buildings and cabins that survive today at the state park, offering rest for anglers burdened by heavy stringers of fish. This is where I learned to tie a fly, although I never mastered the art of the fly rod. The trout are safe around me.

A View from Under the Bridge

The back entrance to Waynesville is guarded by Fort Leonard Wood. But the sentry along the east approach is the world's greatest frog, if size means anything. Sure, to most observers it looks like a giant rock outcropping, but to the tattoo artist who painted the rock green and yellow, it's a frog. His best side faces the traffic coming downhill on old Route 66. The highway department erected a "Frog Crossing" sign. Somebody bitched about the expense of the sign. But the sign is well worth your tax dollars for two reasons. First, the frog is a roadside attraction like no other, including that world's largest ball of twine in Kansas. Second, it causes every passing eyeball to look for live toads crossing the road. So drivers tweet less for fifty yards or so, until they spy this brightly-painted twenty-ton hopper, poised to jump across the highway from its perch four stories above the road, or perhaps flick its ninety-foot igneous tongue to zap passing traffic. And toad found, driver smart phones come out like lightning bugs, turning selfie angles. The end is near.

———— ✺ ————

There are a lot of ways to see Route 66. This view is the lowest: Afternoon thunder roared in the distance as we unloaded three kayaks and prepared to launch into Roubidoux Creek. My floating buddies Cork and Gary paused to look up, not so much at the storm clouds poised to strike a glancing blow, but at the giant piers supporting twin bridges over this creek.

The bridges, sixty feet above our heads, carry traffic along I-44, and they're the granddaughters of the Route 66 bridge we'd float beneath downstream, the route of the frog crossing.

On this day, the navigable part of Roubidoux Creek begins here, beneath I-44 amid the concrete pillars sprayed with graffiti and littered with trash. We spent a few minutes deciphering the prose and picking up trash.

Then we hit the water.

As we launched our kayaks, over our heads we heard a hundred cars pass, their passengers unaware we were floating Missouri's second-most overlooked stream.

For almost a mile the water twists and braids past brush piles and gravel bars and blue herons thick as mosquitoes around their rookeries. We flowed into the heart of Waynesville. Yet we never really saw the town. Not from the creek. Buildings and buzz and hubbub rose around us on both sides of this waterway. But we were insulated by lush vegetation. From the water our view was pastoral.

Roubidoux Spring gushed at us from the right, roiling from beneath a giant concrete wall where a dozen young brave souls jumped into the frigid waters. The spring doubled the volume of Roubidoux Creek, and lowered the water temperature twenty degrees.

We approved.

A kayak floating Roubidoux Creek is like a blood cell coursing through an artery. A lot of activity happens outside this conduit, but you don't see it. And it doesn't see you.

We paddled past dozens of locals along the stream bank. Kids swimming. Adults relaxing on their lunch break. Off-duty soldiers from nearby Fort Leonard Wood were fishing, right here in this hidden waterway through the middle of town.

And then we looked downstream.

In the distance the old Route 66 bridge arched high over our path, connecting two sides of a deep canyon as it has for eight decades, looking like an old Roman aqueduct. The original mother road courses over the old span's back through the heart of Waynesville. Drivers only catch a fleeting glimpse of us, if they see us at all. I waved at them anyway.

On our right were ball fields and soccer fields and fitness trails. Or so we were told. We saw only green vegetation and clear spring water. We passed a giant pipe pouring thousands of gallons of purified water into the stream. That water once was sewage. But treated, it's drinkable.

It looked clear, smelled good.

We paddled downstream as another thunderstorm shook its fist, blared at us, then twisted off to the north. I became aware we were coursing beside another highway, draped along a ledge a few stories above water level. Occasionally, through the trees, I could see motorists. I waved. They didn't see me. Too busy texting.

During the hundred times I've driven this same stretch of Highway 17, my eyes were always sweeping this creek. I would've seen me. I would've waved back.

Our afternoon float trip ended too soon, abruptly dumping us into the Gasconade River at a picturesque spot beneath a towering bluff. As we carried our kayaks up a steep bank, I turned to promise St. Francis I'll work to help save the mudpuppies—the Ozark hellbenders—who struggle to survive beneath these waters. And I said goodbye to the second-most overlooked stream in Missouri.

Next time you're driving along old Route 66 through Waynesville, look down as you cross Roubidoux Creek. I'll be waving.

Soldiers, Sybill's and Saint Lucy

Deep cuts through Ozark mountains give I-44 a straighter path that slices through meandering Route 66. The two roads reflect a contrast between two types of travelers: The daughter road is about the destination. The Mother Road is about the journey. Sometimes mother's icons are visible as the two roads intertwine.

We pulled up a ramp where a man stood holding a sign: Save the Squids. I cranked down my window to give him something. He leaned into me and said: "The Great Pacific Garbage Patch is a 600,000 square mile floating thatch of trash that's twice the size of Texas." I offered him a dollar and he refused. "Send it to the efforts to clean our oceans."

Moving east from Rolla—east of where the King of the Gypsies died and lies buried beneath a hundred bouquets—I spied a familiar friend from childhood, a unique physique seen only in the Ozarks. Beside the Mule Trading Post, the charcoal scent lingers from legendary Toky's BBQ. Although Toky's is long gone, the scent was fanned by a giant hillbilly who flails at the air like a windmill. He's a caricature of Ozark culture, standing tall as a tree, painted on both sides with a hillbilly beard and a hillbilly hat and hillbilly overalls and a corn cob pipe, and motorized arms that rotate backwards, so his arms pinwheel in perpetuity, making him seem like he's logrolling, always about to fall down.

He never falls, but if he was suddenly smashed to bits by an 18-wheeler, I'd call in the Attack O Matic vacuum cleaner, a proud possession of the area's foremost cleanup crew, the Vacuum Cleaner Museum in Saint James. Yep, the world's only vacuum cleaner museum and factory outlet hides just off Route 66 behind the Saint James Veterans Home. Just like your old Kirby, you gotta do a little digging to find this pay dirt. The museum is a hoot. Before you enter, get over the suck jokes that spring to your mind. They've heard them all. The displays include a vacuum from Air Force One, and some ancient models with headlights, so when your grandmother screwed the power cord into the light bulb socket, she wasn't sweeping in the dark.

The residents of the Saint James Veterans Home know about those old sweepers. Sadly, most visitors to the vacuum museum don't stop to say thanks to the old vets sitting on the porch. There's a waiting list to get one of the home's beds. Shame on this nation for making elderly veterans wait. Thanks, indeed.

On recommendations from everybody, I found Sybill's, a century-old farmhouse on the north edge of town, reborn as a restaurant. Sybill Scheffer cut her culinary skills at the elbows of her parents at the legendary Zeno's in Rolla. The rejuvenated farmhouse draws diners from hundreds of miles away. In a country estate setting, the service is relaxed and unhurried. The servers even write their own comments on the restaurant's web page—lots of team player references and sports metaphors. "I strive to go the extra mile." "I never take my guests for granted." In a food industry plagued with employee turnover that rivals changing underwear, it's refreshing to see service and product at the top of their game. Sybill and staff don't miss the opportunity to offer shopping while you wait. Candles, florals, purses and paintings, "...beautiful objects that help us fulfill everyday needs." If I'm Maslow, I'm only slightly annoyed by the concept, realizing that if people are waiting for a table, they have two choices: Drink or shop. I demurred on both, and the maitre d' showed me to a quiet corner. I immersed in maple Dijon scallops and a beet & goat cheese salad. *Syblime.*

After dinner we drove rings around Saint James looking for an Adopt-A-Highway sign from the vacuum cleaner museum. Hope they're sweeping up a few miles of roadside somewhere.

———— ⋘ ————

Millions of travelers trust their Mother Road to deliver them safely through these beautiful hills and valleys, never knowing that ravenous industrials raped and stained the land years ago.

One stain felt the healing hands of a saint.

South of Saint James at the bottom of a steep Ozark valley lie the remains of one of the earliest industries in the Ozarks, now surrounded by Maramec Springs Park. It cost me five bucks to enter the park, and I invoked some saint's name, muttering an inane comment about the fee. I only showed my ignorance. This visit was enlightenment, a lesson in ecology, a primer in restoring Mother Nature to a position of respect.

The park's centerpiece is Maramec Springs, which pumps enough liquid out of the ground daily to fill 1.1 billion little plastic water bottles...if it were so inclined. But the spring doesn't bottle its water, mercifully allowing it to flow as the headwaters of the Meramec River, which waits to get choked with plastic a few miles downstream, when floaters with rectal-cranial inversions toss their trash in the river.

It's puzzling that the springs are spelled Maramec, the river Meramec. Zeb Pike might know why.

As a kid I'd visited Maramec Springs Park, not really understanding the significance of the spot. Oh, I knew they smelted iron ore almost two centuries ago, in a stone furnace the size of a modest Mayan pyramid. Closer inspection revealed layers of love for this land, and a privately-funded effort to keep the park's nearly 2,000 acres a pristine example of Ozarks topography and culture. It wasn't always pristine.

The iron works operated for fifty years, burning a billion local trees to feed the smelter's roaring fire. The nearby open pit mine is a scar tissue reminder of the conflagration.

The ironworks harnessed the springs, transforming the daily power of a hundred million gallons of gushing water into kettles and plows and hoe blades, and pig iron ingots for the railroads. But the remoteness of this Ozark spring was the downfall of the business, when transportation costs ate into profits, and the ironworks went bust in 1876. The granddaughter of the ironworks founder bought the land, and when she died, her will instructed that "As this is considered to be the most beautiful spot in Missouri, it is my great hope that you will arrange that it may ever be in private, considerate control, and ever open to the enjoyment of the people." It's a refreshing sentiment, after her grandfather had usurped the land so dramatically. Lucy James is an angel.

The James Foundation now owns the park and operates two museums, one dedicated solely to farm implements, hundreds of reapers and sowers, anvils and blowers, growers and planters and shuckers and such. Another museum displays hands-on scale models explaining how the old ironworks operated. Or you can visualize it yourself as you walk through the remnant stone chimneys and drop towers, almost medieval in their distance from our modern culture.

A trout hatchery flourishes here, producing enough fish to feed the habits of thousands of anglers, its successive pools fattening fry into fine future filets. The cold spring water moves swiftly through successive trout pools, each pool holding a school of fish who share the same birthday. For a quarter you can buy a handful of fish food from a dispenser and make the trout whip into a frenzy like a crowd getting new cars from Oprah.

Boeuf Berger on a Clothesline

Down the road, there's always something. Maybe not a saint, but a golly just the same. We traced Highway 47, crossing the Missouri River into Washington's movie star face, a gorgeous riverbank town with chiseled features, church spires and storefronts peeking from under a brow of hills draped in nature's thick mane of hardwood forests. The town smiles with art shops and antiques and festivals, and along the tracks where Amtrak stops, Washington revels in its marriage to the Missouri River.

I couldn't take my eyes off the steel road for long, because this old bridge, like most of its sisters, requires nerve and skill and keen attention to avoid a sideswiping succession of 18-wheelers, coming at us like they're pumped from a pitching machine. Most of this bridge's old river sisters have been replaced by wider, safer spans. Soon this ninety-year-old sister will retire, too.

From Washington, Highway 100 stretches toward Hermann like a clothesline, draping over bluffs and peeking down ravines at your road's companion, the Missouri River. The river was the major highway when John Colter traveled upstream with Lewis and Clark. Later, Colter settled on a farm near what became New Haven. The town sits undisturbed by our plastic fast-food culture. Even mighty Amtrak doesn't slow down as it splits the town in half, shaking windows with the blast of its fearsome whistlehorn when it barrels past. The railbed creaks and vibrates the ground and everything around.

The John Colter Memorial is the town's centerpiece. Or maybe the centerpiece is the pair of museums, or the old Central Hotel Bed and Breakfast. But for me the town's centerpiece is the art-deco ambiance of the Walt Theatre, an eighty-year-old movie house refurbished to its 1940s glory, with the original towering movie marquee dressed in neon. In a life-imitates-art moment, the marquee displayed one word: *Sing*. It's an animated movie: "a Koala named Buster Moon has one final chance to restore his theatre to its former glory by producing the world's greatest singing competition."

Picking a sure bet for lunch, Erifnus parked in front of El Ranchito Mexican Restaurant, and I put another notch in my bandolier, maybe my 500th Mexican restaurant. Maybe more.

On cue the Amtrak whistle sounded from a mile away. Stashing the leftovers from El Ranchito into the passenger seat, I climbed into Erifnus and fired her engine. As we pulled out of the parking space and headed to the end of the street to cross the tracks, Amtrak's Missouri River Runner bore down on the intersection. The crossing guard arm started to come down. I thought about trying to beat the train. Erifnus is old, and it wasn't fair to turn her into scrap metal after a historic run. Worse, if we failed, the engineer and conductor and passengers would sustain injury from the impact and suffer post-traumatic distress. They would be delayed while emergency personnel cleared the wreck and packed my bloody body parts into a bag.

We waited for the train to pass, and we lost twenty seconds we'll never get back.

This old river road is the attic route to Berger. And like an old attic, antiques dot the landscape. Antique farmhouses and barns, antique tools, antique shops. Maybe the most fabled antique from these river bluffs is the world's greatest riverboat gambler, Captain Bill Massie, born near Berger, bonded by a bullet to Bill Hickok, and buried at Bellefontaine Cemetery downriver in Saint Louis.

Driving from Berger past Berger Creek, near Big Boeuf Creek and Little Boeuf Creek, Erifnus sensed a theme, so we circled back to Highway 50 and stopped for a hamburger at Buck's Hilltop Lounge. Buck's has braved the hilltop in New Haven for eighty years, and the aroma of grilled burgers permeates the place. It's comfort food, fuel for this road winding through pastoral beauty, through countryside settled by German and Swiss immigrants, through tidy Owensville, and tiny Drake with its hexagonal Dutch Mill, a quaint old building, a waymark for all my life, that lately suffers the gaudy accessories of modern marketing. Unevenly spaced across its frontage, a succession of beer signs, ice dispensers and soda pop machines stand like pawns guarding the old mill from an errant rook. The neighboring gas station's mansard awning looms so close to the mill that in a big west wind the roof might become airborne and shear the top off the old Dutch Mill. The end is near.

A squirrel ran in front of Erifnus. I braked but the thump told us the animal had been hit. We stopped and I looked in my rearview mirror at a twitching tail, shifted Erifnus in reverse and euthanized the poor creature. I made a promise to Saint Francis, then resumed through the forest.

Erifnus slowed to 45 miles per hour, the speed limit through the miniscule town of Swiss. Its population struggles to reach forty, including pets, according to the folks who work in the town's dominant industry, Swiss Meats and Sausage Company. I assume the farm animals they butcher aren't included as pets. The town looks like any other sleepy rural village, even with the Swiss Meats storefront. But behind that facade, they're processing more pork than Congress, and they custom process bison, elk, ostrich, emu and venison. I resisted the temptation to go back and salvage the dead squirrel from the road. She'll be buzzard pizza.

We tightroped the highway down a ridge to Frene Creek, descending into a community bypassed by time. A unique set of events isolated Hermann, and allowed its old ways to survive largely intact. Settled in the 1830s by German immigrants who moved west from Pennsylvania, the town is a living museum of German culture preserved in brick architecture nearly two centuries old. Two wars against Germany ensured this town remained ostracized for much of the twentieth century.

Isolation wasn't Hermann's biggest survival challenge.

Before the wars, Hermann produced more wine than any American city but one. Hermann and her neighbors even saved the French wine industry. When a microscopic nematode infested grapevine roots in France and decimated French vineyards, Missouri vintners in the Hermann area shipped tons of hardy nematode-resistant Missouri Norton rootstock to France. Viticulturalists grafted the French vines to the healthy new roots, and the Champagne and Bordeaux flowed again.

But in America, Hermann's reward was prohibition. It could have been the end of the world for a village so deeply rooted in wine. But the town's pluck was strong as its brick. Hermann hunkered down for half a century, enduring the temperance movement, and anti-German intemperance. Within the past few generations Hermann has rebounded.

Nowadays the vineyards and the crowds keep growing.

For a while, Hermann became a victim of its own success. Or excess. Festivals in Hermann became so popular that hordes of revelers would bus and train and drive into town. Many would get snot-slinging drunk, and vomit all over other people's shoes. Motorcycle gangs roared into town and scared the residents, even though the motorheads were more courteous than most other revelers. Some of the merchants and at least one winery took steps to mitigate the debauchery, limiting wine sales to one bottle per esophagus, or butthole. It seems to have worked, and for the most part, folks behave themselves. The town seems comfortable with this new persona, comfortable enough that somebody promoted a poker run road rally called "Girls with Their Tops Down." Here we go again.

The big draw to town is Oktoberfest, a series of fall weekends when Hermann celebrates the grape harvest. At the Grape Stomp, entrants compete to mash the most grapes with their bare feet. They dance to honky swamp swing music, stomping furiously in their own big white oak half barrels. Something about human feet makes grapes taste better. Blame it on the yeast.

I holed up for the night in the Captain Wohlt Inn, a bed and breakfast named for a fearless steamboat pilot from this area. It was the second time I'd spent an overnight in the Wohlt house, always an experience because I'm intimidated by the delicacy of bed and breakfast bedrooms, decorated with antiques and heirlooms and fine things ripe for my destructive ham hands. I'd probably be more suited to sleep on the cargo deck of one of Captain Wohlt's ancient steamers, if any had survived. My room was within walking distance of the local pleasures—bars, wineries, festhalles, restaurants—but I spent the afternoon paging through giant photographs of shipwrecks in the River Room of the old German School Museum. It's a stark contrast: on one hand, the museum represents the well-preserved brick masonry of these Hermann buildings, the well-preserved lifestyle of a culture that proudly resists assimilation into modern McLife; conversely, the photographs show wrecks dashed against the rocks and drowned in the river, proud old riverboats that knew their lives were counted in weeks and months when they entered the treacherous currents and snags of the Missouri River. These old shipwreck photos kept me captive, evoking the same human curiosity that causes traffic to slow to a crawl as gapers pass a car wreck. Each shipwreck photo represents hundreds of stories, families whose westward progress ended, often tragically. The soft cushion of time makes it easier to view the wrecks, knowing that those tragedies have long since subsided, and the scars have turned to dust.

Looking upriver from the Hermann bluff, I could almost see Sonora Chute. It was a cold February day in 1856 when Captain Bill Terrill ran his sidewheeler Sonora through ice floes near Portland,

Missouri. At 363 tons, the Sonora was a good size, but her wooden hull was no match for the ice, which smashed her hull and she sank. For years after that, the wreck of the Sonora was visible at low water. In 1916 her machinery and brass were removed, and finally, in 1940, the dredge Keokuk removed the wreckage.

It's hard to imagine 400 shipwrecks buried beneath this riverbed. But they're there.

The Cow with Five Legs and Six Feet

Back when the Lake of the Ozarks was pristine, nestled among forested hills unspoiled by civilization, I took my first ride in an automobile. Erifnus was fifty years in the future. I was a newborn riding from a Jefferson City hospital to our home in Eldon.

In those early years, gaudy lake attractions were sparse. Between Eldon and the lake, one ancient tourist icon stabs my memory.

Max Allen's Zoological Garden was a serious attempt at a zoo, even though the billboards on the highway lured visitors with lurid phrases like, "See the cow with five legs and six feet." Yikes.

Max Allen Nickerson was born into a family of promoters, most famous for spawning those red-roofed Nickerson Farms stores along Midwestern interstates. Max expanded the family's Ozark Reptile Gardens to include the fishy poopy aroma of sea lions and parrots and monkeys. My mom never let me enter the monthly drawing to win a monkey. The zoo gave them away as a tourist draw. But I did ride George, the 400-pound Galapagos turtle who was older than my dad, and was born with the unfortunate affliction of being slower than trappers and kids. Sorry, Saint Francis.

The zoo has been closed for decades now. Max went off to school to become a respected herpetologist. He co-wrote a book called *Hellbenders: North American Giant Salamanders,* considered an important work in the effort to save the species. He also wrote *Amphibious Behavior in Northern Copperheads.* I recommend the book for bedtime reading. Sweet dreams.

—————— ∞ ——————

In any spot, at any time of day, I react willingly to those three magic words, "Pass the gravy." Friends gathered for a feast outside Lohman, uphill from the LoMo Club—which kicks into high gear on weekends for the Yee Haw set—to sup at Steve's Family Style Restaurant. Steve's is stellar, in a refreshingly low-key way. It's a family operation, serving the best homestyle country ham and fried chicken dinner in the galaxy. Steve's culinary skills drip from the pans of his parents, who operated a legendary eatery called Nick's Homestead. Family style recalls the way humans used to eat, peeling away America's single-serving culture. Servers crowded our tables with platters of chicken and country ham, big bowls of green beans and mashed potatoes. And gravy. I ate until it hurt, lamenting the fact that I'm half-bulimic: I binge, but don't purge, a condition articulated by my friend Nancy Miller.

Leaving Steve's I was swollen but not bleeding, grateful that some children grow up to carry on the family tradition serving homestyle food to their neighbors, even though the preparation means long hours and hot kitchens and sacrificing weekend pleasures.

We drove the backroads, among tiny Catholic parish towns. Argyle and Folk and Koeltztown, Rhineland and Rosati, Westphalia and Taos.

As we approached Jefferson City on Highway 50, a devilish example of highway department humor greeted us. A mileage sign shows distances: Six miles to Jefferson City, 66 miles to Sedalia. This mark of the beast adds to Missouri's extensive roster of references to the Devil.

Erifnus crested a hill and her windshield framed the great Missouri River valley ahead of us. The dome of the Missouri State Capitol rose from the valley below like a giant marble tit. The capitol is an enormous beast, so big it has its own weather system. The building is a treasure, and likely will stay that way since, by my estimation, 400 toilets help move the bad stuff out. Alas, it may not be enough.

The dome grew in our windshield as Erifnus descended into Jefferson City, named for our third president, whose credits include writing the Declaration of Independence.

Thomas Jefferson challenged authority on many levels: political kingdoms for sure, but religious kingdoms, too. Most Missouri residents probably don't realize Jefferson's religious views, and if they did they might storm the capitol and tear down his statue. Or maybe they'd forgive him for his doubts, in the name of the Prince of Peace.

We skirted Thomas Jefferson's statue and the capitol and drove past the walls of another beast, one I'd seen from the inside out, where clout was measured in cigarettes, and love played out in bizarre acts.

The Gas Chamber

A tower guard phoned the warden. "There's a woman standing naked on a balcony across the street." Earlier, a tightly scripted marriage ceremony united a death row inmate and his fiancée. Sent away, the bride reappeared on that balcony, consummating her marriage the best way she could, by standing naked in view of the groom's death row cell.

"Should I call the police?" the guard asked the warden.

"Yeah," the warden responded, "in a half hour."

Back in the '90s I spent time in the Missouri State Penitentiary. As a visitor. With a backstage pass I anticipated some terrifying scenes among the 2,000 inmates crammed into this hellhole.

Amid the hate and violence within these walls, an apple tree shaded a gray flagstone path to the gas chamber. A few stones were painted white in the form of a cross, reminding the condemned to make peace with the Great Conscience. The tree and the painted rocks created a faux Mexican courtyard outside the small stone kill building. The cast iron door groaned a heavy creak as my escort pulled it open. The door to the gashouse hadn't been used for nearly two decades when I clutched it.

My guide, Sergeant Smith, led me into the gas chamber through a small bulkhead, into a Jules Vern-ish cylindrical iron diving bell-like capsule set upright and rounded at top, riveted like a boiler, with a bulkhead door and square windows spaced evenly around. Outside each small window, fixed steel chairs accommodate witnesses. Few gas chamber execution witnesses remain around town since the last cyanide gas execution in 1965.

The chamber's steel furnishings sat snug together, two metal chairs side by side, with perforated seats to allow the gas to waft up to the condemned nostrils when the cyanide pellets slid into the crocks of sulfuric acid beneath the chairs. This two-seater was built in 1934, when cyanide gas replaced the noose as the state's lethal dose of preference.

Thirty-eight men took their last painful gasps here, including at least one man innocent of the crime for which he was convicted. Adam Richetti was no saint. Authorities fingered Richetti and Pretty Boy Floyd as principal shooters at the Kansas City Massacre, killing four law enforcement officials and one prisoner. But evidence suggests Richetti, an alcoholic, was sleeping off a drunk during the time the massacre took place. No matter, guilt by association—a bullet casing from a gun once owned by Floyd (who died in a shootout before he could be brought to trial)—was enough for a jury to convict Richetti and send him to die in this chamber. It's not the only time American citizens rushed to judgment.

But sometimes the evidence is strong.

A week before Christmas 1953, the only woman executed in Missouri, Bonnie Brown Heady, sat in this gas chamber next to Carl Austin Hall in a double execution for the kidnaping and murder of young Bobby Greenlease, child of a prominent Kansas City auto dealer. The motive was ransom, but the child died at the hands of his captors. They were executed here because the federal government had no setup to execute condemned prisoners. Missouri's only other double execution was the first ever in this chamber in 1938, when two inmates were gassed simultaneously for two different murders. On two other occasions, the chamber was used twice in one day, the execution staff careful to vent the deadly vapors through the forty-five-foot pipe that towers over the kill building.

My guide flipped on the switch to the lone light bulb dangling shadeless from the ceiling by its cord. He sat in one of the steel chairs. I sat in the other. Smoke from his cigarette rose to the chamber's low rounded ceiling and cascaded downward.

Enough for me. We ducked out of the chamber, flipped off the light and emerged into the courtyard, sun shining through the apple tree onto the white flagstone cross.

We walked into the Death Row cellblock and mingled freely with a pair of death row inmates mopping the cellblock floor. "Hey, Smitty!" Alan Bannister shouted. A towering figure, Bannister leaned on his mop handle and grinned, "What are you doing with the keys to the gas chamber?" Observant. The state convicted Bannister for the contract killing of a man in a Joplin trailer court. He was executed in 1997, a few years after my visit here.

We finished a thorough tour of this bloody prison, talked about its carnage. Bigger than all the atrocities within these walls, this prison will always be shamed as the place that let James Earl Ray escape. He later assassinated Reverend Martin Luther King, Jr. On the way out, I saw a faded painting on the prison wall bordering the exercise yard. A former heavyweight boxing champion of the world, and Missouri State Penitentiary alum Sonny Liston, boxing gloves on, crouched ready to strike.

The memory of that prison visit sent me downtown for a drink. Erifnus drove down the street to Bones, a local watering hole that starts its charm offensive by facing an alley. Only a few blocks from the capitol, this bar helps keep the political process well oiled. Nothing wrong with that. It's a relief valve for the high pressure and high stakes of lawmaking, and Bones does a good job easing stress. Most of the time. I've spent good times there, played music on its ample rooftop patio, watching nighthawks dive through the floodlights illuminating the giant American flag atop a nearby bank building. I've sat eavesdropping on governors, inebriated on spirits and ego, telling stories about brazen senators. I've heard senators, inebriated on spirits and ego, telling stories about themselves. I've listened to lobbyists laughing at those stories, knowing there is a price after all. On this evening, the bar was quiet, three or four tables felt the elbows of patrons huddled in negotiation. Nobody at the bar. The bartender leaned over to hear my order.

"*Uno* Busch Beer, *por favor*," I said cheerfully, holding up one index finger.

"What?" he snapped. I repeated my request, suspecting I'd just jangled his jingo nerve, the one that ran between his brain and his asshole. "We only speak American here," he barked.

Rather than adjusting my patriotism to his Neanderthal level, I mustered a smile at this pitiful creature, and left. I walked down the alley to Madison's Café. Entering the lounge, I relaxed as the bartender greeted me with a smile, "Whaddaya have?"

"*Uno* Busch Beer, *por favor*," I said cheerfully, holding up one index finger.

"*Uno momento!*" said Marvin the bartender, and he fetched a bottle of Belgian brew. Marvin has worked at Madison's for at least a third of my life. And like the rest of the folks at this restaurant, he practices congeniality. I ordered a chicken Marsala with a side salad whose artichokes, onions, dressing and cheese combine to make one of the best Italian salads this side of Maria Callas.

Walking out of Madison's Café I snagged a toothpick, because an after-dinner toothpick becomes more than a toothpick. It's a memory chip, a reminder of a satisfying meal. On the street I heard a train whistle, and my mind went back to a bizarre encounter at Jefferson City's Amtrak Depot.

The train was late. That didn't matter to seven men awaiting its arrival.

"I've learned to be patient," said Mason, sitting next to me in his prison issue gray trousers and white T-shirt.

Earlier that morning, seven inmates had been released from three area Missouri correctional institutions. Guards gave them a lift to the depot. Two parolees awaited a train to Kansas City. Five were headed home to Saint Louis.

Three prison guards milled around the depot, not particularly mindful of their charges. Why should they be? The parolees were free men as of nine o'clock that morning. The guards handed each parolee a one-way ticket and a box of belongings, and waited around to ensure the parolees boarded their trains and left town.

Mason was going home after successfully completing substance abuse treatment at Fulton Diagnostic Center. "I had a UA [urine analysis] today, right before they let me out. I had a clean drop."

My grade school-aged grandsons sat beside me, not appearing to pay much attention. This was their first train trip; I had brought them here to experience a ride on a mode of transportation that dangles on life support. The younger grandson asked why we didn't just drive to Saint Louis. At seven years old he was too practical for nostalgia or history or anything rail related. "You will love trains," I predicted.

The interlude with newly-released inmates was a bonus experience.

"How long were you in?" I asked Mason.

"Five months."

"Got work?"

"Yes sir. *Post-Dispatch*."

"I applied there once. They rejected me," I told him, thinking in some perverse logic that he'd feel better, knowing that. He smiled.

Bad news. The train was running even later, an hour away. It didn't faze the group of new parolees. "The air smells fresh," Mason told me.

Six parolees still wore prison garb. The seventh wore brand new clothes. Joe looked crisp in his bright striped shirt, stuffed into blue jeans that shone, and Easter-white sneakers. "I've waited twelve and a half years for this day," he beamed. His family would pick him up at Union Station in Saint Louis.

Stacked near the tracks were six cardboard boxes and two brown paper bags, all hand-marked with last names and six-digit numbers. One box was marked "TV." Those boxes and bags represented the entire belongings of five men on their first day of freedom.

Mason said he didn't want to cause any more trouble for his family. His father, a retired auto worker at the General Motors plant, would pick him up in downtown Saint Louis. And soon he would see his two children. He was proud of his kids. "They like jazz," he told me. "Miles Davis. Coltrane. Learned to like it from their grandpa. I don't know much about jazz, but they do. My daughter told me she went to a haunted house. She said it was hideous. Hideous. My eight-year-old used a word I never did. They got better schools than I had."

"Ever been to the capitol?" I asked, nodding to the dome of the Missouri State Capitol, visible above the buildings behind us.

"Nope."

"It's got my favorite room in the world," I gushed. "A giant mural on all four walls of an entire room, with pictures of Frankie and Johnnie, and Staggerlee." He'd never heard of them. I explained they were real characters who lived in the old Saint Louis tenderloin district, long since replaced by a giant football stadium.

"Ever been to Columbia?" I asked him.

"Nope."

As the train approached the station, I wished Mason well. We boarded separate ends of the same coach. As we waited to climb onto the car, my oldest grandson asked about the man I had been talking to. I told him.

Aboard the train, I watched the behavior of the men who were free at last. Perfect gentlemen.

Mason had paid his debt to society. Now as he prepared to enter the next phase of his life, his outlook reflected the practicality of surviving from minute to minute. His philosophy was uncomplicated when I asked him who paid for the ticket. "They brought me here. They can take me home."

At Kirkwood we left the parolees sitting on the train. In less than an hour, they'd be dumped onto the streets of Saint Louis. I hope they're ready.

Growing up in Jefferson City, I remember no homeless people, no street people. More than once as a kid, I heard that when inmates walked out of the Missouri State Penitentiary, officials told them they weren't welcome here. "You're welcome in Columbia," the officials said.

The Details in the Devils

After my Madison's meal, chewing on my memory chip, home was my destination. Erifnus wheeled my pulsing gut through Jefferson City. It was dark, and a full moon busted orange over the horizon. We crossed the Missouri River. On this moonlit night, I diverted my eyes from the bridge to look at the river below. The wind earlier had whipped the water's surface into white caps, but as the moon rose the wind died, and the froth of the river's braiding currents glistened like slug trails in the moonlight. Funny how we cross a bridge a thousand times before we really see what we're crossing. The bridge deposits its vehicles to the other side of the river at a wide spot called Cedar City, a once-thriving community based around a gauntlet of flood-plain gas stations.

Two 1,000-year floods within two years wiped Cedar City off the map. The first flood, in 1993, claimed another venerable institution, Cedar City's lonesome neighbor, Renz Prison Farm.

As Erifnus motored past, the old abandoned Renz Prison sat spooky and silent under the full moon. I could see the old prison for three full minutes, even at 70 miles per hour, because it sat alone, naked, one big white two-story building surrounded by nothing but a chain link fence and a thousand acres of fallow Missouri River bottomland.

In the shadow of the bridge, a half mile from the prison, a skeleton stands on the bank of the Missouri River, a lone cedar tree twenty feet tall, its dead limbs stripped and replaced with mileage signs for towns up and down the river. Hermann 45 miles. Rocheport 43 miles. Yankton, SD 662 miles. The signpost informed prison escapees how far they had to follow the riverbank to reach Omaha.

The prison stood vacant for nearly two decades. For some reason nobody tore it down. On this night, the moonlight illuminated the building's whitewashed facade, its four dozen windows stared back, black and void. A tree grew out of the roof.

Years ago I visited the prison to pick up a print job. A young receptionist at the print shop greeted me cheerily. She was sweet, pretty, young, didn't fit the profile of a criminal. She was convicted for her role as the getaway driver in a bank robbery, an exciting job for a youngster weaned on Bonnie and Clyde movies. She drove down a path that ended badly. So Renz Prison became her home for eight years.

Next time I returned, she wasn't at the counter. I asked the shop foreman what happened to her. He said a few weeks ago, a pair of female inmates took her into the print shop basement and raped and beat her to a bloody pulp.

Some people make bad choices. Others have bad choices thrust upon them. Some get the double whammy. I drove on, under a full moon, feeling its gravitational pull, and its pock-faced promise that the end is near.

On a back road to Hartsburg, which sits on the Missouri River, the moon lit my surroundings like a cosmic refrigerator light. In town a juke joint called the Hartsburg Hitchin' Post—no bigger than a country church—parlayed honky swamp swing music into dancing on the pool table and hanging from the rafters. The Hitchin' Post has the two most important qualities for a dance hall: wood floors and Stag Beer. Sometimes the only reason I do things is for Stag Beer. Stag and happiness are hard to find. But they're out there, in real taverns.

Hartsburg attracts eclectics, down the blacktop road that ends in the middle of town, beside a legendary river that drains half a continent. Big levees break occasionally under the strain of big floods that simultaneously cleanse and trash the town.

Even the mention of Hartsburg causes nods and smiles, eyes fixed faraway to good times spent there. A bicycle shop hopes for business from its perch near the Katy Trail. A winery sits like a Saint Bernard ready to revive trail riders.

And hiding within spittin' distance are a billion pumpkins. Some grow big as washing machines. The pumpkins take center stage at a fall festival that accomplishes the solitary feat of clogging the artery descending into town, causing a massive single-file traffic jam stretching five miles back to the highway, thus offering a good hike for otherwise sedentary folks who must park on the road's shoulder, and walk a few miles downhill to the pumpkin fest. The return hike uphill is less enjoyable, especially for those lugging pumpkins to the car.

With no pepitas, Erifnus easily fled Hartsburg's charm for the backroad leading to Columbia. We skirted along the edge of the Mark Twain National Forest, a natural treasure which never gets anywhere near Mark Twain's stomping grounds. But Mark Twain would approve, since the forest is his namesake, a ready cache of trees to be transformed into more copies of *Life on the Mississippi*, should the forest ever be sold. For now the Mark Twain National Forest still exists, having rebuffed attempts to sell it for quick cash.

On our late-night journey home, the refrigerator moon had set. A heavy curtain of clouds rolled overhead. No rain. No wind. Just darkness on a desolate road. I could see only what Erifnus's headlights allowed. A dozen miles ahead we'd pass Devil's Icebox, a cool fissure hiding in the dark. My mind wandered past the headlights, into the darkness, and the long list of geologic formations given satanic names.

Devil's Well. Devil's Elbow. Devil's Tongue.

In our travels, Erifnus took me to some truly dangerous spots, places called "don't go there."

One chilling hellhole was Snake Pit Cave, off Route 66, near Leasburg. The sinkhole from this collapsed cave has sheer walls down to the bottom of a pit twenty-five feet deep. If I ever had to dungeonize a vile transgressor with no hope of salvation, I would dump the cretin into Snake Pit Cave. According to a guy named Rimbach who climbed into the sinkhole, there's no way out of the pit except by ladder. Any animal who falls into the pit must survive its last days eating other trapped animals. Most of them are snakes. Dozens of snakes. Guess who eats.

This Bible Belt obsession with devil names is unsettling. Aside from the snake pits and steep fissures, most of the Devil's caves and crannies don't seem particularly dangerous, not nearly as dangerous as the descendants of the folks who named them.

An intrepid crew once braved the bottom of Slaughter Sink to dredge seven dozen automobile tires, three freezers and a ton of trash from this sixteen-story-deep hole, proof that relatives of Beelzebub use this spot as Devil's Dump.

Erifnus has shuttled me past Devil's Hole, Devil's Hollow, Devil's Boot, Devil's Chute, Devil's Raceground, Devil's Rockpile, Devil's Sugar Bowl, Devil's Washboard, Devil's Washpan and Devil's Dick, proving that Missouri is a leader in invoking the name of the Prince of Darkness, and exporting the handiwork of that most fearsome beast. Civil War historians know. Missouri's biggest export before the Civil War wasn't hemp. It was Hell. Some people forget that. Or maybe they never knew. Missourians know. Kansans know. The proof peeks from the crags and crevasses throughout the state, where many of our most vivid geological wonders bear the name of Satan.

Consulting the works of authorities on Devilish eponyms in Missouri, their reports vary in scope and intensity. Geologists appreciate the vivid descriptions. Historians admire the pioneer accounts. Evangelists point to the Devil's outcroppings for props and allegories. Some of these scholars have passed into the unknown. Regardless of their whereabouts, one common theme pervades their work: There are more Devil's comfort zones in Missouri than you can shake a snake at. It only makes sense. If Hell is historically Missouri's major export, good marketing dictates you need ample retail outlets.

Driving through the dark, I added to my mental list of Lucifer's hangouts. We've crept up on the Devil's Jack O' Lantern, slid down the Devil's Race Course, and survived the Devil's Rake, a satanic system of snags on the Missouri River described by Lewis and Clark, but forgotten by steamboat pilots until they struck the rocky rake and sank. Farther south the Devil's Tea Table waits to entertain a royal wedding. The Devil's Bake Oven got its name "perhaps, because it does not powerfully resemble anybody else's bake oven," according to one leading authority on deviltry in Missouri, Mark Twain.

Irish and Scottish pioneers seemed obsessed with naming odd geologic formations as testaments to Beelzebub's prowess. The Ozarks is the Medusa of Lucifer's spines: no less than two dozen Devil's Backbones jut out from Hell on Missouri's backside.

He's a hungry devil, haunting Devil's Ice Box dead ahead, ten miles from the edge of Erifnus's high beam headlights.

Visitors to the Show Me State might smile if they saw the slogan "Devil's Living Room" on a Missouri license plate, especially if they watched *Ozark* or *Winter's Bone* or *Three Billboards Outside Ebbing, Missouri*. That slogan and those movies are fictitious. But if...

A low whine startled me out of my thoughts. The whine grew into a muffled drumbeat as Erifnus resisted my steering and slowed. I maneuvered her to the road's narrow shoulder, grabbed my flashlight from the glove box, jumped out onto the black roadway and pointed to the culprit: left front tire flat. At least I could change this tire without worrying about traffic. I opened the trunk and pulled out the donut spare, savior on two dozen occasions during our long journey. I found a cup-sized rock from the ditch, and placed the flashlight against the rock to project a dim light onto the wheel well. I set the jack, took the tire tool that doubled as a jack handle, and began to crank, unaware at first that from miles away a car was approaching from behind.

As Erifnus's shoulder slowly raised off the ground I sensed distant headlights and heard the high whine of a speeding car. As it closed in on Erifnus the whine dropped dramatically in pitch. Thank goodness this driver won't barrel past at breakneck speed and cause a wake that might tip Erifnus off her jack.

The car slowed and pulled behind us, clicking its headlights on high beam as I crouched at the wheel well. I didn't move from my stance, from my duty, figuring that the driver would make contact with me, maybe yell, or exit the car. Nothing. At least I had a tire tool for defense, and a cup-sized rock. Grateful for the flood of light, I pulled off the damaged tire and replaced it with the trusty donut, glancing occasionally into the blinding headlights. The driver, still a mystery, must be a Samaritan, maybe an off-duty cop. But a cop would exit the car. Maybe it was an elderly woman returning a good deed for a time she was stranded by the side of the road. Maybe they were carjackers, waiting for me to do the dirty work before they stole my car at gunpoint. But why would they steal an old car, worthless to anybody but me? Robbery would be a likelier motive.

I worked fast. With donut spare securely attached, I released the jack and rose to put the damaged tire into the trunk. The attendant car slowly pulled from behind me onto the roadway. As the car passed and gained momentum, its passengers remained a mystery. But the car's make was unmistakable: a jet-black '56 Cadillac Coupe de Ville, long and sleek with a front bumper shaped like Barbarella's bra, and tailfins that hoisted bordello-red brake lights.

Watching the Cadillac speed away I waved thank you with the tire tool, then shut the trunk, happy I didn't end up inside it. Erifnus limped toward home.

We drove north through the late-night dark. Good luck filled our windshield as a shooting star blazed diagonally through the sky and split into two burning bottle rockets.

I made a wish.

Epilogue: 300,001: A Road Odyssey

Should've planned it better. Some exotic background like Mount Rushmore or the Golden Gate Bridge. It sneaked up on us as we left the city limits, so we took an exit ramp off I-70 and into an abandoned parking lot where I made Erifnus Caitnop turn in circles until she reached a milestone. 300,000 miles. It was an insensitive thing to do to an old horse who has served so well. But I wanted photos, and not on the shoulder of I-70.

I stopped in the lot to savor the moment and got out of the car. An old Cadillac limousine pulled up. The backdoor window lowered and a mellifluous voice resonated the car: "Need a ride?"

I demurred, shaking my head, peering into the shadowy backseat. The face looked a lot like Elvis, hiding age behind aviator sunglasses and a jet-black pompadour. I almost asked him if we'd met a fortnight ago on a dark deserted backroad. Or in the bleachers at Busch Stadium. Instead I just replied, "Thank you. Thank you very much."

He nodded. The window cranked up. The Cadillac sped away.

Acknowledgments

The end of all knowledge should be service to others.

—Cesar Chavez

Love and thanks to the pair who share my mutant travel gene: Dad and sister Susan. A wave to six million Missourians I drove past, and to their ancestors who didn't see me coming.

I found 32,314 stories on the road. Thanks to storytellers Dave Lineberry, Gerry Mandel, Stephen Andsager, Jordan Yount, Vance Heflin and others quoted in these pages.

Editor Mary V. Helsabeck helped me sift and select and stay focused.

Thanks to local historians and researchers who keep the flame, and guides Byron Nicodemus, Janeen Aggen, Angela Da Silva, Alan Peters and Maryellen McVicker.

Thanks to detailed histories: Switzler's 1889 *Illustrated History of Missouri*, Walter Williams's 1913 *History of Northeast Missouri*, BlackPast.org, and to the Missouri Division of Historic Preservation, storykeeper for properties on the National Historic Register.

Special gratitude to the University of Missouri graduate students who did remarkable legwork compiling Robert L. Ramsay's *Missouri Place Names 1928-1945,* housed at the State Historical Society of Missouri: Orvyl Guy Adams, Bernice E. Johnson, Fauna R. Overlay, Mayme L. Hamlett, Nadine Pace, Cora Ann Pottinger, Anne Atchison, Gertrude M. Zimmer, Anna O'Brien, Esther Leech, Ruth Welty, Eugenia L. Harrison, Frank Weber, Martha Ewing, Robert Lee Meyers, Margaret E. Bell, and Katherine Elliott.

I tapped the well of three great geologists: Jerry Vineyard, Wally Howe, and Tom Beveridge's *Geologic Curiosities and Wonders of Missouri.* Jo Schaper directed me to some great geological wonders.

Archaeologist Timothy E. Baumann conducted and wrote "The Du Sable Grave Project in St. Charles, Missouri." *The Missouri Archaeologist.* 59–76 (December 2005).

Chantal Allen gave me insight into my grandfather in her book, *Bomb Canada and Other Unkind Remarks in the American Media.* Larry Melton and the Sedalia Ragtime Archive personnel guided me through the story of Jelly Settle.

Thanks to the State Historical Society of Missouri's S. Fred Prince Collection regarding Marvel Cave, and especially to the *Missouri Conservationist* article, Dec 02, 1998 and Nov 03, 2010 by Suzanne Wilson.

Bless the librarians everywhere, especially the Wolfner State Library. Bill Caldwell, librarian at *The Joplin Globe*, told the story about Neck City.

Beth Pike, Steve Hudnell and Peg Craft filmed Erifnus's good side, and won her an Emmy Award.

For the Civil War I consulted Jim Robertson, Hank Waters, Rudi Keller and Robert Hawkins.

More than musicians, Big Smith and the Ozark Mountain Daredevils gave me a deeper understanding of chickens.

Cheers to the · underappreciated workforce at Missouri's Departments of Transportation, Conservation, Natural Resources, Divisions of Parks, Tourism, and the Board on Geographic Names.

Thanks to the 256 newspapers of the Missouri Press Association. Thanks to magazines *Show Me Missouri, County Living, Rural Missouri, Missouri Life and Inside Columbia* for allowing me to recount bits and pieces of my past articles from their pages.

Most important, my loving gratitude to Cheryl and our children and grandchildren for excusing my absences.

Erifnus thanks University Garage, her car spa. They think she'll make it to 500,000 miles. I do too.

I dedicate this work to Sandy. Good dog.

And Mom.

CPSIA information can be obtained
at www.ICGtesting.com
Printed in the USA
BVHW070839230119
538283BV00032B/564/P

9 781942 168881